Edexcel
Success through qualifications

THE SCHOOLS HISTORY PROJECT
·S·H·P·
OFFICIAL TEXT

Medicine
for Edexcel

an SHP study in development

THE SCHOOLS HISTORY PROJECT
· S·H·P ·
OFFICIAL TEXT

Success through qualifications

CORE TEXTS
FOR GCSE

Medicine
for Edexcel
an SHP study in development

IAN DAWSON

IAN COULSON

Edexcel consultants:
Angela Leonard
Christopher Culpin

JOHN MURRAY

The Schools History Project

The Project was set up in 1972, with the aim of improving the study of history for students aged 13–16. This involved a reconsideration of the ways in which history contributes to the educational needs of young people. The Project devised new objectives, new criteria for planning and developing courses, and the materials to support them. New examinations, requiring new methods of assessment, also had to be developed. These have continued to be popular. The advent of GCSE in 1987 led to the expansion of Project approaches into other syllabuses.

The Schools History Project has been based at Trinity and All Saints College, Leeds, since 1978, from where it supports teachers through a biennial Bulletin, regular INSET, an annual conference and a website (www.tasc.ac.uk/shp).

Since the National Curriculum was drawn up in 1991, the Project has continued to expand its publications, bringing its ideas to courses for Key Stage 3 as well as a range of GCSE and A level specifications.

Note: the wording and sentence structure of some written sources have been adapted and simplified to make them accessible to all pupils, while faithfully preserving the sense of the original.

Words printed in SMALL CAPITALS are defined in the Glossary on page 208.

© Ian Dawson, Ian Coulson 1996, 2001

First published in 1996 as *Medicine & Health Through Time* by
John Murray (Publishers) Ltd
50 Albemarle Street
London W1S 4BD

This revised edition first published 2001

Reprinted 2002 (twice)

Layouts by Black Dog Design
Artwork by Art Construction, Linden Artists, Janek Matysiak, Steve Smith
Printed and bound in Spain by Bookprint, S.L., Barcelona

A catalogue entry for this book is available from the British Library

ISBN 0 7195 7727 6

Contents

What is a study in development?

A STUDY IN DEVELOPMENT is a study of how things have changed over a long period of time.

Periods

In this study in development you will be examining how medicine and health have changed over many centuries. You will look at at least three different periods. Source 1 shows families from different periods.

Causes of illness

You will be investigating what people thought caused diseases and illness in these periods. Source 2 shows healers from different ages and some of their ideas.

The ancient civilisations of Egypt, Greece and Rome
The first doctors

Life expectancy: women 38; men 40

The Medical Renaissance (AD1350–1750)
Many new discoveries about the body

Life expectancy: women 38; men 41

1900 to the present day
Rapid progress in preventing and curing many diseases

Life expectancy: women 78; men 72

The Middle Ages (AD500–1350)
Very little medical progress

Life expectancy: women 36; men 37

The eighteenth and nineteenth centuries
Discoveries about the true causes of disease

Life expectancy: women 49; men 45

Timeline: 2000, 1000, BC / AD, 500, 1000, 1350, 1500, 1750, 1900, 2000

Note: timeline not to scale

God has made you ill because he is angry with you.

Your body contains four HUMOURS (liquids). You are ill because your humours are out of balance.

You are ill because of GERMS. They are all around you and some of them have gone inside you and your body is reacting to them. That is why you are ill.

SOURCE 1

SOURCE 2

1. Look at the various causes of illness in Source 2. Which of the people in Source 1 do you think might have believed in each cause?
2. Which of these ideas are still believed today?

Methods of treating illness

In this study in development you are going to see how in different periods people used different methods of treating illness.

3. Look at the various treatments in Source 3. Which of the people in Source 1 do you think might have used each method of treatment?
4. Which of these methods of treatment are still used today? Which are not?

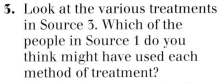

The only thing you can do is pray to God that he will take away your illness.

Carry this charm with you wherever you go. It has magic powers and will stop you getting ill.

You are ill because the channels of your body are blocked.

This tablet will kill the INFECTION which is making you ill.

You are ill because this week the planet Jupiter was in conjunction with the constellation Sagittarius.

To get your humours back into balance I must drain some of the blood from you.

I have gathered and mixed a potion of many different herbs. You must drink it. It will heal you.

You'll only be healthy if we clear away all the awful dirt in this town.

I will cut out the infection.

You are ill because of the smells and bad air (MIASMA) which come from the rubbish in the streets.

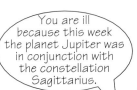

SOURCE 3

Factors causing change

In this study in development you will find out how different factors have affected medicine and health. Sometimes these factors hold up progress, sometimes they speed it up.

Attitudes and beliefs
Example: In the 1940s there was widespread support for the idea that no one should have to pay to see a doctor. The government set up the National Health Service to provide free treatment for all.

War
Example: The Second World War speeded up the development of PENICILLIN.

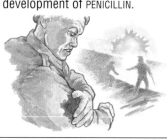

Governments
Example: When the British government made smallpox VACCINATION compulsory in the nineteenth century, deaths from smallpox plummeted.

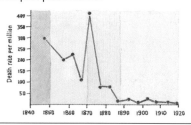

Individuals
Example: Pasteur devised a famous experiment to prove that there are MICRO-ORGANISMS (called BACTERIA or germs) which cause disease.

Science and technology
Example: The technology of glass-making improved in the nineteenth century. This meant better lenses could be made for microscopes, which surgeons could then use to study the micro-organisms that cause disease.

Improved communications
Example: When printing was invented new medical ideas such as Vesalius' ideas about ANATOMY could be spread much more quickly than before.

Factors causing change

■ TASK

Write each factor from the spider diagram above as a heading on each of the last six pages of your exercise book. Write the examples given in the diagram under the appropriate heading. As you work through this study in development, use these pages to record any further examples you find of these factors affecting medicine and health.

Important terms

Medicine and health have their own specialist vocabulary. You cannot talk about medicine and health without using words like dissection or anatomy – which you may not have come across before. We have included them in the Glossary on pages 208–9, and every time an important new term appears in this book it is DISPLAYED LIKE THIS.

■ ACTIVITY 1

Work in groups to look up the following terms in the Glossary on pages 208–9 or in your own dictionary. They are all terms you will come across in Chapter 1 of this book. Look up at least two words each and write your own clear definition of what they mean.

- physician
- plague
- Asclepion
- anatomy
- embalm
- dissection
- gangrene
- remedy.

Key questions

Remember that throughout your study of the history of medicine and health you will be looking for historical explanations for change:

- **When did things change? Why?**
- **When did things stay the same? Why?**
- **When did things change very quickly? Why?**
- **When was there regression (things getting worse)? Why?**
- **Did change always mean progress?**

These are key questions which you will be asked within each period. By the end of the book you should be asking them yourself without any prompting from us.

■ **ACTIVITY 2**

Can you suggest any answers to the questions on the graph below?

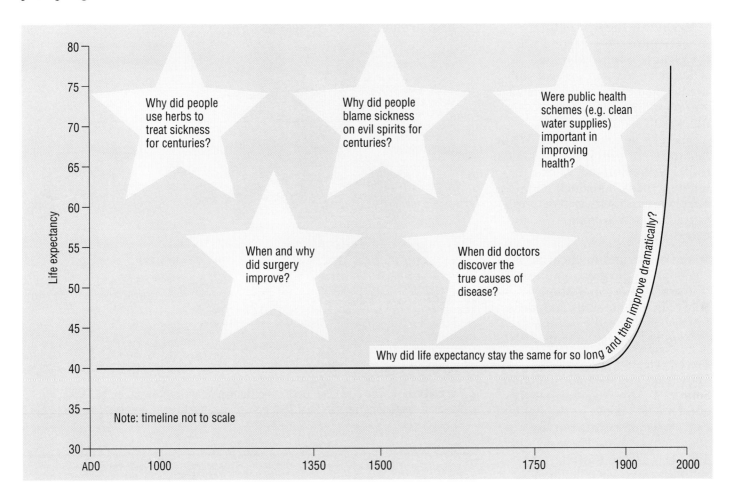

Life expectancy

Why did people use herbs to treat sickness for centuries?

Why did people blame sickness on evil spirits for centuries?

Were public health schemes (e.g. clean water supplies) important in improving health?

When and why did surgery improve?

When did doctors discover the true causes of disease?

Why did life expectancy stay the same for so long and then improve dramatically?

Note: timeline not to scale

AD0   1000   1350   1500   1750   1900   2000

MEDICINE AND HEALTH IN THE ANCIENT WORLD AND THE EARLY MIDDLE AGES 3000BC–AD1350

Egypt, Greece and Rome: the great empires

THIS CHAPTER COVERS a very long period of time – around 4000 years. It begins in **Ancient Egypt** around 3000BC, when skilled builders were erecting massive pyramids to house their dead rulers.

Egypt was the first of three great empires. The second was the **Greek** empire. At a time when the early Britons had still not learned to write, the Greeks were building cities with universities and libraries.

Then came the **Romans**. While Britons were still living in isolated hillforts, the Romans were building roads, aqueducts and sewers across their great empire.

You are now going to investigate:

- the health and medical skills of people in the great empires of Egypt, Greece and Rome
- whether their skills and ideas survived after the Roman empire came to an end.

Before you start, use your own knowledge and the information in Sources 1–3 to suggest answers to questions 1–3 above on the right. Don't worry if you are not sure about the answers. These are only first ideas and you will have a chance to improve them or even change your mind once you start looking in detail at Egypt, Greece and Rome.

1. What kinds of evidence do you think will tell us about medicine in ancient times?
2. a) What were the two kinds of doctor in these ancient empires?
   b) What ideas about the causes of sickness did these different kinds of doctor have?
3. a) What was the average life expectancy of people in these empires?
   b) Think about the answer to 3a. Do you think that doctors could help people who were sick?

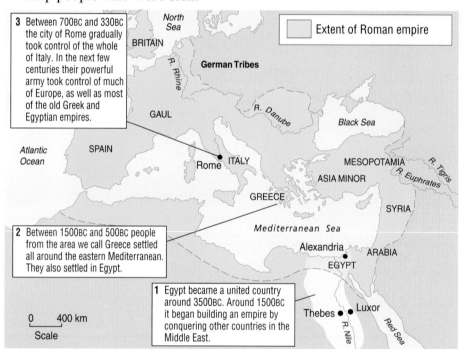

3 Between 700BC and 330BC the city of Rome gradually took control of the whole of Italy. In the next few centuries their powerful army took control of much of Europe, as well as most of the old Greek and Egyptian empires.

2 Between 1500BC and 500BC people from the area we call Greece settled all around the eastern Mediterranean. They also settled in Egypt.

1 Egypt became a united country around 3500BC. Around 1500BC it began building an empire by conquering other countries in the Middle East.

SOURCE 1 The Egyptian, Greek and Roman empires grew up in the region around the Mediterranean Sea. This map shows the Roman empire in AD120

BRITAIN		Stonehenge	
EGYPTIAN EMPIRE	The pyramids		
GREEK EMPIRE			
ROMAN EMPIRE			

3000BC   2000BC

HOME REMEDIES

Wives and mothers learned cures for illnesses and how to use herbs as medicines from older members of their families. They also acted as midwives when babies were born.

Who helped the sick?

Priests said prayers and used charms to drive away the evil spirits that they believed caused disease.

Physicians looked at symptoms and used treatments and simple surgery recorded in books.

DOCTORS

SOURCE 2 The people who treated the sick in ancient times

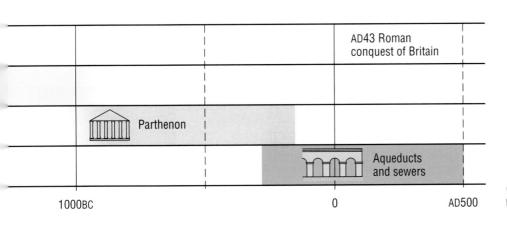

			AD43 Roman conquest of Britain	
Parthenon				
		Aqueducts and sewers		

1000BC   0   AD500

SOURCE 3 Timeline of the great empires

How did life in Egypt affect medicine?

■ ACTIVITY

1. Use the information and sources on pages 8–9 to make notes explaining how Egyptian life affected Egyptian medicine. Include the following features:
   - ■ wealth
   - ■ trade
   - ■ improved writing
   - ■ religion
   - ■ the Nile and farming.

2. Choose one feature that you think was particularly important and write a paragraph to explain your choice.

A wealthy country

Egypt was a wealthy country, with powerful rulers, international trade, large cities and writing. It was the most advanced civilisation the world had known.

Egypt's wealth was based on the River Nile. When the river flooded every year it covered the surrounding land with fertile soil which gave rich harvests of good crops. Farming was so successful that landowners in Egypt became rich.

Egypt's wealth led to improvements in medicine.

Specialist doctors

The rich employed doctors to look after them. For example, the ruler (the Pharaoh) had his own PHYSICIAN. These specialist doctors spent much of their lives trying to improve their understanding of medicine and health.

Metal workers

Rich Egyptians could also afford to employ specialist craftsmen such as metal workers to make tools or jewellery for them. These skilled craftsmen also made fine bronze instruments for the doctors, so Egyptian doctors worked with better medical instruments than healers in prehistoric times.

SOURCE 1 A tomb painting showing Egyptian farmers at work

SOURCE 2 'Vulture Collar' necklace made for the Egyptian pharaoh Tutankhamun. The outlines of all the feathers, the head and limbs were made of gold. The feathers themselves were encrusted with precious stones

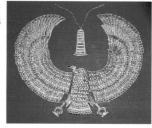

Trade

Egypt had widespread trade links. Ships and merchants arrived from India, China and parts of Africa, bringing new herbs and plants with them. Many of these herbs and plants were recommended as medicines, so Egyptian healers built up a wide knowledge of herbal medicines.

Improved writing

The Egyptians also developed PAPYRUS (a kind of paper made from reeds) and a simpler, quicker form of writing, which together made writing easier and more convenient than before.

Doctors benefited from these developments. Treatments and REMEDIES could be written down and passed on accurately to other healers.

Religion

Religion helped to increase medical knowledge. Egyptians believed that people had a life after death and that they would need their bodies in the afterlife. Therefore, the bodies of important people were EMBALMED ready for the afterlife. Parts of the body, such as the liver, were taken out and preserved. The rest of the body was embalmed, which involved treating it with spices and wrapping it in bandages to make a mummy.

The Nile and farming

Egyptian doctors began to think hard about the reasons why people became ill. They got some of their ideas from the River Nile itself. The Nile was so important to the health of their farmland. The irrigation channels dug by the farmers brought life to the farmland. Egyptian doctors began to think of the body as having many channels inside it which, if they became blocked, could cause a person to be unhealthy.

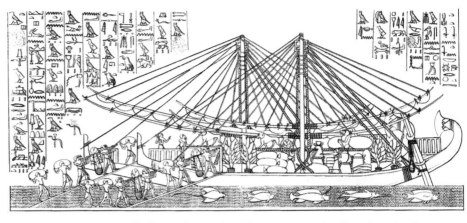

SOURCE 3 A wall carving showing Egyptians loading a trading ship for a voyage to Arabia. The Egyptians greatly improved the design of their ships so they could sail long distances across the Mediterranean

SOURCE 4 A modern African farmer opens an irrigation channel to let water flow onto his crops. This same method of irrigation was used by ancient Egyptian farmers around the River Nile

---

Summary

River Nile ⟶ rich crops ⟶ wealthy people ⟨ specialist craftsmen: metalworkers and doctors

trade: new herbs and plants

writing

How did the Egyptians treat illness and injuries?

1. Sort Sources 1–7 into the following categories:
   - the use of herbs
   - the use of surgery
   - the use of magic or charms
   - other treatments (list them).

2. Egyptian doctors were developing rational cures like that in Source 3. Why do you think they still used the type of treatments described in Source 4?

3. Why might the cure for a diseased eye in Source 2 have worked? Use Source 9 to help you explain.

SOURCE 1 The Greek historian Herodotus visited Egypt around 450BC and recorded this information

❝ Each Egyptian has a net. He uses it to fish by day, but at night spreads it over his bed to keep off mosquitoes. ❞

SOURCE 2 From the Ebers Papyrus

❝ For a diseased eye
To clear up the PUS: *honey, balm from Mecca and gum ammoniac.* To treat its discharge: *frankincense, myrrh, yellow ochre.* To treat the growth: *red ochre, malachite, honey.*

For diseases of the bladder
Bread in a rotten condition. The doctor must use it to fight the sickness – not to avoid the sickness. ❞

SOURCE 3 From the Edwin Smith Papyrus, a collection of Egyptian medical documents written around 1600BC. The papyrus lists 48 cases of surgery, each with a careful description of examination, symptoms, diagnosis and treatment

❝ Instructions for treating a broken nose
Examination
If you examine a man whose nose is disfigured – part of it squashed in, the other part swollen and both his nostrils are bleeding.
Diagnosis
Then you should say 'You have a broken nose and this is an AILMENT which I can treat'.
Treatment
You should clean his nose with two plugs of linen and then insert two plugs soaked in grease into his nostrils. You should make him rest until the swelling has gone down, you should bandage his nose with stiff rolls of linen and treat him with lint every day until he recovers. ❞

SOURCE 5 Some ceremonies of ancient Egypt in 750–300BC described by J. Worth Estes in *The Medical Skills of Ancient Egypt*, 1989

❝ … some temples were also associated with healing … The sick could bathe in water that had been sanctified, perhaps in the temple's sacred lake, so that they would be healed … another procedure … required the sick person to spend a night in the SANATORIUM with the expectation that the god would cause him to dream his cure. ❞

This charm will protect you against evil spirits. It is made from evil smelling herbs and garlic and from honey which is sweet for people but horrible for spirits, from a fishtail and a rag and a backbone of a perch.

This is certain to make your hair grow again. It mixes fat of lion, fat of cat, fat of crocodile, fat of ibex and fat of serpent.

SOURCE 4 Two treatments which are described in Egyptian medical documents written between 1900BC and 1500BC

SOURCE 6 Written by the Greek historian Herodotus in the fifth century BC

❝ *For three successive days every month they [the Egyptians] purge themselves ... for they think that all diseases stem from the foods they eat... they drink from cups of bronze which they clean daily. They are careful to wear newly washed linen clothing. They practise circumcision for the sake of cleanliness. Their priests shave their whole body every third day so no lice may infect them while they are serving the gods. Twice a day and every night they wash in cold water.* ❞

SOURCE 7 From J. Worth Estes, *The Medical Skills of Ancient Egypt*, 1989

❝ *Skinned whole mice have been found in the stomachs of children buried in an [ancient Egyptian] cemetery, perhaps administered as a treatment of last resort. Mouse fat is recommended in the Ebers Papyrus 'to relax stiffness' and a mouse head to remedy earaches. A rotten mouse is the chief ingredient of a Hearst Papyrus ointment that would keep the hair from turning white. During the reign of Nero (AD54–68), the Greek physician Dioscorides noted that whole mice would dry children's saliva, and that chopped mice were useful for scorpion bites. Two thousand years later, in 1924, skinned whole mice were being used for the treatment of both urinary incontinence and whooping cough in rural England.* ❞

4. Choose either Source 1 or Source 6 and explain why the measures it describes might have helped to prevent disease.
5. Source 7 describes a cure which has been used over a long period. Why might such a cure be used for so many centuries?

■ ACTIVITY

Choose one of the treatments or remedies mentioned on this page and write an advertisement for it. Your advertisement should try to attract people to use the treatment. It should therefore say:

■ what the treatment involves
■ who will provide it and where
■ what the effects will be on the patient.

Did the Egyptian treatments work?

Some of these treatments might seem quite sensible to you, others might look useless. But just because a treatment is different from those we use today does not mean to say it would not work.

SOURCE 8 The most commonly used ingredients in Egyptian medicines as recorded in the Ebers Papyrus

Honey	30.3%
Djaret	14.6%
Frankincense	14.1%
Salt	10.4%
Dates	9.6%

[Historians are not sure what 'djaret' was. Many other ingredients were used, including juniper and figs.]

SOURCE 9 Scientists have analysed and tested some of the ancient Egyptian remedies. This cartoon is based on information in *The Medical Skills of Ancient Egypt* by J. Worth Estes, 1989

What did Egyptian healers know about the body and causes of disease?

The Egyptians knew about the heart, pulse, liver, brain, lungs and the blood. However, they did not understand the proper roles of these parts of the body.

Egyptians believed that the heart was the most important organ in the body. They described how blood flowed through over 40 channels from the heart to every part of the body. The blood carried air and water that were essential for life. Healthy channels were vital for good health. Everyday greetings included 'May your channels be sound'!

In Egypt when someone died the body was embalmed (see page 9). Many of the organs were taken out (only the heart was left inside) and the body was then preserved with spices. Egyptians learned a little about anatomy (the parts of the body) from this, but embalming was carried out quickly for religious reasons and because of the heat. Egyptians also believed that people would need their bodies in the afterlife so DISSECTION of other parts of the body was forbidden.

6. If Egyptian doctors wanted to learn more about parts of the body, how did embalming:
a) help them
b) hinder them?
7. Irrigation was important to Egyptian farmers. If the channels from the River Nile were blocked, the crops would die in the great heat. How do you think the River Nile influenced their ideas about the causes of disease? You may need to refer back to page 9.
8. What other factors might have helped Egyptians arrive at the explanation of disease in Source 10? For example, why might they think that rotting food in the bowel lets off gases?

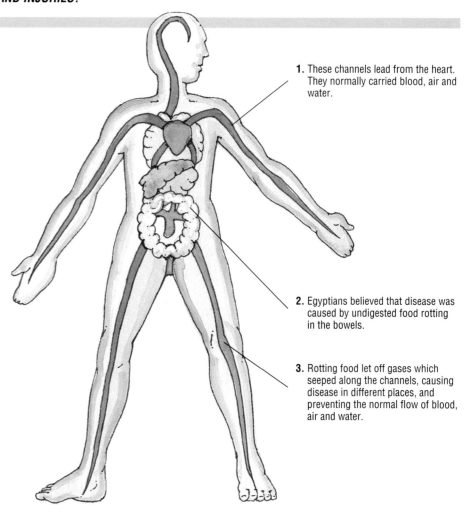

1. These channels lead from the heart. They normally carried blood, air and water.

2. Egyptians believed that disease was caused by undigested food rotting in the bowels.

3. Rotting food let off gases which seeped along the channels, causing disease in different places, and preventing the normal flow of blood, air and water.

SOURCE 10 Egyptian ideas about the causes of disease

■ ACTIVITY

Here are the beginnings of a chart summarising Egyptian medicine. Make your own copy of the chart and use the information on pages 7–12 to complete it.

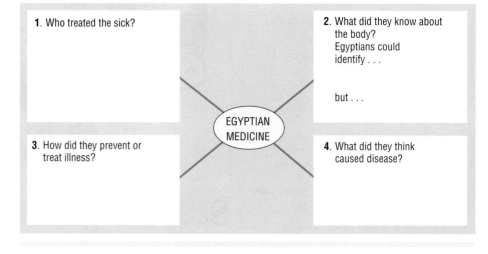

1. Who treated the sick?

2. What did they know about the body? Egyptians could identify . . .

but . . .

EGYPTIAN MEDICINE

3. How did they prevent or treat illness?

4. What did they think caused disease?

From the Egyptians to the Greeks

Egyptian medicine: a summary

Medical knowledge and methods changed when people began to live in cities and became richer. They had specialist craftsmen, including doctors. Trade increased the range of herbs available for use as medicines. They developed writing and they began to learn about anatomy.

They also tried to work out a logical reason why people became ill. Learning from the waters of the Nile, they blamed blocked channels for causing illness.

However, not everything was new. Egyptians used many herbs in the same ways as their ancestors. They still did not understand the function of important parts of the body, such as the liver, and how they kept people healthy.

The Egyptians did not understand the real causes of disease either, despite efforts to find a logical cause. Therefore, they were helpless when sickness spread. That was why Egyptians still believed in evil spirits and protected themselves with AMULETS and other magical charms.

The Greek empire

Now it is time to investigate Greek medicine. Remember that you need to look for changes and continuities from the days of the Egyptians. Look at Sources 1 and 2.

1. Why was Greek medicine likely to be similar to Egyptian medicine?
2. Why might new medical ideas spread easily in the Greek empire?
3. How did Hippocrates influence other Greek doctors?

SOURCE 1 Hippocrates, the most famous Greek doctor. He is thought to have been born in Kos around 460BC. He wrote a number of medical books, advising doctors how to treat their patients. However, we cannot be certain about the details of his life. This bust, produced long after his death, may not even be very like him. You can find out more about Hippocrates on pages 20–21.

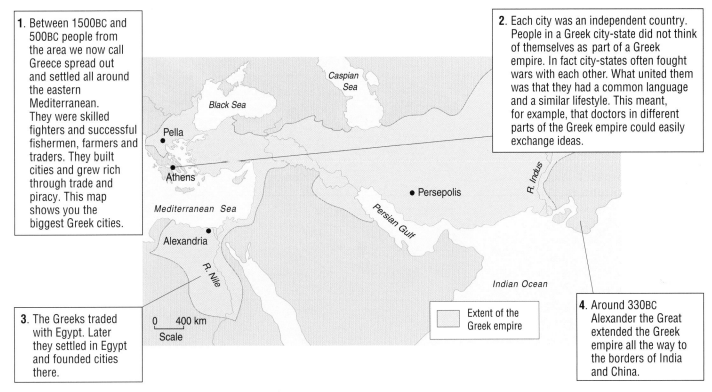

1. Between 1500BC and 500BC people from the area we now call Greece spread out and settled all around the eastern Mediterranean. They were skilled fighters and successful fishermen, farmers and traders. They built cities and grew rich through trade and piracy. This map shows you the biggest Greek cities.

2. Each city was an independent country. People in a Greek city-state did not think of themselves as part of a Greek empire. In fact city-states often fought wars with each other. What united them was that they had a common language and a similar lifestyle. This meant, for example, that doctors in different parts of the Greek empire could easily exchange ideas.

3. The Greeks traded with Egypt. Later they settled in Egypt and founded cities there.

4. Around 330BC Alexander the Great extended the Greek empire all the way to the borders of India and China.

Caspian Sea
Black Sea
Pella
Athens
Mediterranean Sea
Persepolis
R. Indus
Persian Gulf
Alexandria
R. Nile
Indian Ocean

0   400 km
Scale

Extent of the Greek empire

SOURCE 2 The Greek empire in 334BC

Greek medicine: what happened at an Asclepion?

THE ANCIENT GREEKS play a very important part in this story of medicine and health – even more important than the ancient Egyptians. The Greeks had many new ideas about causes of disease and methods of treatment, and these ideas remained important for centuries to come. Over the next eight pages you are going to find out about some of these new ideas. But you are going to start with one which is not so new – the gods.

As you have seen, one of the oldest medical beliefs was that gods could cause and cure disease. Did the Greeks believe that gods affected people's health?

Greek gods

The Greeks had many gods. They had a god of wisdom; a god of wine; even a god of laughing. They believed that gods caused events such as earthquakes or thunderstorms. If there was a rich harvest they said that the gods were pleased. If someone was a great soldier they said the gods favoured him. With all these gods it is no surprise therefore that they also had a god of healing. His name was Asclepius (which is also sometimes written as Asklepios).

1. Look at Source 1. Asclepius had two daughters. Which English words come from the names of his daughters?
2. Both these words have a medical meaning today. What do they mean?
3. Look at Source 2. The ASCLEPION at Epidaurus was surrounded by other buildings which were useful in health care. How might each part of the complex have helped to make a visiting patient healthier?
4. Why would an Asclepion be built in a quiet place?

SOURCE 1 A relief of Asclepius, the Greek god of healing. He was helped by his daughters, Panacea and Hygeia. People believed that if they went to sleep in the Asclepion at night, the god and his daughters would come to heal them

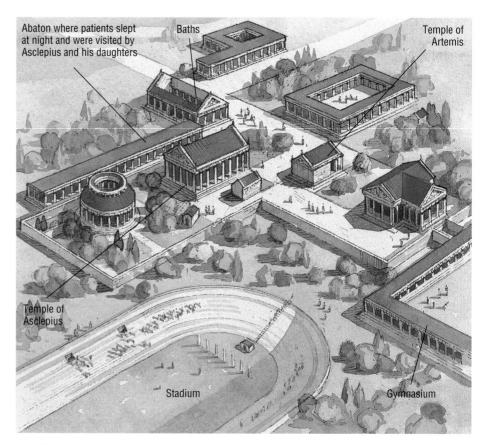

SOURCE 2 From about 600BC temples called Asclepeia (one temple is called an Asclepion) were built in quiet places. Some were very simple temples. This reconstruction drawing shows the Asclepion at Epidaurus. This was the most important Asclepion. It was built around 400BC

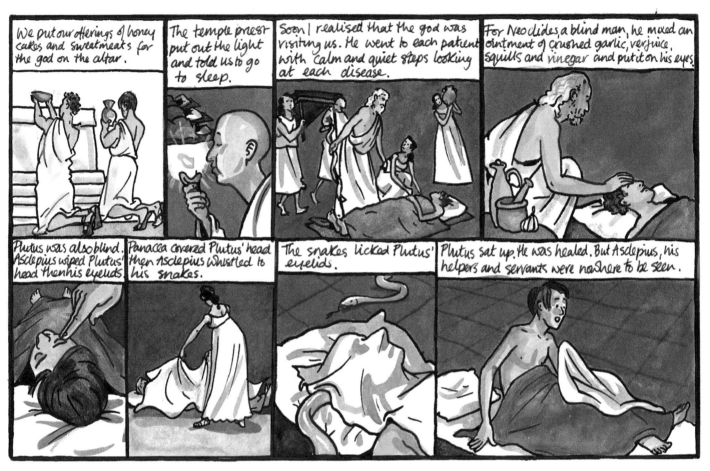

We put our offerings of honey cakes and sweetmeats for the god on the altar.

The temple priest put out the light and told us to go to sleep.

Soon I realised that the god was visiting us. He went to each patient with calm and quiet steps looking at each disease.

For Neoclides, a blind man, he mixed an ointment of crushed garlic, verjuice, squills and vinegar and put it on his eyes.

Plutus was also blind. Asclepius wiped Plutus' head then his eyelids.

Panacea covered Plutus' head then Asclepius whistled to his snakes.

The snakes licked Plutus' eyelids.

Plutus sat up. He was healed. But Asclepius, his helpers and servants were nowhere to be seen.

SOURCE 4 An inscription from the Asclepion at Epidaurus in Greece. Grateful visitors paid for and left inscriptions on stone columns at the temple. Four of these columns have been found during excavations

66 *A man with an ABSCESS within his abdomen. When asleep in the Temple [of Asclepius] he had a dream. It seemed to him that the god ordered the servants who accompanied him to grip him and hold him tightly so that he could cut open his abdomen. The man tried to get away, but they gripped him and bound him ... Asclepius cut his belly open, removed the abscess and, after having stitched him up again, released him from his bonds. Whereupon he walked out sound, but the floor ... was covered in blood.* 99

SOURCE 3 A visit to an Asclepion. The story is based on one told in a play by the Greek writer Aristophanes around 400BC. Aristophanes was a careful observer of people's attitudes and behaviour and he put a lot of realistic description into his plays

■ **ACTIVITY**

Many people who visited the Asclepion believed that the gods cured them. They went home excited, determined to tell their friends about the wonderful cure.

Your task is to write a letter about your healing at an Asclepion. Your friend is suffering from the same medical problem as you. Tell your friend the story of your visit, and how you were healed. Try to persuade him or her to go to an Asclepion to be cured.

You need to include:

■ a description of your medical problem
■ what the Asclepion is like
■ what happened at the temple
■ who you saw and how you were cured
■ what you did when you left.

Use Sources 1–4 to help you write your letter.

The Greeks' big idea – the theory of the four humours

THE HISTORY of medicine and health is full of surprises. The Greeks are one of them. Many Greeks sought Asclepius' help and believed that he had healed them. Yet at the same time as people were flocking to Asclepeia, other Greeks were gradually developing new theories about disease and treatment. Their ideas suggested that gods such as Asclepius had nothing at all to do with health or disease. They began to believe that diseases actually have natural causes. They claimed that people's belief in magic and the gods prevented effective medical treatment.

The theory of the four humours: the Greeks' big idea

Greek thinkers believed that the body contained four important liquids, which they called humours. They were:

- phlegm
- blood
- yellow bile
- black bile.

If these humours stayed in balance then a person would remain healthy, but if the humours became unbalanced (if there was too much of one humour and not enough of another) this could make a person ill (see Source 1).

It is important to understand this theory because:

- it was the basis for many Greek treatments
- doctors continued to believe in the theory of the four humours for well over 1000 years and so it affected the way people were treated throughout that time.

SOURCE 1 Hippocrates explains the Greek theory of the four humours

How did the Greeks find time for all this thinking?

Like the Egyptian empire, the Greek empire was rich. Its wealth came from farming and trade and from the hard work done by slaves and the poor. This allowed the wealthy classes to spend their time becoming educated and discussing new ideas. Trade also helped, bringing knowledge and methods from other civilisations.

Why did the Greeks develop the theory of the four humours?

The Greeks had enquiring minds. They did not just have ideas about medicine – they had theories about everything! Many Greeks went on believing in the old ideas about gods or spirits controlling everything, but a small number of Greeks were interested in finding more rational explanations. They wanted to understand how and why things worked. Greek thinkers investigated mathematics, geometry, science, astronomy, philosophy and politics, as well as medicine.

Observation

Greek thinkers and doctors tried to understand what caused disease through careful observation of people who were ill. They saw that when someone was ill there was usually a liquid coming out of the body, for example, phlegm from the nose or vomit from the stomach. They decided that these liquids (which they called humours) must somehow be the causes of illness. The liquid or humour must be coming out of the body because there was too much of it. The humours had got out of balance with each other.

Was it a step forward?

It is easy to laugh at ancient ideas about illness. Rotting food sending gases round the channels – mad! The body's humours are out of balance – ridiculous! Or is it? This idea led the Greeks to do everything in moderation – not eating too much; not exercising too much – and so it did help to make them more healthy.

The idea is important for another reason – in those far-off times people had started to search for the causes of illness, instead of simply saying, 'It's the gods. We must pray to them.'

While people still believed that natural events like disease were caused by gods or spirits they would never find the real causes. However, if they looked closely at what they saw, as the Greeks were doing (and as the Egyptians had done with their idea of blocked channels), and tried to explain it rationally and logically then eventually they might find the real causes.

The theory of the four humours was a far cry from blaming illness on evil spirits. Hippocrates, the most famous Greek doctor, who developed the theory of the four humours, told his students that all diseases could be treated without using any magic. He said that all they had to do was to discover the nature of each disease. Then they would be able to treat it. You can find out about the treatments they came up with on page 18.

1. How did wealth help to improve medical ideas?
2. What was a humour?
3. According to the theory of the humours, what made people sick?
4. Why was this theory a big step forward in medicine?
5. Why was this theory so important in the history of medicine?
6. Look at your answer to Question 3. How do you think a Greek doctor would try to cure someone who was sick?

A Big Idea that lasted a very long time!

Roman doctor *c.*AD200

We believed in the theory of the humours, too!

Medieval doctor *c.*1300

So did we!

Stuart doctor *c.*1650

And us – that Greek idea really lasted a long time!

How did Greek doctors prevent and treat illnesses?

Observation

Greek doctors were trained to diagnose illnesses carefully. They observed symptoms and recorded each stage of an illness. Sometimes they wrote up what doctors today would call a case-history of the patient.

SOURCE 1 A patient's case-history which is included in a book called *On Epidemics,* part of the Hippocratic Collection (see page 20)

66 Silenus began with pains in his abdomen, heavy head and stiff neck.

First day: he vomited, his urine was black, he was thirsty, his tongue dry and he did not sleep.

Second day: slightly delirious.

Sixth day: slight perspiration about the head, head and feet cold, no discharge from the bowels, no urine.

Eighth day: cold sweat all over, red rashes, severe DIARRHOEA.

Eleventh day: he died – breathing slow and heavy. He was aged about twenty. 99

1. Read Source 1. List which of the following techniques of observation the doctor probably used:
   - inspecting urine
   - inspecting FAECES
   - feeling temperature
   - listening to breathing
   - asking the patient questions.

2. Why would such a case-history be written down in a book?

Advice

Silenus, the patient in Source 1, may have died, but by their observation doctors knew that many diseases cleared up on their own without any help from a doctor. So a lot of the time they simply gave advice to patients on how their disease might develop (a PROGNOSIS). This was based on their knowledge of earlier patients whom they had treated with similar symptoms.

They also offered advice on avoiding illness altogether. They instructed their patients on what they should eat, on taking exercise, and on keeping clean.

Treatments

Once they had established how the patient's humours were unbalanced, the main task of Greek doctors was to try to help nature restore the proper balance – by making the patient vomit, PURGING their bowels, or BLEEDING them.

Doctors knew there were some illnesses they could not cure. In these cases they could see nothing wrong with a visit to an Asclepion – a miracle might happen!

3. The treatments and advice on preventing disease in Sources 2, 3 and 5 are based on the theory of the four humours. Explain how each one would help restore the balance of the humours.

SOURCE 2 From a book in the Hippocratic Collection, *On the Treatment of Acute Diseases,* 400–200BC

66 If the pain is under the diaphragm, clear the bowels with a medicine made from black hellebore, cumin or other fragrant herbs.

A bath will help PNEUMONIA as it soothes pain and brings up phlegm. 99

SOURCE 3 From *A Programme for Health,* one of the books in the Hippocratic Collection

66 In winter, people should eat as much as possible and drink as little as possible – unwatered wine, bread, roast meat and few vegetables. This will keep the body hot and dry. In summer they should drink more and eat less – watered wine, barley cakes and boiled meat so that the body will stay cold and moist. Walking should be fast in winter and slow in summer. 99

SOURCE 4 Adapted from a book by a Greek doctor, Diocles of Carystus, who lived in Athens c.390BC

66 After awakening he should not arise at once but should wait until the heaviness of sleep has gone. After arising he should rub the whole body with oil. Then he should wash face and eyes using pure water. He should rub his teeth inside and outside with the fingers using fine peppermint powder and cleaning the teeth of remnants of food. He should anoint nose and ears inside, preferably with well-perfumed oil. He should rub and anoint his head every day but wash it and comb it only at intervals. Long walks before meals clear out the body, prepare it for receiving food and give it more power for digesting. 99

SOURCE 5 A bleeding cup, used to draw blood from a patient. It was heated and placed over a scratch. The warmth drew blood to the surface of the skin and out through the scratch. Doctors used bleeding in the spring and summer when it was thought that people had too much blood because they often became hot and red

4. Read Source 4. List the ways in which this advice would help someone stay healthy.
5. Do you think that all Greeks would be able to follow the advice in Sources 3 and 4?
6. Are there any treatments on the opposite page that you know were practised in ancient Egypt?
7. Hippocrates and his followers used some methods that are still used today. What are they?

Surgery

From around 1200BC the use of iron and steel gave doctors stronger and sharper instruments. Greek surgeons developed good techniques for setting broken bones and also, in extreme cases, AMPUTATION (the cutting off of a leg or an arm). However, very few operations were done inside the body. One exception was the draining of the lungs – performed if a patient had pneumonia. This operation was frequently and successfully undertaken, thanks to doctors' careful observation of the symptoms and pattern of the illness.

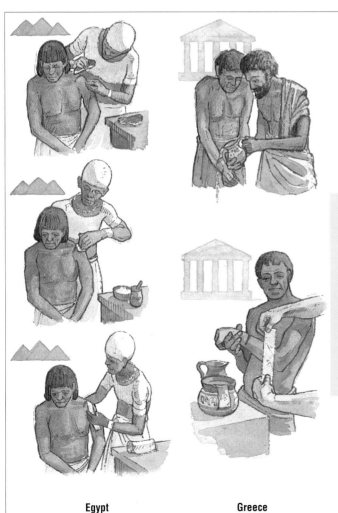

Egypt   Greece

SOURCE 6 An extract from the *Iliad*, Book 11, written by the Greek poet, Homer. The *Iliad* is the story of the Greek war against the Trojans

   'My lord,' replied the wounded man, ... 'I want you to cut out this arrow from my thigh, wash off the blood with warm water and spread soothing ointment on the wound. They say you have some excellent prescriptions... I cannot get help from our surgeons for one of them is lying wounded in our camp while the other is fighting the Trojans in the battle ... '

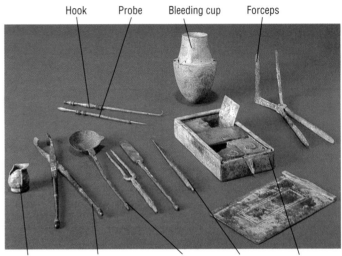

Hook   Probe   Bleeding cup   Forceps

Mixing container Small shears Measuring spoon Scalpel Medicine container

SOURCE 7 A set of Greek surgical instruments

SOURCE 8 Adapted from H. von Staden, *Herophilus, The Art of Medicine in Early Alexandria*, 1989

  The three most common 'non-magical' Egyptian techniques of wound care – putting a slab of fresh meat on a wound; applying a SALVE of honey and animal fat; applying adhesive linen tape – are not among the techniques that dominate Greek wound care.
  The Greeks instead washed the wound with wine or vinegar – a basic antiseptic procedure apparently ignored in Egypt. Sometimes they bandaged wounds with linen soaked in wine.

8. What technological improvement helped Greek surgeons?
9. Read Source 6. How might war have helped Greek doctors improve their skills and knowledge?
10. Read Source 8. What new treatment did the Greeks use which the Egyptians had not used?
11. Was this treatment likely to be successful?

Key individual: Hippocrates – the greatest doctor of them all?

IN THE LAST few pages you have read a good deal about Hippocrates. He is an important figure in the story of medicine and health. These two pages summarise some of the reasons why.

1. Which parts of Hippocrates' work and ideas helped to:
a) improve his patients' health
b) improve medical knowledge?
2. What was new about Hippocrates' work?
3. For all his skills, Hippocrates did not understand the true causes of diseases. Why not?
4. Why is Hippocrates important in the history of medicine?

The Hippocratic Oath
The HIPPOCRATIC OATH (see Source 1 below) is still used today. It makes clear that doctors are not magicians. They have to keep high standards of treatment and behaviour and work for the benefit of patients rather than to make themselves rich.

SOURCE 1 From the Hippocratic Oath, which was created by Hippocrates to give people confidence in doctors

66 *I will swear by Apollo, Asclepius and by all the gods that I will carry out this oath. I will use treatment to help the sick according to my ability and judgement but never with a view to injury or wrongdoing. I will not give poison to anybody … whatever I see or hear professionally or in my private life which ought not to be told I will keep secret.* 99

Why was Hippocrates important?

Books
The Hippocratic Collection contains books which doctors used for centuries. Hippocrates may not have written all of these books and historians simply cannot tell who did write them.

However, this collection is important because it is the first detailed list of symptoms and treatments. Doctors continued to use the theories of Hippocrates as the basis of their own work for hundreds of years.

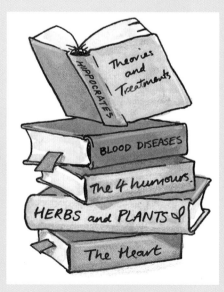

Observing and recording

Hippocrates showed how important it was to observe and record carefully the symptoms and development of diseases.

This had two advantages. Doctors were more likely to choose the right cure if they took care to find the cause of the problem. These notes could also be used to help with the diagnosis and treatment of future patients.

Causes of disease

Hippocrates developed the theory of humours to explain the causes of disease. We now know that this theory was wrong but it dominated medical treatments for many centuries.

Natural treatments

Hippocrates encouraged people to look for natural treatments for illnesses rather than going to the gods for help.

Was the Roman empire different from the Greek empire?

FROM AROUND 300BC the Greek empire was growing weaker. At the same time, the new Roman empire was steadily growing stronger. By AD120 Rome controlled most of the Mediterranean lands and western Europe (see Source 1 on page 6).

The Romans took over almost all the Greeks' old empire and, as you might expect, the two empires were very closely connected (see Source 1). These connections affected Roman medicine. However, there were also important differences between the two empires (see Source 2) which affected medicine, too.

In the next section you will investigate:

■ which ideas the Romans borrowed from the Greeks
■ why the power of the empire helped them develop their own new big idea.

1. Look at Source 1. Why might treatments and theories stay the same?
2. Look at Source 2. The Romans built huge PUBLIC HEALTH schemes. How do the features described here help to explain why they did this?

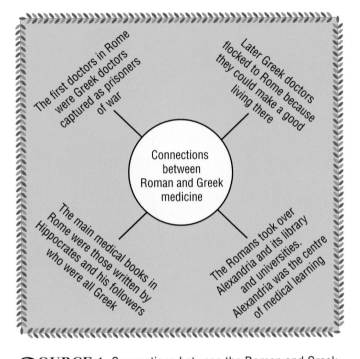

The first doctors in Rome were Greek doctors captured as prisoners of war

Later Greek doctors flocked to Rome because they could make a good living there

The main medical books in Rome were those written by Hippocrates and his followers who were all Greek

The Romans took over Alexandria and its library and universities. Alexandria was the centre of medical learning

Connections between Roman and Greek medicine

SOURCE 1 Connections between the Roman and Greek empires

Greek empire	Roman empire	
Mostly small cities – fewer than 20,000 people – which did not pose health problems.	Large cities – Rome itself had a million people. Many people living in cramped conditions posed health problems.	
Not very centralised. Each city was independent. Ideas spread slowly.	Very centralised with strong government. Quick communication around the empire. New ideas and treatments spread quickly. So too could diseases.	
Greek philosophers were famous for having ideas and theories about everything.	Romans were less interested in theories. They were efficient, well-organised people who liked practical solutions to illness as well as to everything else.	
Had only a small army for each city, which got together only when there was a war.	The Roman army had hundreds of thousands of soldiers, permanently stationed all over the empire. The army was frequently at war. The government provided the army with the best medical care as it depended on the army to control the empire.	
There were wealthy people who could afford to pay for doctors to care for them.	There were even more wealthy people than in the Greek empire.	

SOURCE 2 Contrasts between the Greek and Roman empires

A Roman army hospital

'Best amputate, whilst he has some strength.'

Historical novels can be a very good way of learning about the past, simply because reading novels doesn't feel like hard work. History can be fun! However, you only learn about the past if the story describes the real ideas, clothes or houses of that period. *The Silver Pigs* is a carefully researched novel. The author has worked hard to ensure that her historical detail is accurate. The extract in Source 1 is about medicine.

The story is set in AD70 and it is told by Marcus Didius Falco, a 'private informer' employed by the Emperor Vespasian to uncover details of a plot to smuggle silver from Britain to Rome. Falco goes to Britain ('the province out beyond civilization') but, working undercover as a slave in a silver mine, he breaks his leg and several ribs and has to be rescued …

1. Read Source 1. Describe the impression it gives of Roman surgery. You could use some of these words: skilful, hygienic, gentle, painful, dirty, brutal.
2. What actually happened to Falco?

■ TASK

1. a) Read Source 1. Make a list of all the phrases and sentences that refer to doctors.
   b) Look at Sources 2–8 on pages 24–25. If a source provides evidence to support a phrase or sentence in your list write the source number against it.
2. Do the same activity for:
a) medical methods and instruments
b) hospitals.

SOURCE 1 From *The Silver Pigs* by Lindsey Davis (reproduced with permission from Arrow Books)

66 I was lying on a high, hard bed in a small, square room at a legionary hospital. Unhurried footsteps sometimes paced the long corridor round the courtyard at the back of the administration block. I recognized the evil reek of ANTISEPTIC turpentine. I felt the reassuring pressure of neat, firm bandaging. I was warm. I was clean. I was resting in tranquillity in a quiet, caring place …

Their opium had ebbed away. When I moved pain shot back. A red tunic, brooched on one shoulder with the medical snake and staff, loomed over me, then sheered off again when I stared him in the eye. I recognized the complete absence of bedside manner: must be the chief (medical) orderly. Pupils stretched their necks behind him like awestruck ducklings jostling their mother duck.

'Tell me the truth, Hippocrates!' I jested. They never tell you the truth.

He tickled me up and down my ribs like a moneychanger on an abacus. I yelped, though not because his hands were cold.

'Still in discomfort – that will last several months. He can expect a great deal of pain. No real problems if he avoids getting pneumonia …' He sounded disappointed at the thought that I might. 'Emaciated specimen; he's vulnerable to GANGRENE in this leg.' My heart sank. 'Best amputate, whilst he has some strength.' I glared at him with a heartbreak that brightened him up. 'We can give him something!' he consoled his listeners. Did you know, the main part of a surgeon's training is how to ignore the screams? …

The surgeon was called Simplex … Simplex had spent fourteen years in the army. He could calm a sixteen-year-old soldier with an arrow shot into his head. He could seal blisters, dose DYSENTERY, bathe eyes, even deliver babies from the wives the legionaries were not supposed to have. He was bored with all that. I was his favourite patient now. Among his set of spatulas, scalpels, probes, shears, and forceps, he owned a shiny great mallet big enough to bash in fencing stakes. Its use in surgery was for amputations, driving home his chisel through soldiers' joints. He had the chisel and the saw too: a complete toolbag, all laid out on a table by my bed.

They drugged me, but not enough. Flavius Hilaris wished me luck, then slipped out of the room. I don't blame him. If I hadn't been strapped down to the bed with four six-foot set-faced cavalrymen grappling my shoulders and feet, I would have shot straight out after him …

'Stop it at once!' cried Helena Justina. I had no idea when she came in. I had not realized she was there. 'There's no gangrene!' stormed the senator's daughter. She seemed to lose her temper wherever she was. 'I would expect an army surgeon to know – gangrene has its own distinctive smell. Didius Falco's feet may be cheesy, but they're not that bad!' Wonderful woman; an informer in trouble could always count on her. 'He has chilblains. In Britain that's nothing to wonder at – all he needs for those is a hot turnip mash! Pull his leg as straight as you can, then leave him alone; the poor man has suffered enough!'

I passed out with relief. 99

3. Some references to medicine in Source 1 are not supported by Sources 2–8. Do you think that they are likely to be based on other sources? Explain your answer.
4. Is Source 1 an accurate description of medical treatments in Roman Britain? Explain your answer.
5. Do you think that historical novels are a better way of learning history than textbooks or lessons in school?

SOURCE 4 A tombstone found at Housesteads, one of the major forts on Hadrian's Wall. It reads 'To the spirits of the departed [and] to Anicius Ingenuus, medical orderly of the First Cohort of the Tungrians: he lived 25 years'

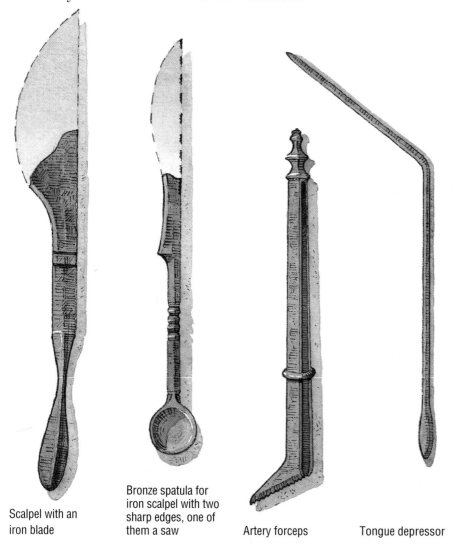

Scalpel with an iron blade

Bronze spatula for iron scalpel with two sharp edges, one of them a saw

Artery forceps

Tongue depressor

SOURCE 2 A Roman doctor's surgical instruments found in Britain. The dotted lines show reconstruction

SOURCE 3 Celsus, *De Medicina*, Book V. Celsus was a Roman doctor. These are instructions for making opium, a sedative used in surgery

66 *... take a good handful of wild poppy-heads when just ripe for collecting the juice and put into a vessel and boil with water sufficient to cover it. When this handful has been well boiled there, after being squeezed out it is thrown away; and with its juice is mixed an equal quantity of raisin wine and heated ... when the mixture has cooled, pills are formed ... they procure sleep.* 99

SOURCE 5 From *De Medicina*, Book VII, part of an encyclopaedia compiled by the Roman doctor Celsus in the first century AD.

66 *When gangrene has developed ... the limb ... must be amputated. But even that involves very great risk; for patients often die under the operation ... It does not matter, however, whether the remedy is safe enough, since it is the only one. Therefore between the sound and the diseased part, the flesh is cut through with a scalpel down to the bone, but this must not be done actually over a joint, and it is better that some of the sound part should be cut away than that any diseased part should be left behind ... the bone is then to be cut through with a small saw ...* 99

SOURCE 6 Celsus, *De Medicina,* Book VII, concerning the training of surgeons

" *... a surgeon should be youthful or at any rate nearer youth than age; with a strong and steady hand which never trembles, and ready to use the left hand as well as the right; with vision sharp and clear, and spirit undaunted; filled with pity, so that he wishes to cure the patient, yet is not moved by his cries, to go too fast, or cut less than is necessary; but he does everything just as if the cries of pain cause him no emotion.* "

SOURCE 7 Pliny the Elder, *Natural History,* Book XX, written in the first century AD

" *A hot application of [turnips] cures chilblains, besides preventing the feet from being chilled. A hot decoction of it is good even for gout, and raw turnip, pounded and mixed with salt, for every ailment of the feet.* "

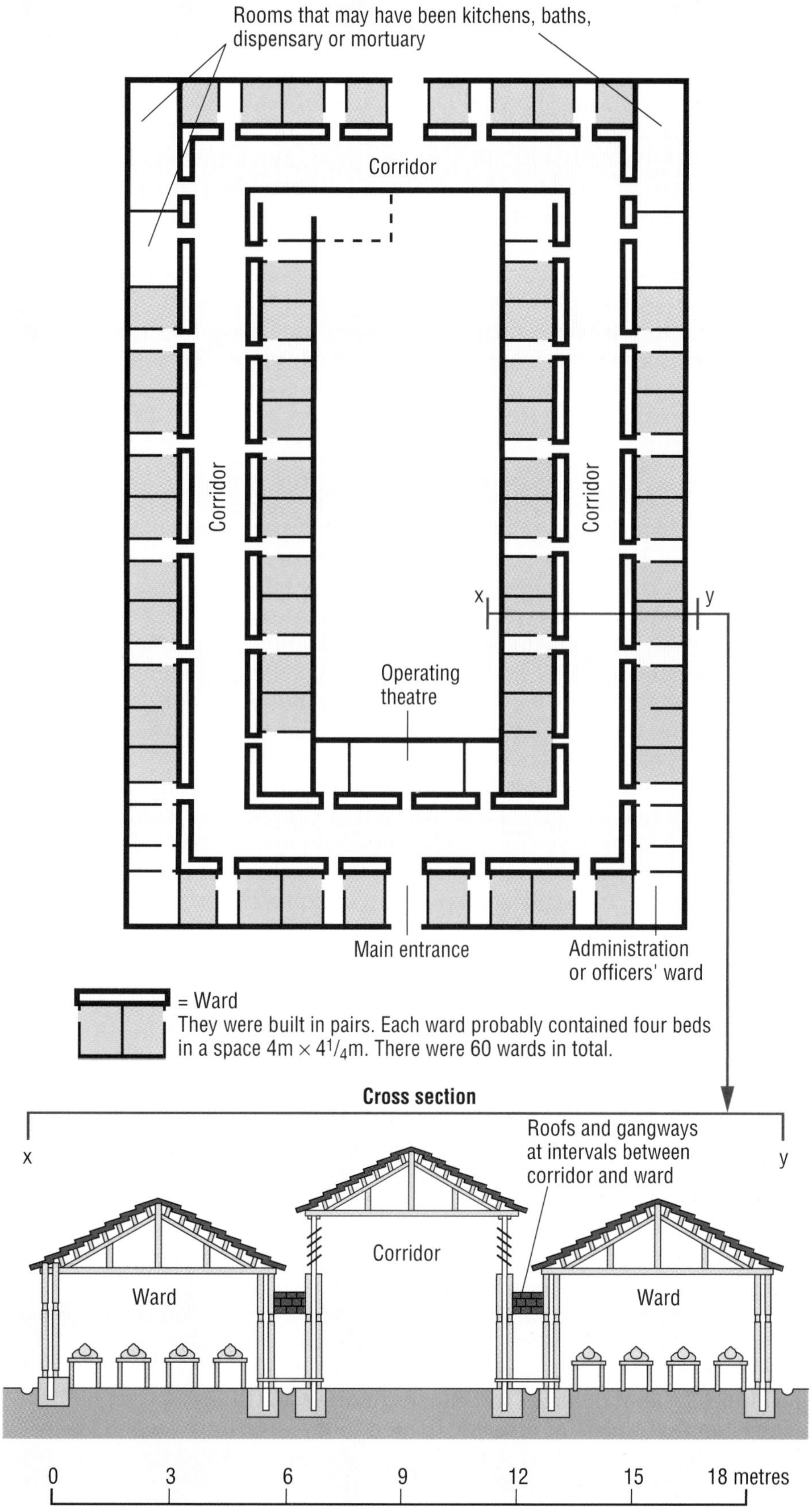

Rooms that may have been kitchens, baths, dispensary or mortuary

Corridor

Corridor

Corridor

Operating theatre

x ┤ ├ y

Main entrance

Administration or officers' ward

= Ward
They were built in pairs. Each ward probably contained four beds in a space 4m × 4¼m. There were 60 wards in total.

Cross section

Roofs and gangways at intervals between corridor and ward

x

y

Corridor

Ward

Ward

0   3   6   9   12   15   18 metres

SOURCE 8 A plan of the hospital at the Roman fort of Inchtuthil, Perthshire, which was excavated in the 1950s. There were separate roofs over the outer row of wards, the corridor and the inner wards

How did the Romans try to cure the sick?

The gods

In 295BC the people of Rome were in grave danger – from PLAGUE. Normally illnesses were treated within the family, using remedies passed down from parents and grandparents. While some Romans tried these age-old remedies, based on herbs and vegetables, others appealed to their gods, chiefly Salus, the goddess of health. The gods did not hear them. In desperation, the Romans turned to an outsider – they built a temple dedicated to Asclepius, the Greek god of healing. The plague ebbed away.

Few Romans were surprised by the power of Asclepius. Gods were part of their everyday life and were expected to be powerful. When medical treatment was costly, risky, uncertain or painful, there was good reason to use every means available to help protect against illness. Asking for the help of the gods would often have been a first, not a last resort.

Treatments

Like the Greeks, Roman doctors used three main methods of helping their patients. They recommended more exercise, changes in diet or prescribed herbal medicines as 'opposites' (see page 28).

Most Romans agreed with Hippocrates that people should take daily exercise to stay fit. Many took exercise with trainers at public baths or the gymnasium. Celsus wrote: 'He who has been engaged in the day, whether in domestic or on public affairs, ought to keep some portion of the day for the care of the body. The primary care … is exercise, which … ought to come to an end with sweating.'

Roman families used herbs and vegetables in medical treatments. Roman doctors used opium as a weak ANAESTHETIC. Turpentine and pitch were used as antiseptics. Around AD64 Dioscorides, a former army doctor, wrote a huge book listing 600 herbal remedies. Modern doctors have calculated that 20 per cent of these remedies would have been effective. There were also many like the one in Source 2 that were less useful!

Theories about disease

The most common surgical treatment was bleeding. Roman surgical instruments, as you can see from Source 2 on page 24, were very similar to those of the Greeks. Internal operations were still rare because they were so risky without effective antiseptics, anaesthetics or more detailed anatomical knowledge. However, there were amputations; TREPHINING was used to relieve pain in the head, and cataracts were removed from eyes using fine needles. The greatest danger in eye operations came from the patient moving.

Despite the influence and ideas of Greek doctors in Rome, there was a major difference between the two empires in their attitude to medicine. The Romans were not as interested as the Greeks in developing theories about the causes of disease. Galen (see page 27) suggested that 'seeds of disease' floated in the air. However, he knew that this idea did not help cure illnesses and so he spent little time on it, preferring to collect more practical knowledge.

SOURCE 1 Drawing of a Roman altar found at Chester. It is dedicated to Asclepius and shows his snake winding round surgical instruments

SOURCE 2 A remedy recorded by Pliny the Elder

❝ The best of all safeguards against serpents is the saliva of a fasting human being, but our daily experience may teach us yet other values of its use. We spit on epileptics in a fit, that is, we throw back infection. In a similar way we ward off WITCHCRAFT and the bad luck that follows meeting a person lame in the right leg. ❞

■ TASK

1. Why did Romans ask the gods for help in curing the sick?
2. List three ways in which Roman treatments were similar to Greek treatments.
3. 'The Greeks and Romans were equally interested in discovering the causes of disease.' Explain why you agree or disagree with this statement.

Key individual: Galen – what made him famous?

THE PIG SQUIRMED on the table. Galen cut into its neck and found the nerves. The pig squealed. 'Watch,' said Galen to his audience, 'I will cut this nerve but the pig will keep on squealing.'

He cut. The pig kept squealing. Galen cut another nerve. Again the pig squealed.

'Now,' said Galen, 'I will cut another nerve which controls the pig's voice. It will not squeal.'

Galen cut the nerve. The room was silent.

Galen had just arrived in Rome. He wanted to win fame and fortune. His public experiments were his way of attracting the attention of other doctors. In this experiment Galen proved that the brain controlled the body, not the heart.

Where did Galen come from?

Galen was born in AD129 in Greece. He began studying medicine at the age of sixteen and spent twelve years travelling to improve his knowledge, including a visit to the famous medical school at Alexandria in Egypt.

He gained practical experience as a surgeon at a gladiators' school. Gladiators were trained to fight with other gladiators and with wild animals in amphitheatres around the Roman empire. They suffered stab wounds, broken bones, and other major injuries, yet they were usually very healthy and fit young men. The school was an ideal place for a young ambitious surgeon to learn his craft.

In AD162 he travelled to Rome. He soon became famous as doctor to the Roman emperor and as a teacher of other doctors.

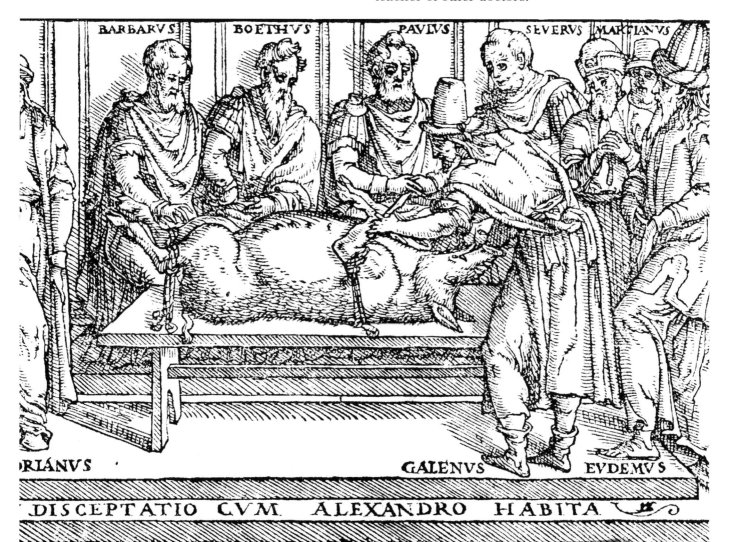

SOURCE 1 A medieval illustration showing Galen's famous experiment

What were Galen's ideas and methods?

Observation

Galen emphasised the importance of Hippocrates' methods. He told doctors to observe, record and use their experience of past cases to decide how to treat an illness.

The four humours

Like Hippocrates, Galen believed in the theory of the four humours and that treatments should restore the balance of the humours. However, Galen did not just copy Hippocrates.

Galen believed in using 'opposites' to balance the humours. If the symptom was too much phlegm then the patient's problem was caused by cold. Galen recommended an opposite treatment – a hot treatment such as taking pepper.

Galen also followed Greek ideas in telling people who were weak to take physical exercise.

Dissection

Galen dissected human bodies in Alexandria to increase his knowledge of the body. In Rome, however, he usually had to make do with animals for his experiments. This meant that some of the detail of his work was wrong. However, much of it was very precise. He proved that the brain, not the heart, controlled speech and that ARTERIES as well as veins carried blood.

Although he used animals for dissection, he proved that animals' anatomy is different from that of humans, and he told his students that they should dissect human corpses whenever possible.

SOURCE 2 From Galen's *On Anatomy*, AD190

❝ *Human bones are the subject which you should first get to know. At Alexandria this is very easy, since the physicians in that country let their students inspect human bodies for themselves. Try to get to Alexandria. But if you can't manage this it is not impossible to get to see human bones. I have often had the chance to do this where tombs have been broken. Once I examined the skeleton of a robber lying on a mountain-side. If you don't have the luck to see anything like this, you can still dissect an ape. For this you should choose apes which most resemble men. In the apes which walk and run on two legs you will also find other parts as in man.* ❞

Writing
What really made Galen famous were the 60 books he wrote. They combined Greek ideas with what he had learned from his own work in Alexandria and Rome. He presented it all so convincingly that his books became the basis for medical teaching and learning for the next 1500 years. For most of that time nobody dared to say that Galen was wrong!

Careful observation

The four humours
• Hippocrates' ideas
• His own ideas about 'opposites'

Dissection and surgery
Knowledge of anatomy

Galen wrote 60 books on medicine. They were the main books used by medical students for over 1500 years

SOURCE 3 Galen's work

Design
Galen tried to show his students how different parts of the body all fitted together into a well-designed whole. This idea was particularly important in later centuries because the Christian Church saw that Galen's explanations of the body fitted in with the Christian belief that God created human beings.

■ ACTIVITY

Galen is applying for a job as the Roman emperor's doctor. Write a CV for him, using the information on pages 27–29.

What was the Romans' big idea?

Public health

Public health means action taken by governments to improve the health of their people.

Even though the Romans were not so interested in theories about the causes of illness, their practical skills produced the best public health schemes yet seen anywhere in the world. These did much to protect people against disease.

In the crowded city of Rome sewers were essential if the city was to be fit to live in. But the Romans didn't limit their schemes to Rome. Throughout the empire fresh water was supplied to major towns along aqueducts and brick conduits. Sewers were built to take away sewage from private houses and public toilets. Even small towns had public baths, open to anyone on payment of a quadrans, the smallest Roman coin. The baths helped rid people of fleas which spread disease. Public toilets were also built in towns. Up to twenty people could be seated at once around three sides of the room. Individual cubicles were rare. Other public health measures included rules about burying the dead, and preventing fires.

Engineers took great care over the siting of towns, forts and villas as Source 1 (below) makes clear.

SOURCE 1 Marcus Varro, writing in his book on country life

66 When building a house or farm especial care should be taken to place it at the foot of a wooded hill where it is exposed to health-giving winds. Care should be taken when there are swamps in the neighbourhood because certain tiny creatures which cannot be seen by the eyes breed there. These float through the air and enter the body through the mouth and nose and cause serious diseases. 99

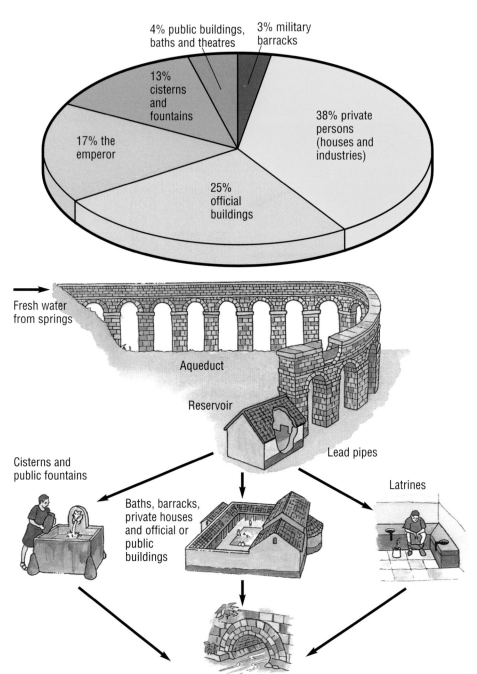

SOURCE 2 Water supply and sewage system in ancient Rome. People did not have equal access to clean water. Even in homes which had a water supply, the water could not reach the upper floors. The pie chart shows how the water supply was shared out

(Pie chart labels: 4% public buildings, baths and theatres; 3% military barracks; 13% cisterns and fountains; 17% the emperor; 38% private persons (houses and industries); 25% official buildings)

(Diagram labels: Fresh water from springs; Aqueduct; Reservoir; Lead pipes; Cisterns and public fountains; Baths, barracks, private houses and official or public buildings; Latrines; Sewers emptying into the River Tiber)

■ ACTIVITY

You have been asked to write a leaflet promoting the Romans' public health schemes. It should summarise the main measures taken, the reasons for them, and the effects they have had.

Use evidence from Sources 1–5 to draw up your leaflet.

In Rome water commissioners were appointed to ensure good supplies of clean water. One of them, Sextus Julius Frontinus (who held the post in AD97), wrote of the improved health of the city:

SOURCE 3

66 ... as a result of the increase in the number of works, reservoirs, fountains, and water-basins ... the air is purer; and the causes of the unwholesome atmosphere, which gave the air of the City so bad a name ... are now removed ... With such an array of indispensable structures carrying so many waters, compare, if you will, the idle Pyramids or the useless, though famous, works of the Greeks. 99

Frontinus exaggerated. Toilets were still built in kitchens, and sewage pits dug near wells. There was also no clear understanding of how dirt caused disease. However, the improvements did help, especially in the Roman army.

To help the legionaries stay fit, each fort had a bath house with drains and fresh water and also a hospital carefully sited in the quietest part of the camp. The military writer, Vegetius, added:

SOURCE 4

66 Soldiers must not remain for too long near unhealthy marshes. A soldier who must face the cold without proper clothing is not in a state to have good health or to march. He must not drink swamp water. 99

SOURCE 5   K. Branigan, *Roman Britain: Life in an Imperial Province*, 1980

66 **The baths**
In Britain, in towns like Chichester, Leicester and Wroxeter in Shropshire, probably as many as 500 people a day used the [public baths], even if they only visited them once a week. One of the finest suites of public baths in Britain was at Wroxeter, which also included an outdoor swimming pool and a massive exercise hall.
Water supply
... Water in most large towns in Britain was supplied by aqueduct – contoured channels dug in the ground and perhaps lined with clay. The most impressive surviving example is the one running into Dorchester; an eight-mile [13km] channel, 5 ft [1.6m] wide and more than 3 ft [1m] deep.

The aqueduct at Wroxeter could deliver two million gallons of water each day, distributed through the town by a complex system of timber and lead pipes. Mains ran along the principal streets to side channels from which sluices diverted the water into individual buildings.

If, during a drought, the level of water in the mains dropped below 7 in. [18cm], then the supply to private houses was automatically cut off. Householders often supplemented their needs with wells, lined with stone or with old topless and bottomless barrels.
Drains and sewers
Timber-lined drains were constructed in many towns, and substantial stone-built sewers have been found beneath the streets of Roman Colchester and York...

Main sewers collected water from the public baths, and recycled it to flush the latrines. These were usually built within the bath-house, though at Wroxeter a very large public latrine next to the baths was flushed by water that had already coursed through another lavatory in the market hall. The original source was rainwater collected from the roof of the market... 99

■ TASK

1. Make a list of the public health schemes which protected people against disease.
2. How did public health schemes help the army?
3. Read Source 3. Why did the Romans feel superior to the Greeks?
4. Look at factors a)–e) below. How does each of these factors help to explain why the Romans had such good public health schemes?
a) The Romans had a large, unpaid workforce – **slaves**.
b) Rome had a very large and **wealthy empire**. Tax collecting was efficient.
c) The emperors knew that a **healthy, fit army** was vital for keeping control of the empire.
d) The army and government officials kept close **control** over towns throughout the empire.
e) The government made **improving public health a priority**. It made sure there was enough money to spend on public health and organised schemes right across the empire.

Will you survive in ancient Rome?

THIS IS A game – but a game with a purpose. By playing it you can revise or learn about some of the main features of Roman medicine.

Your objective is to survive by finding a cure for your illness! This is how you play.

1. Get into pairs. You will each need a counter – a rubber or a coin will do as long as it is different from your opponent's.
2. Choose one of the **people** from Box A, one of the **ailments** from Box B and one of the **healers** from Box C.
3. On the board opposite start by putting your counter on the number your healer instruction tells you to.
4. Take turns following the instructions in your square. At each turn note down the square, treatment and result.
5. If you die (or recover) before your partner, try the game again either as a different person, or using a different healer.

Good luck!

Box A: People

Marcus Decimus, a wealthy Roman senator, and his wife Helena Rubina.

Julius Camillus and Silvia Priscilla, shopkeepers.

Gaius Fabius and Julia Claudia, who scratch a living as best they can. When they are ill they cannot afford to stop working to rest.

Box B: Ailments

1. You have a sharp headache that has lasted for several days. It is stopping you sleeping.
2. You have been vomiting all day and you cannot eat without being sick again.
3. You have a pain in your side that hurts more as you walk. In fact, you can hardly stand because of the pain. It has lasted for a couple of days.

Box C: Healers

The temple of Asclepius.

If you choose this option start at square 11.

Trebonius, a well-qualified and wealthy doctor. You will need to pay him a high fee. If you choose this option start at square 9.

Brutus, a retired legionary doctor. He is now the town doctor and will treat you without charging a fee. If you choose this option start at square 13.

Buying a potion from a local shop. If you choose this option start at square 21.

You could simply stay at home to be treated by your own family. If you choose this option go to square 19.

1

The remedy contains opium and eases the pain. You feel more relaxed lying down at home. Go to 16.

2

If you have a headache, the purging makes you feel weaker. Go to 24. If you have a pain in your side or you are vomiting, the purging makes you feel worse. Go to 22.

3

You wake up feeling better. The vomiting has stopped. Your stomach feels more settled. Go to 16.

4

Trephining. The doctor drills carefully into your skull. Was this a good idea? Toss a coin. Heads go to 12. Tails go to 23.

5

The visit to the temple has relaxed you, but you need more rest. If you can afford time off work, then go for a walk, get some fresh air and go to 16. If not, choose another healer so that you can get back to work and earn some money quickly.

6

If you are vomiting, the doctor offers you a herbal remedy. If you take it, go to 10. If not, go to 17. For a side-pain the doctor recommends rest and then exercise. If you agree, go to 14. If not, go to 17. For a headache the doctor suggests trephining. If you agree, go to 4. If not, go to 17.

7

Sadly you have just died.

8

You wake up feeling even worse. Your arm is swollen where the blood was taken and you feel feverish. You feel sicker and sicker. Go to 7.

9

You can only see this doctor if you are the senator or his wife. If you are, go to 6. If you are not, choose another healer.

10

Herbal remedy. If you have a side-pain the remedy has no effect. Go to 17. If you are vomiting, take the remedy, then go home and fall asleep. Go to 3.

11

At the temple you get a good night's rest. You feel better but a few hours later the problem returns. If you have a headache, go to 5. If you are vomiting or have a side-pain, go to 17.

12

The trephining seems to have worked. You feel better and the small hole gradually heals. Go to 16.

13

For a headache the doctor suggests trephining. If you agree, go to 4. If you do not, go to 17. For vomiting the doctor suggests bleeding or purging. If you decide on bleeding, go to 18. If purging, go to 2. If neither go to 17. For a side-pain the doctor suggests a herbal remedy. If you agree, go to 10. If not, go to 17.

14

Rest, fresh air, exercise and a better diet. If you have a headache, you feel better after a few days. Go to 16. If you have a side-pain the treatment does not help. Go to 17.

15

This quack remedy has weakened your body and made the problem worse. Go to 7.

16

The symptoms have disappeared and you have recovered.

17

Either you do not like the treatment or the cure you chose has not worked. Choose again.

18

Bleeding. This makes you feel weaker. Go home and sleep. Toss a coin. Heads go to 20. Tails go to 8.

19

At home you take a herbal remedy that your family has used for years. It contains honey, rhubarb and lots of other ingredients. Then lie down to sleep. If you have a headache, go to 1. If you are vomiting, go to 3. If you have a side-pain, go to 22.

20

You wake feeling better. Perhaps rest was all that was needed. Go to 16.

21

At the shop you buy Plautus' Remedy for All Ailments. Sounds good! It will certainly purge your bowels. Go to 2.

22

This wasn't the right treatment. It might have worked for another illness, but you feel worse – and worse. Go to 15.

23

You feel better for a day but then a fever begins. Perhaps the instruments were not clean. Go to 7.

24

The purging has made you feel weaker but at least it hasn't made the headache worse. You're still alive. Go to 17.

Egyptian, Greek and Roman medicine – a summary

	EGYPT	**GREECE**	**ROME**
WHAT DID THEY KNOW ABOUT THE BODY?	They could identify some parts of the body but they did not understand what those parts did.	They could identify some parts of the body and had begun to understand some of its workings, e.g. that the brain controls the body.	They could identify some parts of the body and had begun to understand some of its workings, e.g. that the brain controls the body.
HOW DID THEY TREAT AND PREVENT ILLNESS?	Herbal remedies Simple surgery Charms and spells Personal hygiene	Careful observation Herbal remedies Charms and spells Rest, diet and exercise Personal hygiene Bleeding	Careful observation Herbal remedies Charms and spells Rest, diet and exercise Personal hygiene Bleeding Theory of opposites Public health schemes
WHAT DID THEY THINK CAUSED DISEASE?	Gods Food rotting in the channels of the body	Gods The humours in the body getting out of balance	Gods The humours in the body getting out of balance
HOW HEALTHY WERE PEOPLE?	In all three societies, the wealthy probably lived longer than the poor because they ate more and lived in cleaner conditions. This meant, for example, that women in wealthier families were likely to have stronger babies who were less vulnerable to infection. Egyptians, Greeks and Romans had similar life expectancy.		

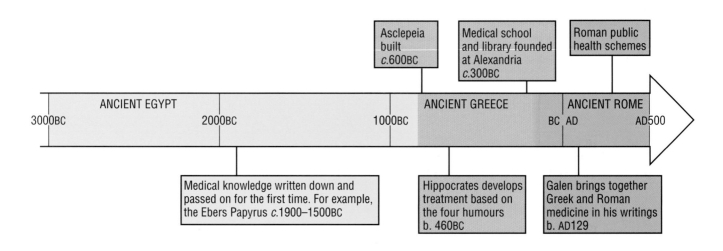

■ TASK 1

1. Which of the developments shown in the timeline was the most important in improving medicine and health? Explain the reasons for your answer.

2. Explain which of these statements you most agree with:
   a) There were very few changes in medical treatments and ideas in this period.
   b) There were a few important changes in medical treatments and ideas, but they mostly stayed the same.
   c) There were many important changes in medical treatments and ideas in this period.

■ TASK 2

FACTOR 1: WAR
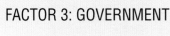

Source 6, page 19

Source 4, page 31

FACTOR 2: ATTITUDES AND BELIEFS
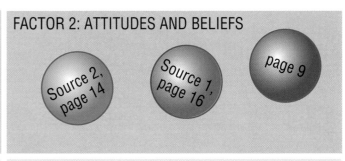

Source 2, page 14

Source 1, page 16

page 9

FACTOR 3: GOVERNMENT

Source 5, page 31

Source 2, page 30

FACTOR 4: TRADE AND COMMUNICATIONS

Source 3, page 9

Source 1, page 22

Source 2, page 13

Each of the squares above tells you about one factor which has affected the history of medicine. You just have to look up the page and references on the balls.

1. Look up each example and add it to your 'factor' list at the back of your exercise book.
2. For each example, explain whether this factor helped to change medical ideas and treatments or helped to keep them the same.

3. Of the four factors here, which factor do you think did most to change ideas and treatments?
4. Which factor did most to keep them the same?
5. Were other factors, such as technology or individuals, more or less important than these four in causing change?

■ TASK 3

Choose one of the following essay writing tasks:

a) Explain whether you agree or disagree with this statement: 'Women played a more important role than men in the early history of medicine.'
b) Did ancient healers and medicines help the sick?

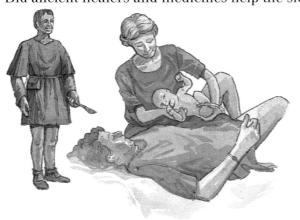

THE FOUR HUMOURS MUST BE KEPT IN BALANCE TO AVOID DISEASE

The health jigsaw: AD200

This is a picture of Galen. The drawing is trying to show how far healers had succeeded in solving the problem they have all struggled with – how to improve the health of their patients and to give them a longer life. The pieces show the ideas and skills that Galen and his contemporaries had available to finish the jigsaw.

1. Why can't Galen complete this jigsaw? Take each jigsaw piece in turn and explain why it was important to a Roman doctor.
2. Looking ahead, do you expect that a doctor 1000 years later will be able to do more of this jigsaw than Galen?

■ ACTIVITY

Galen and Hippocrates are two of the most influential people you have studied in this chapter.

Write an obituary for each of them explaining when they lived, what they did and why they are famous. Use the information on pages 20–21 and 27–29 to help you.

Did medicine grow worse after the Romans?

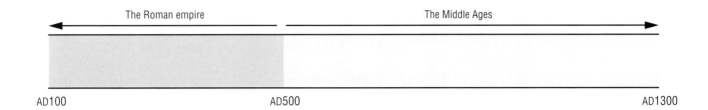

The Roman empire		The Middle Ages	
AD100	AD500		AD1300

THE LEGIONARIES WERE going home. All over Europe, centurions shouted orders and looked at maps. Legionaries packed their kits, said goodbye to their unofficial wives and families and began to march. Rome was in danger and the legions had been recalled to defend the city.

It was all in vain. In AD410 tribes called the Goths pillaged Rome and by AD500 the Roman empire in western Europe had disintegrated. In its place there was a mass of small kingdoms with ever-changing borders.

What has all this to do with medicine and health? Remember that the Roman army had played a very important part in spreading medical knowledge and providing practical skills. Now it was gone. In the largest towns there were collections of medical books filled with effective herbal remedies, advice on diet and fitness, and instructions on diagnosing and treating illnesses, but the tribes who followed the Romans could not read them.

The next six pages investigate what happened to medical ideas and knowledge after the collapse of the Roman empire. There are two case studies:

- How was medical knowledge recorded and transmitted to the Muslim world?
- Did the Roman public health system collapse?

Case study 1: How was medical knowledge recorded and transmitted to the Muslim world?

Alexandria: the centre of all medical knowledge

One of the most famous Greek doctors was Herophilus who lived around 250BC. His most important discovery, thanks to his careful dissections, was that the brain controls the body. Herophilus was successful partly because of his hard work and his genius. However, another reason was that he was working in Alexandria. Alexandria had become a centre of medical knowledge after the Greeks built a university and library there. The library collected together writings not only from Greek medical writers such as Hippocrates, but also from doctors in India, China, Egypt and Mesopotamia. It was said that the library eventually contained 700,000 different items.

Herophilus was not the only great doctor working in Alexandria. Another was Erasistratus, who almost made an even greater discovery. Erasistratus was busy dissecting a heart when he noticed it had four one-way valves. Why? What did this mean? He made the link to a new invention – the pump. Perhaps the heart was a kind of pump?

Erasistratus was one of the few Greeks who did not believe in the theory of the four humours. His views must have been unpopular among doctors, and no one took up his idea about the working of the heart. It was to be another 1800 years before he was finally proved to be correct – that the heart was indeed a pump, sending blood around the body (see pages 62–63).

The influence of Alexandria

Alexandria was the centre of medical ideas and knowledge. Eager medical students from around the Mediterranean travelled to Alexandria to learn. One was a young man called Galen who became the most famous doctor in the Roman empire. However, Alexandria became even more important after the end of the Roman empire.

While western Europe collapsed into disorder, a new civilisation based on the Islamic faith was growing in the Middle East. Islamic scholars picked up and developed the ideas of the ancient Greeks, whom they greatly admired. Many of the books they read came from the great library in Alexandria, which was now part of the Muslim world. Alexandria thus played a vital part in:

■ the recording of medical theories and treatments
■ the spread of those theories and treatments around the Mediterranean region and beyond.

Egypt was conquered by the Greeks in the fourth century BC.
The Greek leader, Alexander the Great, founded the city of Alexandria in 331BC.
Medical writings were brought to the library from India, China, Mesopotamia, Egypt and Greece.

SOURCE 1 The flow of medical knowledge into Alexandria. The library continued to attract medical students until it was burned down in AD391

Why did Arab medicine become famous in the Middle Ages?

The Koran, the holiest book of Islam which contains the words of Muhammad, tells Muslims that taking care of the sick and needy is a vital part of the Muslim faith. This helps to explain why large hospitals were built in Baghdad, Cairo and other cities. Muslims also admired educated people. Arab noblemen had large libraries at a time when very few English or French knights could read. This interest in learning led Arab scholars to collect and study manuscripts containing the work of Hippocrates, Galen and other classical medical writers. These books were translated into Arabic and were read by medical students.

The result of these developments was that Arab doctors were very knowledgeable.

Ibn Sinna (980–1037) was a Muslim who lived in Spain. He wrote a million-word textbook covering all aspects of medicine. In Europe he was known as Avicenna. Other Arab doctors also made important discoveries. Rhazes (852–925) wrote the first accurate descriptions of measles and smallpox. Ibn Nafis dared to disagree with Galen about how blood flows around the body.

However, in other ways Islam did not encourage new developments. Islamic law forbade the dissection of human bodies. Muslims also believed that the Koran contained all important knowledge so there was no point in trying to make new discoveries. Their attitude to the Koran also meant that they were unwilling to criticise other ancient books, such as the writings of Galen. Many influential Arab doctors believed that understanding theory was more important than practical experience. Even great doctors like Rhazes and Avicenna thought that doctors should not dabble in surgery.

1. Why was Alexandria important in medicine during the Greek and Roman empires?
2. Identify one important discovery made in Alexandria.
3. How did Muslim doctors learn about Greek and Roman medical ideas?
4. How did the Koran both help and hinder the development of medicine?

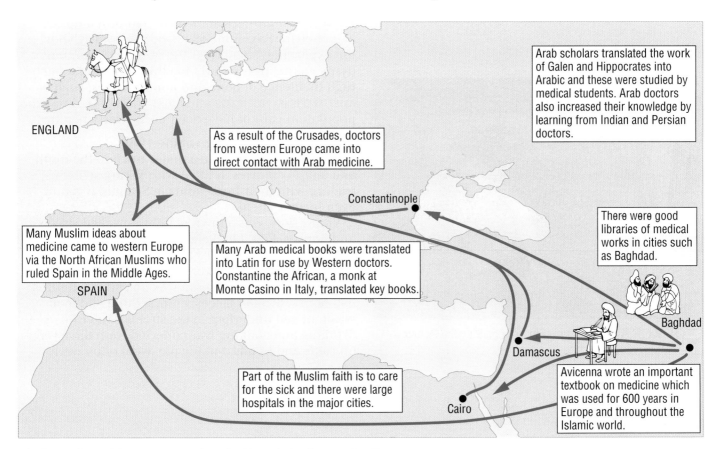

Arab scholars translated the work of Galen and Hippocrates into Arabic and these were studied by medical students. Arab doctors also increased their knowledge by learning from Indian and Persian doctors.

As a result of the Crusades, doctors from western Europe came into direct contact with Arab medicine.

Many Muslim ideas about medicine came to western Europe via the North African Muslims who ruled Spain in the Middle Ages.

Many Arab medical books were translated into Latin for use by Western doctors. Constantine the African, a monk at Monte Casino in Italy, translated key books.

There were good libraries of medical works in cities such as Baghdad.

Part of the Muslim faith is to care for the sick and there were large hospitals in the major cities.

Avicenna wrote an important textbook on medicine which was used for 600 years in Europe and throughout the Islamic world.

ENGLAND · Constantinople · SPAIN · Damascus · Baghdad · Cairo

SOURCE 2 The movement of medical knowledge from and to Europe

Case study 2: Did the Roman public health system collapse?

THE ROMANS HAD an excellent public health system, even in the furthest regions of their empire. What happened to this public health system after the end of the Roman empire? Here you can find out, using evidence from the city of York in northern England.

Roman York – Eboracum

Roman York was a legionary headquarters. The soldiers had a bath house and latrines flushed by sewers. Fresh water was brought to York by an aqueduct and lead pipes carried it to individual buildings. The civilian population also lived in stone buildings which were heated, drained by sewers and supplied with water from wells and pipes. Skeletons from this period show no evidence of rickets or other diseases caused by poor diets. The Roman citizens of York were well supplied with wheat, beef and other foods including imported figs, olives and grapes. Despite this, many of them still died at an early age because it was impossible to protect people, especially the newborn and young, from infectious diseases.

SOURCE 3 A stone sewer in York built by the Romans

Saxon York – Eoforwic: AD400–800

Most of York was probably abandoned after the Roman legions left, although the stone buildings stood for centuries as reminders of the Roman past. Then in the 600s York gradually grew once more, becoming an important centre for the Church. The middle of the city became densely populated but, within a few hundred metres, there was rough grassland and patches of woodland.

One of York's most famous citizens was Alcuin, a scholar renowned throughout Europe. Alcuin lived from around 732 to 804 and spent nearly all his life in York. He wrote the description of the city in Source 4.

> **S**OURCE 4 Alcuin's description of York
>
> 66 *The city is watered by the fish-rich Ouse*
> *Which flows past flowery plains on every side;*
> *And hills and forests beautify the earth*
> *And make a lovely dwelling-place, whose health*
> *And richness soon will fill it full of men ...* 99

Pleasant though this sounds, the living conditions in York at this time were not healthy. M.L. Cameron, author of *Anglo-Saxon Medicine*, summed up the evidence for Saxon life as revealing 'a fairly short life expectancy, a high INFANT MORTALITY, women dying young, particularly in childbirth, and a fairly high incidence of bone and joint diseases, such as RHEUMATISM, ARTHRITIS and RICKETS. The Anglo-Saxon population cannot have been particularly healthy.'

Viking York – Jorvik: AD800–1066

York once again became a major town in the ninth and tenth centuries. It filled with Viking settlers, trading with their homelands in Scandinavia and even further afield.

Viking York was a town of tightly-packed streets and houses. Pigs, chickens and other animals roamed freely. As the city grew, rubbish and dung were at first put in wicker-lined pits, but the city grew so fast that soon there was no control. Rotting fish bones, human faeces, animal dung and food waste mixed underfoot in the streets. Water for drinking and cooking was collected from the river, on roofs and in pits, but the pits were often next to CESSPITS.

SOURCE 5
A reconstruction of an Anglo-Saxon house, based on archaeological evidence. Most dwellings were small, dark, dank and smoky. They had just one room and were also draughty

Water was collected from a nearby stream or well

Waste matter was taken away from the house to a cesspit

Rats, mice and flies infested the town; hawks, falcons and ravens scavenged amongst the rubbish. One archaeologist has described York as 'a town composed of rotting wooden buildings, covered by decaying vegetation, surrounded by streets and yards filled by pits and middens [piles] of even fouler organic waste'.

Despite this the diet of many citizens was varied and nutritious. They ate plenty of fish, oysters and other shellfish, beef, chicken, cereals, fruits (including apples, plums, bilberries and raspberries) and vegetables. Unfortunately, most people also suffered from WORMS and other PARASITES, thanks to the way water was collected from pits dug near cesspits. Some of these worms may have measured 30 centimetres in length. In such conditions health did not improve and neither did life expectancy!

SOURCE 6 A sewer in York built during the Viking period

■ TASK

1. Draw a spider diagram recording the different parts of the public health system in Roman York.
2. Put a tick against the parts that still worked in Saxon and Viking York.
3. What evidence is there that people in Saxon and Viking York were less healthy than the people of Roman York?
4. The Roman public health system:
a) stayed the same
b) changed a little
c) collapsed
   under the Saxons and Vikings.
   Which of these do you think best describes what happened to the Roman public health system? Explain your answer.

Why did the Roman public health system collapse?

■ TASK

Now you know that the Roman public health system collapsed during the Saxon and Viking periods. The sewers and baths were still there but nobody used them. On this page you can see the differences between the two periods and opposite you can see the reasons why they were so different.

1. Explain in your own words why the Romans had an effective public health system.
2. Explain in your own words why the Saxons and Vikings did not have an effective public health system.
3. Which reason do you think is the most important in explaining why the Roman system collapsed?

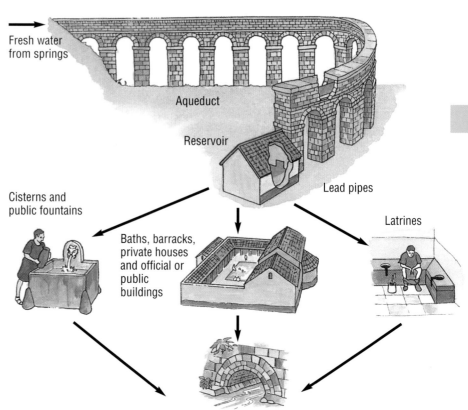

Fresh water from springs

Aqueduct

Reservoir

Lead pipes

Cisterns and public fountains

Baths, barracks, private houses and official or public buildings

Latrines

Sewers emptying into the River Tiber

SOURCE 7 The Roman public health system

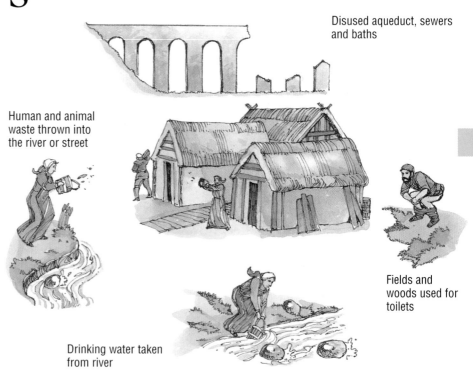

Disused aqueduct, sewers and baths

Human and animal waste thrown into the river or street

Fields and woods used for toilets

Drinking water taken from river

SOURCE 8 Public health under the Saxons and Vikings

Why did the Romans have an effective public health system?

SOURCE 9 Roman senators discuss the public health system

Why did the Saxons and Vikings NOT have an effective public health system?

SOURCE 10 Viking chieftains discuss their plans

MEDICINE AND HEALTH AD1350–1750

Did the Medical Renaissance improve people's health?

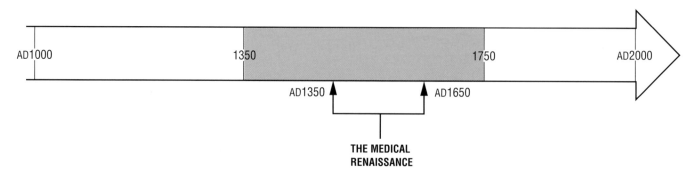

AD1000   1350   1750   AD2000

AD1350   AD1650

THE MEDICAL RENAISSANCE

LOOK AT THE cartoon. Ridiculous, isn't it? Important scientific discoveries were made and yet they did not affect the way people lived. Can this be true? Your task in this chapter is to investigate whether these discoveries did change the way doctors and healers treated their patients or whether the news vendor in the cartoon was right.

You are going to investigate a period known as the Medical Renaissance. Between 1500 and 1650 there were major breakthroughs in anatomy, PHYSIOLOGY (understanding how the body works) and surgery.

Read all about it! Great medical discoveries! Nobody healthier for centuries!

What was medicine like *c.*1350?
pages 45–56

The Medical Renaissance – what were the great discoveries?
pages 57–65

Had medical treatments and health changed by 1750?
pages 66–91

Medicine in the Middle Ages

■ TASK

Use this page to guide you through pages 46–53. Take each topic in turn and read the pages listed. Then complete the following task.

1. Decide whether each statement under each topic is *true* or *false*.
2. a) If it is *true*, explain which evidence proves it is true.
b) If it is *false*, explain which evidence proves it is false and then write a new statement that is true.
3. Make a list of the reasons why life expectancy was much lower in 1350 than it is today.

Disease and the causes of disease

Pages 46–49
a) In 1350 people had effective methods of preventing diseases from spreading.
b) People had many different ideas about the causes of disease but none of them was correct.
c) Doctors still followed the ideas of Galen and other Greek and Roman doctors.

Public health
Pages 50–51
a) Towns were clean and healthy.
b) Governments tried hard to keep towns like London clean and healthy.

Average life expectancy: 40

Treatments
Pages 52–53
a) Many cures were based on herbal remedies and some of them worked.
b) Doctors carried out simple surgery successfully.

NOW BEGIN YOUR STUDY OF MEDIEVAL MEDICINE BY INVESTIGATING THE BLACK DEATH!

The Black Death: a case study in medieval medicine

THE BLACK DEATH was the most terrifying event in the Middle Ages. It began in Asia but soon spread along the trade routes to Europe.

In the fourteenth century trade around Europe was increasing and ships regularly travelled from the Mediterranean to other parts of Europe. In 1348 one ship brought this devastating plague to England. Source 1 describes its arrival.

SOURCE 1 Written by a monk from Malmesbury in Wiltshire, in the 1350s

66 In 1348, at about the feast of the Translation of St Thomas the martyr [7 July] the cruel pestilence, hateful to all future ages, arrived from countries across the sea on the south coast of England at the port called Melcombe in Dorset. Travelling all over the south country it wretchedly killed innumerable people in Dorset, Devon and Somerset … Next it came to Bristol, where very few were left alive, and then travelled northwards, leaving not a city, a town, a village, or even, except rarely, a house, without killing most or all of the people there so that over England as a whole a fifth of the men, women and children were carried to burial. As a result, there was such a shortage of people that there were hardly enough living to look after the sick and bury the dead … 99

According to modern historians, Source 1 underestimates the effects of the BLACK DEATH. It is now estimated that over 40 per cent of the people in England died. Towns and ports were hardest hit. Villages and farms high in the hills were safest. Further outbreaks of plague came in 1361, 1369, 1374 and 1390. The Black Death killed the rich and poor alike, and it killed quickly and painfully.

We now know that the Black Death included two kinds of pestilence.

- **Bubonic plague** made people suddenly feel very cold and tired. Painful swellings (buboes) appeared in their armpits and groin and small blisters covered their bodies. This was followed by high fever and severe headaches. Many lingered unconscious for several days before death. This form of the Black Death was spread by fleas.
- **Pneumonic plague** attacked the victim's lungs, causing breathing problems. Victims began to cough up blood and died more rapidly than those who had bubonic plague. This form of Black Death was spread by people breathing or coughing germs onto one another.

SOURCE 2 King Death, an illustration in a French book of prayers

SOURCE 3 Black Death graves at Hereford cathedral, recently excavated. In many places new burial grounds were opened and in London, according to one chronicler, 'they dug broad, deep pits and buried the bodies together and, reducing everyone to the same level, threw them into the ground – treating everyone alike except the more eminent'

SOURCE 4 These words were scratched on a church wall in Ashwell, Hertfordshire: '1349 the pestilence. 1350, pitiless, wild, violent, the dregs of the people live to tell the tale.'

How did people react? Panic? Horror? Shock? Anger? Probably in all these ways and more. Most simply waited, hoping against hope that they and their families would survive. However, others took action.

The king and his bishops sent out orders for churchmen to lead processions, pleading with God to end the pestilence. Some people made candles their own height and lit them in church as an offering to God. In Barcelona the citizens tried to protect themselves by making a candle seven kilometres long – enough to encircle the city.

A Londoner called Robert Avesbury describes in Source 5 how a group of men called the Flagellants, responded.

SOURCE 5 The group Robert Avesbury is describing had recently come from Flanders, to London

66 *They went barefoot in procession twice a day in the sight of the people ... their bodies naked except for a linen cloth from loins to ankle. Each wore a hood painted with a red cross at front and back and carried in his right hand a whip with three thongs. Each thong had a knot in it, with something sharp, like a needle stuck through the middle of the knot ... and as they walked one after the other they struck themselves with these whips ... three times in each procession they would all prostrate themselves on the ground, with their arms outstretched in the shape of a cross.* 99

SOURCE 6 Advice written by John of Burgundy in 1365, on how to avoid the plague. His was one of the first books to be written about the plague

66 *First you should avoid too much eating and drinking and also avoid baths which open the pores, for the pores are the doorways through which poisonous air can enter the body.*
In cold or rainy weather you should light fires in your room, and in foggy or windy weather you should inhale perfumes every morning before leaving home.
If however the epidemic occurs during hot weather you must eat cold things rather than hot and also drink more than you eat. Be sparing with hot substances such as pepper, garlic, onions and everything else that generates excessive heat and use cucumbers, fennel and spinach. 99

SOURCE 7 Galen was the most famous doctor in ancient Rome (see page 27). He was born in AD129, over 1300 years before the Black Death appeared. Galen agreed with the Greek doctor Hippocrates about the causes of the disease. They believed that people became sick when the four humours (or liquids) in the body became unbalanced. Galen used the treatment of 'opposites'. That meant, for example, using hot treatments or medicines if the patient was cold.

1. Look at Source 3. Why did people bury Black Death victims in this way?
2. Read Source 5. Why do you think the Flagellants behaved as they did?

3. What evidence is there in Source 6 that John of Burgundy knew the works of Galen (Source 7)?
4. Do Sources 1–6 suggest that people understood what caused the plague or how it spread?

What did people think caused the Black Death?

■ ACTIVITY

Amidst the chaos and fear caused by the Black Death some people tried to explain why the pestilence had come.

The diagram on the right shows the most common medieval explanations for the Black Death. These explanations also appear in some of Sources 8–16.

1. Read through each source to decide if it matches one of the explanations in the diagram.
2. a) On your own copy of the diagram write the number of the source which matches each explanation.
   b) If the source adds anything further to the explanation summarise it by adding notes around the diagram.
3. Some of Sources 8–16 give additional explanations for the Black Death. On your own copy of the diagram, add drawings or notes to summarise them.
4. Use these notes to write your own account of the explanations of the Black Death. You should include the following details:

   ■ what the main explanations were
   ■ whether similar explanations were also used to explain disease in earlier times
   ■ whether any of the explanations were accurate (see page 46)
   ■ why people believed in these explanations if they were not accurate.

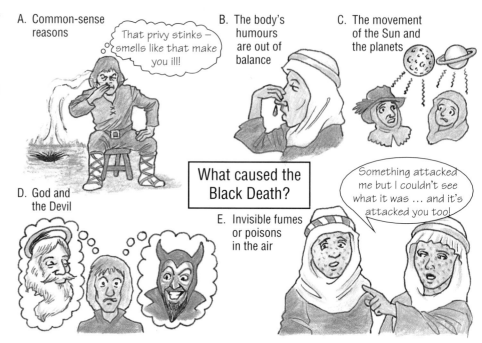

SOURCE 8 From an account by a fifteenth-century Swedish bishop, who based his studies on a work written in the 1360s by John Jacobus, a royal doctor and Chancellor of Montpellier University, which had a renowned school of medicine

66 *Sometimes [the pestilence] comes from … a privy [toilet] next to a chamber or any other particular thing which corrupts the air in substance and quality … sometimes it comes of dead carrion or the corruption of standing waters in ditches …* 99

SOURCE 9 Part of a letter from the Prior of the abbey of Christchurch, Canterbury, to the Bishop of London, 28 September 1348

66 *Terrible is God towards the sons of men … He often allows plagues, miserable famines, conflicts, wars and other forms of suffering to arise, and uses them to terrify and torment men and so drive out their sins. And thus, indeed, the realm of England, because of the growing pride and corruption of its subjects, and their numberless sins … is to be oppressed by the pestilences …* 99

SOURCE 10 From an account of the pestilence written by a French doctor in 1349

66 *This epidemic … kills almost instantly, as soon as the airy spirit leaving the eyes of the sick man has struck the eye of a healthy bystander looking at him, for then the poisonous nature passes from one eye to the other.* 99

SOURCE 11 From the writings of John of Burgundy, who wrote one of the earliest books about the Black Death in 1365

Many people have been killed, especially those stuffed full of evil humours. As Galen says in his book on fevers, the body does not become sick unless it already contains evil humours. The pestilential air does no harm to cleansed bodies from which evil humours have been purged.

SOURCE 12 Guy de Chauliac, one of the most famous doctors in the 1300s

... whatever the people said, the truth is that there were two causes, one general, one particular. The general cause was the close position of the three great planets, Saturn, Jupiter and Mars. This had taken place in 1345 on 24 March in the 14th degree of Aquarius. Such a coming together of planets is always a sign of wonderful, terrible or violent things to come. The particular cause of the disease in each person was the state of the body – bad digestion, weakness and blockage, and for this reason people died.

SOURCE 13 A German woodcut showing the burning of Jews in Germany. The Jews were blamed for the Black Death by some people. This is what one German friar wrote in 1348–49: 'Some say that it was brought about by the corruption of the air; others that the Jews planned to wipe out all the Christians with poison and had poisoned wells and springs everywhere. And many Jews confessed as much under torture ... men say that bags full of poison were found in many wells and springs ...'

SOURCE 14 From a chronicle written by a monk at Westminster

1344 ... the English have been madly following outlandish ways, changing their grotesque fashions of clothing yearly. They have abandoned the old, decent style of long, full garments for clothes which are short, tight, impractical, slashed, every part laced, strapped or buttoned up, with the sleeves of the gowns and the tippets of the hoods hanging down to absurd lengths, so that, if truth be told, their clothes and footwear make them look more like torturers, or even demons, than men ... The sin of pride must surely bring misfortune in the future.

SOURCE 15 From an account of the causes of the pestilence by an unknown German author, written *c.*1350–80

It is a matter of scientific fact that earthquakes are caused by the exhalation of fumes enclosed in the bowels of the earth ... I say that it is the vapour and corrupted air which has been vented ... in the earthquake on St Paul's day 1347 ... which has infected the air above the earth and killed people in various parts of the earth ...

SOURCE 16 Written by an unknown churchman in the early 1360s. The pestilence in 1361 had a severe impact on children and young people

If your father and mother come to want and mischief by age or misfortune you are bound to help them both with your body and help with your possessions ... And if they are dead you are obliged to pray night and day to God to deliver them from pain ... it is vengeance of this sin of dishonouring and despising fathers and mothers that God is slaying children by pestilence.

What did they do about public health in fourteenth-century London?

Descriptions

1. Butchers were put in the pillory for selling 'PUTRID, rotten, stinking and abominable meat'. The meat was burnt in front of them.
2. 1301 – four women butchers were caught throwing rotten blood and offal into the street.
3. 1343 – butchers were ordered to use a segregated area for butchering animals.
4. Wide streets had two gutters, one at each side. Narrow streets had one gutter in the middle.
5. By the 1370s there were at least twelve teams of rakers with horses and carts, removing dung from the streets.
6. In 1345 the fine for throwing litter in the street was increased to two shillings. In 1372 anyone who had filth outside their house could be fined four shillings. Anyone throwing water from a window was fined two shillings.
7. There were open sewers carrying refuse to the river.
8. By the 1380s there were at least thirteen common privies (public conveniences) in the city. One on Temple Bridge was built over the Thames.
9. Houseowners living next to streams built latrines over the streams.
10. Houses away from streams sometimes had their own latrines. In 1391 a latrine built in a house cost £4. The mason dug the pit, and used stone, tiles and cement to line it.
11. Butchers carried waste through the streets, loaded it onto boats and threw it into the middle of the river at ebb tide.
12. Wells for fetching water and cesspools for dumping sewage were often close together. Regulations said that cesspools had to be built two and a half feet (76 centimetres) from a neighbour's soil if walled with stone, three and a half feet (106 centimetres) if walled with earth.
13. 1364 – Two women were arrested for throwing rubbish in the street.
14. 1307 – Thomas Scott was fined for assaulting two citizens who complained when he urinated in a lane instead of using the common privy.

1. What evidence is there here of governments taking measures to make London healthier?
2. What evidence is there of ordinary people trying to make London healthier?
3. Explain whether the measures shown here would help prevent the spread of the Black Death.
4. Does the evidence in this picture suggest that people understood:
a) what caused disease
b) how to make London a healthier place?

■ ACTIVITY

This illustration shows London in the fourteenth century. Match the descriptions 1–14 with events shown in the picture. Each description is based on a real event, recorded in London.

How did they treat the sick?

Were herbal remedies useful?

Whatever people believed were the causes of disease, the treatment for most illness was herbal potions. Doctors used them, and women healers in villages and towns possessed a large store of knowledge about the use of herbs to treat everyday illness.

Many locally grown plants were used, although foreign herbs became increasingly popular. Sugar was believed to be particularly effective and was imported in large quantities by the 1400s.

Were these remedies useful? Medical historians who have studied many of them say they were. Plaintain was an ingredient in 48 remedies in the Anglo-Saxon *Leechbooks*. It was recommended for boils in the ear, dog-bites, cuts and wounds. Modern analysis shows that plantain is an ANTIBIOTIC and in 25 of the 48 remedies would have helped to stop infection. The diagram below shows how the remedy in Source 1 might work. Source 1 comes from *Bald's Leechbook*. This Anglo-Saxon book contained herbal remedies with sensible advice from Greek and Roman medicine. It included remedies designed to balance the body's humours.

SOURCE 1 From *Bald's Leechbook*

66 *Make an eye-salve for a* STYE: *take onion and garlic, equal amounts of both, pound well together, take wine and bull's gall, equal amounts of both, mix with the onion and garlic, then put in a brass vessel, let stand for nine nights in the brass vessel, strain through a cloth and clear well, put in a horn and about night-time put on the stye with a feather.* 99

SOURCE 2 One of the most common treatments was bleeding. Doctors believed that bleeding restored the balance of the four humours in the body by removing the excess blood which was making the patient ill.

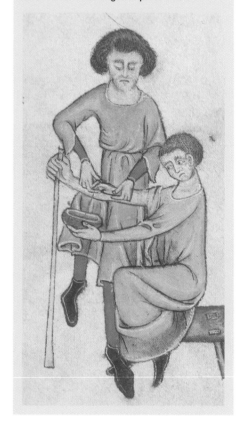

■ TASK

1. What evidence is there that some herbal remedies were successful?
2. Why did doctors bleed patients?
3. 'In the Middle Ages medicine was still mainly based on Greek and Roman ideas.' Explain why you agree or disagree with this statement.

The medieval remedy

1	2	3	4	5	6
Take onions and garlic	Pound them together	Mix with wine and bull's gall	Stand for nine nights in a brass vessel	Strain mixture through a cloth	Apply to stye with a feather

The modern verdict

| Onion and garlic kill bacteria | Bull's gall also attacks bacteria | Wine contains acetic acid which reacts with copper in the brass vessel to form copper salts which also kill bacteria | The result: a practical cure |

Was surgery improving in the Middle Ages?

Surgery was not usually taught in the universities. People became surgeons by being apprenticed to another surgeon, watching his or her work and copying it. There were guilds of surgeons who controlled entrance to the profession. Master surgeons needed to have licences and sometimes had to pass lengthy tests. Women could become surgeons and a number did.

1. According to Sources 3–6 how did surgeons cope with the problems of:
 a) pain during an operation
 b) infection after an operation?
2. Surgery is one area of medicine that is often advanced by war. Is there evidence that this happened in the Middle Ages?
3. Why did doctors use zodiac charts?
4. 'Surgeons in the Middle Ages did not heal their patients.' What evidence is there for and against this statement?

SOURCE 3 Battlefield surgery: an operation on a wounded soldier (fourteenth-century Italian painting)

SOURCE 4 From the writings of Theodoric of Lucca, a thirteenth-century surgeon. His father, Hugh, who was also a famous surgeon in Italy, had travelled to Egypt with a Christian army to fight against Muslims

66 … every day we see new instruments and new methods being invented by clever and ingenious surgeons. 99

66 Ancient surgeons and their disciples teach (and almost all modern surgeons follow them) that pus should be generated in wounds. There could be no greater error than this. For pus hinders the work of nature, prolongs the disease, prevents healing and the closing up of wounds … My father used to heal almost every kind of wound with wine alone and he produced the most beautiful healing without any ointments. 99

[The idea of 'praiseworthy pus' was preached and used by the Greeks, by Galen and by the Arabs. Theodoric's ideas went against Galen. They did not win much support .]

SOURCE 5 A recipe for an anaesthetic from the late Middle Ages

66 To make a drink that men call dwale to make a man sleep while men carve him: Take three spoonfuls of the gall of a boar, three spoonfuls of hemlock juice, three spoonfuls of wild nept, three spoonfuls of lettuce, three spoonfuls of poppy, three spoonfuls of henbane and three spoonfuls of vinegar and mix them all together and boil them a little … and put thereof three spoonfuls into half a gallon of good wine and mix it well together … let him that shall be carved sit against a good fire and make him drink until he falls asleep and then you may safely carve him … 99

[This mixture of hemlock, henbane and wine would certainly have sent patients to sleep and, if the dose was too strong, they may never have woken up.]

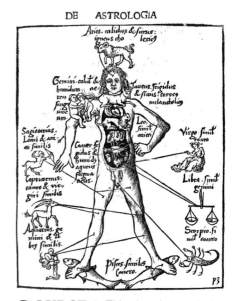

SOURCE 6 This chart is popularly called a Zodiac Man. It gave details about when each part of the body was affected by the planets and stars. If the stars told the surgeon not to open wounds or bleed the patient in that area then he would not do so for fear of causing death. Such charts were in common use

Why were doctors still reading Galen in 1350?

MEDIEVAL DOCTORS STILL used the books of Galen even though they had been written 1200 years earlier. They believed that his ideas were correct and that it was nearly impossible to improve on his work.

Even in universities in the 1200s, students were not expected to have their own ideas. They simply had to learn what Galen and other doctors had written down. Why was Galen still so important?

Reason 2: The growing power of the Christian Church

Christianity was the religion of the Roman empire. Surprisingly, it did not decline when the Roman empire fell apart. Instead it grew stronger. Within a few centuries there were thousands of churches and monasteries all over Europe.

The Christian Church was the only strong, centralised organisation to survive the collapse of the Roman empire. It was very powerful throughout the Middle Ages. It kept Galen's books in libraries in monasteries. When universities began to train doctors, Galen's books were there for them to read.

Reason 1: Chaos in western Europe

With the collapse of the Roman empire, western Europe was gradually split into many much smaller countries and tribes. The following factors made it impossible for new medical ideas to spread.

War
War destroyed many of the Romans' achievements.

- These countries and tribes were often at war with each other.
- War destroyed the Roman public health systems. It also destroyed medical libraries.
- The rulers of the small kingdoms built up defences and armies rather than improving medical skills or public health.
- War disrupted trade so countries became poorer.
- Travel became more dangerous thus reducing communication between doctors.
- Education and the development of technology were disrupted.
- In Europe the training of doctors was abandoned. Copies of Galen's books were either lost, or hidden away for safety.

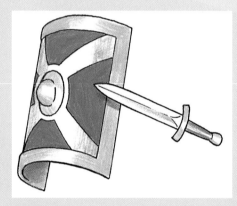

Government
Central government collapsed. Small kingdoms fought with each other. Governments did not think that public health schemes were a priority.

Trade
Trade and travel decreased.

Churches
Each village had its church and priest who told people what to believe and how to behave.

Tradition
People believed and respected what was written in the Bible and other ancient books. People were not encouraged to think for themselves or challenge old ideas. For example, although bodies were sometimes dissected to teach students about anatomy, this was done to prove that Galen's ideas about the body were correct, not to challenge them.

Education
Monasteries controlled education.
Priests and monks were often the only people who learned to read in this period.
The monasteries also controlled what people read. The only libraries were in monasteries. The Church sometimes banned books that it did not want people to read.

SUPERSTITION
The ancient Greeks had looked for rational explanations. The Church taught the opposite – that there were SUPERNATURAL explanations for everything. People believed that God, the Devil, or the planets controlled their lives.

But ... was change on the way?

After about 1000, Europe had begun to recover from the period of chaos:

- harvests improved
- trade increased
- scholars travelled more freely
- there was more money around
- the Church also became richer.

By the 1300s:

- the Church had set up universities where doctors could be trained
- armies took trained doctors to war with them where they gained experience as surgeons on the battlefields
- rulers were again taking measures to clean up towns
- merchants and scholars were once again travelling around Europe, spreading ideas
- new ideas were reaching Europe from Arab doctors.

■ TASK

The illustrations and information on these two pages explain some of the factors which influenced medicine and health in the Middle Ages.

1. Explain how each of the following factors helped to cause change or prevent change in the Middle Ages:

   - war
   - government
   - attitudes and beliefs
   - poor communications
   - education.

2. Which factor do you think was the most important in explaining why doctors in 1350 were still reading Galen?

Although doctors in 1350 still read the books of Galen, some people were beginning to think for themselves. Some were doctors; others were artists and scientists.
Gradually they began to challenge the old beliefs. New ideas were on the way!

Medicine in the Middle Ages – a summary

Treatments
Most people used herbal remedies, many of which were effective. However, if the herbs did not work, there was not much anyone could do – except pray! Surgeons could perform simple operations, although there were no safe, effective anaesthetics.

Public health
Governments made some efforts to keep towns clean. However, they did not have the money or the workforce to build pipes to carry clean water and sewers, as the Romans did. More importantly, kings were usually too concerned with other business, such as wars or keeping law and order, to spend time and money on public health.

■ ACTIVITY

Work in pairs. Go back in time to interview a medieval doctor.

1. Make a list of questions to ask him.
2. Swap your list with another pair. Answer the other pair's questions as if you were the medieval doctor.

Galen – still the greatest doctor of them all!

Disease and the causes of disease
Nobody understood the true causes of disease. Doctors believed that people became sick when their humours were out of balance. Many ordinary people believed sickness was a punishment from God, or the work of the Devil.

1543
Vesalius published *The Fabric of the Human Body*, a new study of anatomy

Black Death   Development of printing ——

1350	1450	1550

The Medical Renaissance – what were the new discoveries?

Anatomy – Vesalius

Surgery – Paré

Physiology (how the body works) – Harvey

■ TASK

Read pages 58–63. For each of the three men explain:

- ■ what discovery he made
- ■ how he made the discovery (for example, by experiment? by chance?)
- ■ which old ideas he was challenging
- ■ whether his discovery improved people's health immediately or in the long term.

75
broise Paré published his *Works on Surgery*

1628
William Harvey published his account of the circulation of the blood

1650

AD1750

Key individual: Vesalius – how did he change the way the human body was studied?

Andreas Vesalius

Biography
Born in Brussels in 1514. Studied medicine in Paris and Italy where he met artists who were studying skeletons and dissecting bodies to make their paintings more realistic. Became Professor of Surgery at Padua in Italy. Wrote *The Fabric of the Human Body* (published 1543) with detailed illustrations of the human anatomy. Died in 1564.

SOURCE 1 Vesalius wrote

66 *The jaw of most animals is formed of two bones joined together at the apex of the chin where the lower jaw ends in a point. In man, however, the lower jaw is formed of a single bone … Galen and most of the skilled dissectors after the time of Hippocrates asserted that the jaw is not a single bone. However this may be, so far no human jaw has come to my attention constructed of two bones.* 99

Specialism
Anatomy

Importance
Before Vesalius: doctors believed that the books of Galen and other ancient doctors were completely accurate and contained all the knowledge they needed. Therefore there was no need to learn more about anatomy by dissecting human bodies.

After Vesalius: Vesalius showed that Galen was wrong in some important details of anatomy. He believed that this was because Galen had to rely on dissecting animals. He said it was vital that doctors dissect human bodies to

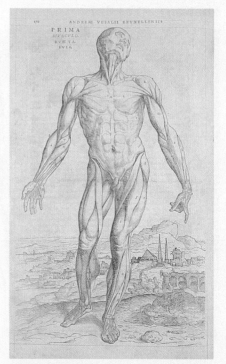

SOURCE 2 An illustration from Vesalius' book

find out about the human structure and exactly how it works. He said doctors needed to test Galen's ideas instead of accepting them uncritically.

An interview with Vesalius
They didn't interview people like this in the 1500s, but if they had done, this is what an interview with Vesalius might have sounded like! The answers are all based on sources from the time.

Question: Why did you want to become a doctor?
Answer: My father was a doctor. What he did always seemed interesting, and I decided to be a doctor, too.

Q: I've heard a story that you once stole a corpse so that you could study the human body. Is that true?
A: Yes. I was still only a boy but I wanted to learn more about anatomy. The only way to do this was to dissect a corpse so I stole the body of a criminal from the gallows. It wasn't easy getting it home!

Q: Where did you study medicine?
A: I went to the university at Paris when I was nineteen. I had heard of Jean Guinter who taught medicine there. He had just translated Galen's works from Greek into Latin so I wanted to study

there to learn from him. After three years in Paris I moved to Padua in Italy.

Q: Was working in Padua as exciting as you hoped?
A: Even better. The university was very good. Nobody tried to stop you thinking and having new ideas. I could get plenty of corpses to dissect, and I found artists who could make excellent drawings of parts of the body.

Q: Was it difficult to get artists to draw such things?
A: No. Some of the artists in Padua and Venice had already carried out their own dissections so that they could learn to draw human bodies more accurately. They were keen to help.

Q: When did you decide to write your book, *The Fabric of the Human Body*?
A: The artists' drawings were so good that I decided to put them together as a kind of atlas of the human body. I knew this would help my students. I wanted every detail in the book to be right and I had to do many more dissections as I was writing it to check that all the drawings were correct.

Q: How was your book produced?

A: Well, it wouldn't have been possible 100 years ago because printing had not even been invented. The artists engraved their drawings onto blocks for the printers to use. It was important to make sure that all the detail on the drawings was clear so I sent the book to the best printers, in Basle in Switzerland.

Q: Many doctors have criticised your book. How do you feel about their criticisms?

A: I expected them to criticise me because I dared to say that Galen was wrong. In fact, most of my work shows that Galen was very accurate, but doctors have been trained to believe that Galen was right about everything. They find it difficult to accept that there were some things he was wrong about.

Q: Are you sure you are right?

A: Yes. I have checked and double checked. And I've dissected human bodies. Galen, of course, often had to make do with dissecting animals. It's not surprising he was sometimes wrong because the bodies of monkeys and pigs are different from those of humans.

Q: Can you give me an example of something Galen got wrong?

A: Yes, the human jaw bone. He said the lower jaw is made up of two pieces but it isn't. It's one piece. Animals have lower jaws made from two bones, but my dissections showed that human lower jaws only have one piece.

Q: But that isn't a very important mistake really, is it?

A: No, but if Galen was wrong about that, then he might be wrong about other things, too.

Q: Well? Have you found other mistakes?

A: Yes. Take this, for example: Galen said that blood moves from one side of the heart to the other through holes in the septum – that's in the middle of the heart (see Source 3).

Q: And what is wrong with Galen's idea?

A: Well, until recently even I did not dare to think that Galen was wrong about something so important, but if you have ever looked at the septum you would know that he was wrong. I have studied many hearts and the septum is always very thick. There are no holes in it. There is simply no way that the blood can pass through the septum – it must move in another way.

Q: And what is that other way?

A: I don't know yet. I will need to do more research to answer that question.

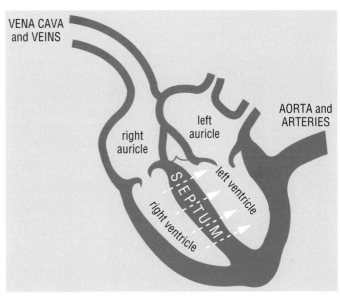

SOURCE 3 Diagram showing Galen's idea about the movement of blood through the heart

Q: What are you going to do in the future?

A: I have been offered a new job, as doctor to the emperor Charles V in Spain. It's well paid and it will be restful after writing three huge volumes in three years. I think I'll enjoy working for the emperor – provided I can still get a supply of bodies to dissect.

1. Why did working in Padua make Vesalius' work easier?
2. Which technological developments helped Vesalius make his work well known?
3. Choose either:
   a) the human lower jaw
   b) the heart
   and explain what Galen got wrong.
4. Vesalius probably knew that Galen was wrong about the heart when he first published his book, but he did not say so. Vesalius added his new discoveries about the heart when the book was republished later. Why do you think he did not show that Galen was wrong when the book was first published?

■ ACTIVITY

Write a review of Vesalius' book **either**:
a) as a doctor who still thinks that Galen is right about everything, explaining why you find it difficult to believe that Galen could be wrong, **or:**
b) as a doctor who believes that Vesalius has made a big breakthrough. Include an explanation as to why his work is so important.

Key individual: Paré – why did he make new surgical discoveries?

Ambroise Paré

Biography
Born in France in 1510. He was apprenticed to his brother, a barber surgeon, and then became a surgeon in Paris at the Hotel Dieu (see page 86). In 1536 he became an army surgeon and spent twenty years on campaign, treating sword and gunshot wounds. He wrote *Works on Surgery*, published in 1575. He died in 1590.

Specialism
Surgery

Importance
Before Paré: wounds were treated by pouring boiling oil onto them. Doctors believed this would help them to heal. They stopped a wound bleeding by sealing it with a red-hot iron. This was called CAUTERISING.

After Paré: Paré discovered that wounds healed more quickly if boiling oil was not used. Instead he put simple bandages onto wounds. He also stopped cauterising wounds. Instead he tied the ends of arteries using silk thread.

Paré's story
Problem 1: helping a wound to heal

It was the young doctor's first battle. Ambroise Paré had been with the French army for only a short time. He had watched the French soldiers begin their attack, but now they were being pushed back by the pikes and guns of the enemy. The wounded began to stagger in for help. Some had to be carried by their comrades.

The old treatment: boiling oil
Paré had never dealt with gunshot wounds before, although he knew how to treat them – in theory. He had read the book by Jean de Vigo called *Of Wounds in General*. Vigo said that gunshot wounds were poisonous and that the only way to stop the poison from infecting the whole leg was to apply boiling oil to the wound, thus killing the poison. This was another method of cauterising a wound.

As the soldiers screamed with pain, Paré checked how the other surgeons were treating the gunshot wounds. 'Go ahead, use the oil,' they said, 'as hot as they can stand. It will save their lives, if they are lucky.'

The crisis: the oil runs out
Paré set to work with boiling oil. He treated one soldier after another until his supply of life-saving oil dwindled and, finally, ran out.

Still the wounded arrived. 'How can I treat them?' thought Paré. 'Something needs to be put on their wounds.'

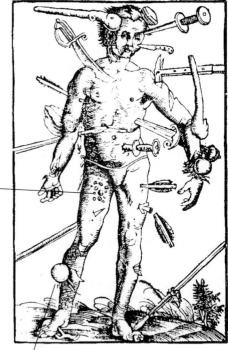

Gunshot wounds

SOURCE 1
This picture of a 'wound man' is from a book on surgery published in 1536. Gunshot wounds were treated with boiling oil

Cannonball wounds

The solution: don't cauterise!
Paré was desperate to help the soldiers so he quickly mixed an ointment of his own. It was made out of egg yolks, oil of roses and turpentine, which Paré knew had been used since Roman times to heal wounds. As soon as the mixture was ready, Paré began to apply it to wounds.

The surprise: healed wounds

That night Paré tossed and turned, worrying about his patients. He was convinced that in the morning the soldiers whose wounds had been cauterised with oil would be well, but that the others – treated with his own emergency mixture – would be dead.

Finally Paré gave up trying to sleep, and decided to examine his patients. He could hear their groans and curses as he walked towards them.

As Paré bent over the first soldier he realised something strange had happened. This was a man whom he had treated with his own mixture. Instead of suffering in agony he was lying back resting comfortably, and his leg wound looked healthy. It was the same with the other men he had treated after the oil ran out. They were all alive.

It was a different story among the soldiers who'd been treated with boiling oil. Their wounds were swollen and red, and they moaned in pain. Some had already died.

Paré decided that he would never again use boiling oil to treat gunshot wounds. It only caused more pain and misery. Instead he would use his own mixture and try to improve it. It would be difficult to go against all the wisdom and beliefs of the great surgeons of the past, but he had to do it.

Problem 2: stopping the bleeding

Paré spent another twenty years as an army doctor. In that time he learned a lot more about how to treat wounds. This included a method of stopping patients' bleeding after an amputation.

The old treatment: red-hot irons

The usual treatment to stop bleeding was to press a red-hot iron, called a cautery, against the stump of the limb. This sealed the blood vessels and stopped the patient bleeding to death but the pain was excruciating. Paré was sure there must be a better way to stop the flow of blood.

The new treatment: ligatures

Paré's answer was to tie silk thread round each of the blood vessels to close them up. These silk threads were called LIGATURES, and they provided a very effective way of stopping bleeding. This meant that Paré could stop using the cautery, which he called that 'old and too cruel way of healing'.

Paré's idea was not totally new, but it had never become popular because it was risky and because surgeons respected tradition. But Paré, like Vesalius, lived at a time when doctors were ready to challenge old ideas. He was also forced to experiment in wartime – it was the only chance he had of saving lives.

When Paré became an experienced and famous surgeon, people began to take notice of what he said but there were many surgeons who did not agree with his methods. In one way they were right, although they did not understand why. Paré's ligatures did stop the bleeding, but they were dangerous because the threads themselves could carry infection into the wound. If Paré had had an ANTISEPTIC to kill the germs then his ligatures would have worked better. Unfortunately, antiseptics were not invented for another 300 years. Nobody in Paré's time knew about germs or exactly how infection spread.

Eventually Paré retired from the army. He became a successful surgeon in Paris, treating three French kings. In 1575 he published his book, *Works on Surgery*. This was written in French, not Latin, and was soon translated into many other languages, spreading his ideas throughout Europe. He also inspired other surgeons to try out new techniques and challenge old ideas.

SOURCE 2 A nineteenth-century painting of Paré at the siege of Metz, tying ligatures on the wounded

1. A number of factors helped Paré to make his discoveries. Explain how each of these played a part in his discoveries and the spread of his ideas:
 a) war
 b) Paré's own intelligence
 c) printing.
2. Which of the factors above was the most important?
3. Why were many other surgeons unwilling to use Paré's methods?
4. Paré wrote his book in French. How did this help to spread his ideas quickly?

Key individual: Harvey – what was his great discovery?

William Harvey

Biography
Born in 1578 in Kent. Studied medicine at Cambridge and Padua. Worked as a doctor in London and then as a lecturer in anatomy. In 1628 he published *An Anatomical Account of the Motion of the Heart and Blood in Animals*. He died in 1657.

Specialism
The circulation of the blood.

Importance
Before Harvey: many doctors still believed in Galen's idea that new blood was constantly being manufactured in the liver to replace blood that was burnt up in the body, in the same way as wood is burnt by fire. This idea had been challenged by a number of doctors but no one had proved exactly how the blood moved around the body.

After Harvey: Harvey showed that blood flows around the body, is carried away from the heart by the arteries and returns to the heart in veins.

He proved that the heart acts as a pump, recirculating the blood, and that blood does not burn up so no organ is needed to manufacture new blood.

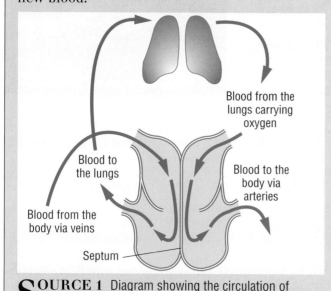

SOURCE 1 Diagram showing the circulation of the blood

How did Harvey prove he was right?

The idea that the heart was a pump had been suggested by Erasistratus 1800 years earlier (see page 38) but he had not been able to prove it. Harvey could prove it.

- He dissected live, cold-blooded animals whose hearts beat very slowly. This meant that he could see the movements of each muscle in the heart.
- He dissected human bodies to build up a detailed knowledge of the heart.
- He tried to pump liquids past the valves in the veins but he could not do so. He also pushed thin rods down veins. This proved that the blood flowed in a one-way system around the body.
- He measured the amount of blood moved by each heartbeat, and calculated how much blood was in the body.
- Whenever he disagreed with Galen or his own contemporaries, he gave clear, detailed proof of his own conclusions, and explained carefully why other doctors were wrong.

What could Harvey not prove?

Between arteries and veins there are tiny blood vessels called capillaries which carry the blood. They are too small to see with the naked eye but even though Harvey could not see them, he said that they must exist.

Later in the 1600s microscopes were developed which allowed doctors to see the capillaries, exactly as Harvey had predicted.

1. Do you think Harvey's discovery will improve his patients' health? Explain your answer.

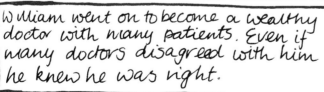

What caused these discoveries?

■ TASK

1. Make your own copy of the chart below.

EXPERIMENTS	WARS	EDUCATION
People were willing to challenge old ideas – by experimenting they could prove whether their theories were correct.	There were many wars in sixteenth- and seventeenth-century Europe.	Literacy was increasing and there were many more schools in the sixteenth and seventeenth centuries.

WEALTH		ATTITUDES AND BELIEFS
Since the Black Death in the 1300s many people had grown wealthier. They had money to spend on luxuries and education.		Many old ideas were challenged. Copernicus said the Earth travelled round the Sun, rather than the Sun travelling around the Earth. The medieval attitude that old ideas must be right was changing.

MACHINERY	ART	ANCIENT LEARNING	PRINTING
There were improvements in clocks, watches, pumps and other machines.	Skilful artists found people to buy their sculptures and paintings.	There was renewed interest in the writings of Roman and Greek thinkers.	From the late 1400s printed books meant that new ideas spread much more rapidly.

2. In the central box write the name of Vesalius, Harvey or Paré, and his specialism.

3. You are now going to try to work out how various developments brought about new discoveries in medicine and health. Look at the developments described in the other boxes. If you think that, for example, printing helped your chosen character to make a new discovery or develop his specialism, then draw a line from 'printing' to the central box. Do this for all the boxes that helped bring about this discovery.

Sources 1–7 opposite will help you, but you will also have to look back through pages 58–63 and think for yourself as well! Some of the connections are less obvious than others.

4. Were there any connections between the developments in the outer ring of boxes? For example, did improvements in education help to improve machinery? If you think so, draw a line between the two boxes. Do this for any other developments that you think were connected.

5. On a separate sheet of paper, list all the developments that helped to bring about your chosen discovery.

6. Finally, write an essay to explain how at least two of the developments worked together to bring about the discovery. Explain why you have made your choice and if you think one of them was more important than the other.

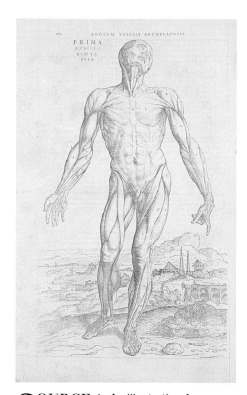

SOURCE 1 An illustration from Vesalius' book, *The Fabric of the Human Body*, published in 1543. In Italy Vesalius found many talented artists who made detailed anatomical drawings

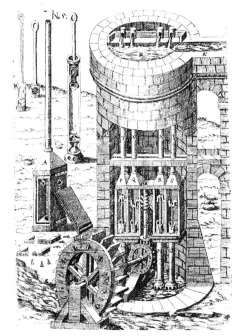

SOURCE 2 A water pump pictured in a book entitled *Various Ingenious Machines*, published in 1588. The valves are shown separately on the left

SOURCE 3 Extracts from Leonardo da Vinci's notebooks, written before 1519. Leonardo da Vinci gave this advice to many ambitious young artists in Italy

66 *The painter who has a knowledge of the SINEWS, muscles and tendons will know exactly which sinew causes the movement of a limb … he will be able to show the various muscles in the different attitudes of his figures …*

You will need three dissections to have a complete knowledge of the arteries, three more for the membranes, three for the nerves, muscles and LIGAMENTS, three for the bones and cartilages. Three must also be devoted to the female body … 99

SOURCE 4 From William Harvey's *On the Circulation of the Blood*, 1649. Harvey's books were reprinted several times before the 1670s

66 *When water is forced through pipes we can see and distinguish the individual compressions of the pump (perhaps at a considerable distance) in the flow of the escaping water. It is the same from the opening of a cut artery…* 99

SOURCE 5 From the writings of Robert Boyle, a leading English scientist, 1663

66 *A human body itself seems to be but an engine wherein almost all the actions are performed mechanically.* 99

SOURCE 6 Written by Ambroise Paré in *Apology and Treatise*, 1585. He is pleading with other surgeons to adopt his methods of tying up arteries after an amputation. His method was not entirely new, but it was Paré's books which made the method widely known

66 *I confess that I used to staunch the bleeding after amputation in a different way, of which I am now ashamed. But what else could I do? I had watched my masters whose methods I intended to follow. They had various hot irons and burning medicines with which they would treat the dismembered part. This cannot be spoken of without great horror, for this kind of remedy could not help giving the patient great tormenting pain.*

I must earnestly beg all surgeons to give up this old and too cruel way of healing, and take up this new method. I think that it was taught to me by the special favour of God, because I did not learn it from my masters. 99

SOURCE 7 A description of some of the technological advancements during the Medical Renaissance

66 *Guns were used increasingly in wars in the sixteenth century. They set a new problem for the surgeons because bullets might carry infection deep into a wound. Around 1600 craftsmen developed the microscope. There had been improvements in glassmaking in the 1500s and in the science of rays of light. In 1661 an Italian professor used an improved microscope to identify the capillaries, the channels along which blood flows from the arteries to the veins. Harvey knew they must exist but had not been able to see them.* 99

Great medical discoveries! No one healthier...

THE DISCOVERIES MADE by Vesalius and Harvey are a vital part of medical history. They proved to doctors that Galen and other ancient writers could be wrong and that careful dissection and experiment were the way to new understanding. Their work inspired others and became the foundation on which later scientists built their discoveries.

However, the discoveries of Vesalius and Harvey, important though they were, did not make anyone healthier at the time! Life expectancy did not increase much. They had not, after all, discovered new and better ways of treating illnesses. John Aubrey, a seventeenth-century writer and gossip, said of Harvey: 'All his profession agree Dr Harvey to be an excellent anatomist, but I never heard any that admired his treatment of the sick. I knew several practitioners in London that would not have given threepence for one of his prescriptions ...'

Ambroise Paré's work was more immediately useful than that of Vesalius and Harvey. Other surgeons could see with their own eyes that his new methods of bandaging wounds (instead of using boiling oil) were successful and helped patients to survive. However, Paré's idea of using a silk ligature or thread to tie arteries instead of sealing them with a cauterising iron was not widely copied. The cautery had helped to stop infection. The ligature could actually introduce germs into the wound and this meant that soldiers were more likely to die from infection. It was not until 300 years after Paré's death that the development of antiseptics meant that his ligature idea could finally be used successfully.

New treatments

In fact it was probably another development altogether which had the greatest impact on treatments. In 1492 Europeans landed in America for the first time. Over the next two centuries they brought back a wide range of new remedies, such as the one in Source 3, which were quickly adopted by herbalists. Once again, trade and communication were playing their part in the development of medicine.

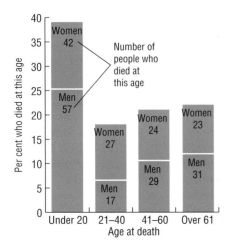

SOURCE 1 This graph shows the age at death of 250 people who were buried at St John's Church, Adel, in Leeds, between 1685 and 1700. Only 20 per cent of people lived beyond the age of 60. Today the vast majority do

Infant and childbirth	21
Consumption (TB)	15
Fever (probably flu)	47
Surfeit	4
Smallpox	17
Wearing	15
Palsy	4
King's Evil	1
Flux	2
Measles	1
Drowned	2
Dropsy	1
Bitten	2
Lost among the bogs	1
Hanged	1

SOURCE 2 This table shows the cause of death for 134 out of the 250 people who were buried at Adel between 1685 and 1700. The biggest cause of death – 'fever' – may well have been influenza. Regular epidemics swept Britain. A quarter of a million people died of it between 1727 and 1731

SOURCE 3 Plants from the Americas were brought to Europe from the 1500s onwards. One was the bark of the cinchona tree, used by native South Americans in many effective remedies. In Europe it was known as QUININE and was particularly used to treat fevers. It was used by Woodforde (see Source 1 on pages 78–79)

■ TASK

Study Sources 1 and 2. Had
a) life expectancy
b) the causes of death
changed since the Middle Ages?

... But ideas and attitudes were changing!

The great discoveries made by Vesalius, Paré and Harvey did not improve people's everyday health but they were a vital stage in the history of medicine. They showed that attitudes to medicine were changing – not for everybody, of course, but for an important group of doctors and other educated people.

How attitudes to medicine changed after the Medical Renaissance

Religion, beliefs and medicine

One important reason for changing attitudes was the great changes in religion that took place in the 1500s and 1600s. During the Middle Ages the Christian Church had both helped and hindered medicine. It helped individuals who were sick but it hindered the development of new medical ideas that would challenge Galen.

■ TASK

Look at Sources 1–6. Make two lists:
a) examples of how the Church helped the sick
b) examples of how the Church hindered the development of new ideas.

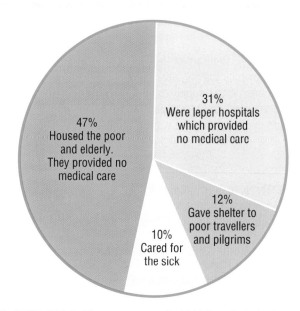

SOURCE 1 Roger Bacon – a thirteenth-century priest. He suggested that a new approach to medicine was needed. He said that doctors should do their own original research instead of learning from the books of ancient writers such as Galen. Church leaders put him in prison for heresy. This nineteenth-century engraving shows him smuggling his work out of prison

SOURCE 2 There were nearly 1200 hospitals in England and Wales in the Middle Ages, but only ten per cent actually cared for the sick. The others were called hospitals because they provided 'hospitality'. You can find out more about hospitals on pages 86–87

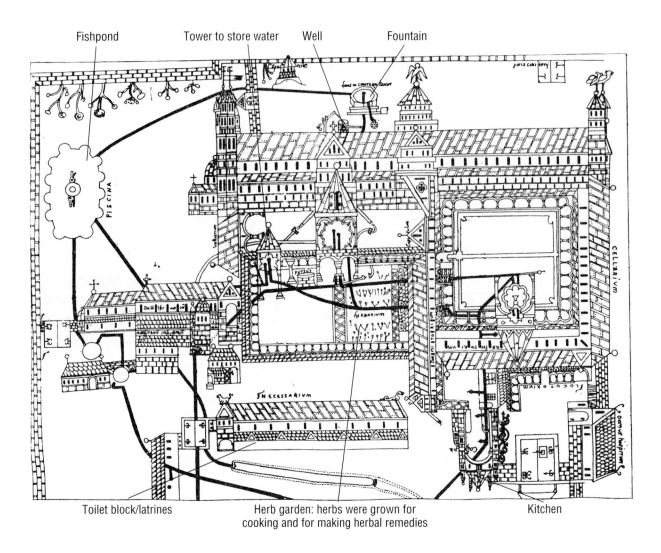

Fishpond | Tower to store water | Well | Fountain

Toilet block/latrines | Herb garden: herbs were grown for cooking and for making herbal remedies | Kitchen

SOURCE 3 Diagram of the water supply to Canterbury Cathedral and monastery, 1153, drawn by the engineer who designed and built the system. All monasteries regarded a fresh water supply as a priority. At Canterbury there were five settling tanks to purify the water. Water was piped to the kitchen, the wash rooms, the brewery, the bakery and the fishpond. The waste water was recycled to flush the latrines

SOURCE 4 A cure for toothache, recommended by John of Gaddesden, a leading English doctor in the early 1300s

Write these words on the jaw of the patient. 'In the name of the Father, Son and Holy Ghost, Amen. + Res + Pax + Nax + In Christo Filio.' The pain will cease at once, as I have often seen.

SOURCE 5 From the rules for Benedictine monasteries AD534

Care for the sick stands before all. You must help them as would Christ, whom you really help in helping them. Also you must bear patiently with them as in this way you will gain greater merit [with God]. Let it also be the chief concern of the Abbot that the sick shall not be neglected at any single point.

SOURCE 6 A medieval illustration showing someone caught illegally dissecting a body. Dissection was only allowed by the Church if it was done to teach students about anatomy

The changing impact of religion – the King's Evil

The Middle Ages
One Christian Church – the Catholic Church. Religion and beliefs were carefully controlled by the Pope from Rome.

The invention of printing
1450s

The Reformation
1500s

The Reformation and the invention of printing

1500–1750
Many Christian Churches developed, including the Protestant Church of England. The Pope still tried to control Catholics but it was much harder to prevent the spread of new ideas once printed books became available.

Religion was very different after the 1500s. Instead of one Christian Church in Europe, there were many. The Catholic Church could no longer stop new ideas spreading, nor prevent doctors and scientists from carrying out dissections and experiments. One example of the weakening power of religion was the way in which people sought to cure a skin disease known as the 'KING'S EVIL'.

SOURCE 8 Charles II, who was king between 1660 and 1685, touching people to cure them of the King's Evil. He treated over 92,000 sufferers in this way. However, by the time of Queen Anne, who died in 1714, the custom had ended. For a thousand years people had believed that the monarch, God's deputy, could cure this disease. By the early 1700s they no longer believed it

SOURCE 7 How people thought the King's Evil could be cured in the Middle Ages

■ TASK

1. How was religion changed by the Reformation?
2. What effects did this have on the spread of new medical ideas?
3. Why do you think people stopped visiting the monarch to be cured of the King's Evil?

New ideas, old ideas

BETWEEN 1350 AND 1750 old attitudes were changing and new discoveries were being made. But that did not mean that everything was new. Pages 71–81 will help you to investigate the balance between new and old in medicine.

When you began this chapter you were looking at the years around 1350 and you studied the following topics:

- plague
- public health
- treatments and surgery
- ideas about the causes of disease.

Now you are going to investigate the same topics for the 1600s and 1700s, after the discoveries of the Medical Renaissance.

■ TASK 1

1. As you work through pages 71–85, fill in a table like the one below. Write down the evidence to show which old and which new ideas were being used and who was using them.

Old ideas	Examples from the 1600s and 1700s
Galen, the four humours, bleeding, treatment by opposites	
Herbal remedies	
Superstitions or magical cures	
Government unable or unwilling to spend money improving public health, e.g. by providing clean water and sewers	
New ideas	
Scientific experiments and willingness to challenge old ideas	
Use of the discoveries of Vesalius, Paré and Harvey	
Government spending money on public health, e.g. by providing clean water and sewers	

2. When you have completed your table, decide which of these statements you agree with and explain why.
a) The Medical Renaissance changed medicine completely.
b) The Medical Renaissance changed most aspects of medicine quickly.
c) The Medical Renaissance changed some aspects of medicine but many things stayed the same.

Case study 1: Public health and the Great Plague of 1665

On pages 46–49 you investigated the Black Death. The plague continued to strike Britain at regular intervals throughout the 1400s and 1500s. Then in 1665 London was hit by the worst outbreak for three centuries.

In London alone more than 65,000 people died out of a population of less than 400,000.

Fifty years later, Daniel Defoe, the author of *Robinson Crusoe*, wrote an account of life in London during the Great Plague. It was called *Journal of the Plague Year: 1665*. He consulted documents from that year and included some in his book. Although parts of his work are imaginary, it provides a dramatic and accurate account of life during the plague. Source 2 contains edited extracts from his book.

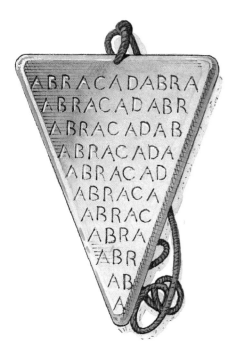

SOURCE 1 Defoe's *Journal of the Plague Year: 1665* describes how people wore charms such as this abracadabra amulet to ward off the plague

SOURCE 2 From Defoe's *Journal of the Plague Year: 1665,* published in 1772

66 *… a blazing star or comet appeared for several months before the plague. The old women remarked that those two comets passed directly over the city, and … imparted something peculiar…*

… astrologers added stories of the conjunctions of planets…, one of these conjunctions … did happen in October and the other in November; and they filled the people's heads with predictions on these signs of the heavens, that they foretold drought, famine and pestilence …

… The Government appointed public prayers and days of fasting, to make public confession of sin and implore the mercy of God to avert the dreadful judgement that hung over their heads…

… When anyone bought a joint of meat in the market they would not take it off the butcher's hand, but took it off the hooks themselves. On the other hand the butcher would not touch the money, but have it put into a pot full of vinegar.

… The infection generally came into the houses of the citizens by means of their servants, whom they were obliged to send for food or physic, and who meet with distempered people, who conveyed the fatal breath into them.

… the calamity was spread by infection, by the breath, by the sweat or by the stench of the sores of the sick persons, or some other way, perhaps, beyond even the reach of the physicians themselves. I cannot but with some wonder find some people talk of its being a stroke from Heaven, which I look upon as ignorance; likewise the opinion of others who talk of infection being carried on by the air, carrying with it vast numbers of insects and invisible creatures, who enter into the body with the breath or even at the pores with the air and there generate or emit most acute poisons or poisonous eggs which mingle themselves with the blood and so infect the body … 99

SOURCE 3 An example of a contemporary treatment for plague

66 *To draw the poison from the plague sore, take the feathers from the tail of a chicken and apply them to the sore. The chick will gasp and labour for life … When the poison is drawn out by the chicken, the patient will recover.*

Wrap in woollen cloths, make the sick person sweat, which if he do, keep him warm until the sores begin to rise. Then apply to the sores live pigeons cut in half or else a plaster made of yolk of an egg, honey, herb of grace and wheat flour. 99

■ TASK 2

1. Using Sources 1–3 make lists of:
   a) explanations for the plague   b) treatments for the plague.
2. For each explanation and treatment, work out whether it was also used at the time of the Black Death (see pages 48–49) or whether it was new.

$\mathbf{S}$OURCE 4 Orders published by the Lord Mayor of London concerning the plague in 1665

- Anyone who falls sick should be shut up in their houses.
- All such houses are to be marked with a red cross and the words 'Lord have mercy upon us'.
- Watchmen to keep guard on these houses to prevent anyone going in or out.

- All householders to sweep clean the streets outside their houses every day. All filth to be removed from the streets daily.
- No animals to be kept in the city and no rotting food to be sold.
- No beggars to be allowed in the streets and no plays, bear-baitings or other public entertainments to be held.

- Women searchers and doctors to examine the bodies and report whether they died of the plague.
- Burials to be after sunset and no friends or relatives to attend funerals.
- All bedding from the homes of the dead to be aired with fire and perfumes before being used again.

The orders in Source 4 were useful in theory, but what really happened?

1. Parliament refused to turn the orders into laws because the members of the House of Lords refused to be shut in their houses.
2. Many people ignored the orders. More than twenty watchmen were murdered by people escaping from houses that had been shut up.
3. The King and his council left London. They only discussed what to do about the plague three times in seven months and two of those discussions were about the safety of the King.
4. Nine men were put in charge of dealing with the plague. Six of them left the city as soon as possible.

■ TASK

1. Choose two orders from Source 4 and explain why they might help to prevent the plague spreading.
2. Why did many people disobey the orders?
3. How concerned were the King and his government to help people deal with the plague?
4. What was **not** being done to improve public health and why?

Exam practice: old and new ideas about the plague

The next three pages give you a typical Paper 2 exam. In Paper 2 you are being tested on your ability to use sources in context. In other words, you need to use your knowledge to understand and evaluate sources.

The questions are printed on this page. The sources are on pages 73–75.

Study Sources A–L and then answer Questions 1–8 below.

1. Study Source A. What can you learn from Source A about actions taken by the City of London authorities to deal with the plague? **(5)**
2. Study Source B and use your own knowledge. Explain why ordinary people used these methods against the plague. Use examples from Source B in your answer. **(8)**
3. Study Sources C and D. Compare the value of Sources C and D for a historian enquiring into the role of the Lord Mayor during the plague. **(8)**
4. Study Sources E, F and G. How far do Sources F and G support Defoe's story about the plague piper? Use Sources E, F and G to explain your answer. **(8)**
5. Study Source H. How can you tell that the author is against the shutting up of infected houses? Use Source H to explain your answer. **(6)**
6. Study Sources H and I and use your own knowledge. Explain why it is difficult to give a complete picture of how people behaved during the plague. **(8)**
7. Study Sources J and K. In what ways does Source J support Paul Slack's view in Source K about the effects of the Bills of Mortality? **(7)**
8. Study Sources B, K and L and use your own knowledge. Do you think people's attitudes to the plague were less influenced by religion and superstition in 1665 than they were in the Middle Ages? Explain your answer, using Sources B, K and L and your own knowledge of changes in ideas about disease and treatment. You can also use any other of Sources A–L you find helpful. **(10)**

(Total: 60 marks)

SOURCE A Drawings published in London in 1665 showing scenes from London during the plague

SOURCE B A letter written in London in 1665 by John Allin to a friend. John Allin was a vicar

❝ 24 August
Death approaches nearer and nearer, not many doors away. Here many wear charms made of poison of the toad to raise a blister and make them well when infection invades.

7 September
This week's Bill of Mortality is increased: 8,252 deaths; 6,978 of the Plague. If you could send a little materia prima* in a letter I should be glad to receive it. For three days coal fires have been made in the streets at every 12th door, but that will not do the work of stopping God's hand. ❞

* materia prima = dust from a plant which grew on sandy soil. Allin believed that extracts from it could cure the plague.

SOURCE C Orders by the Lord Mayor of London, 1665

66 *Women searchers in every parish to report whether the person do die of the Infection.*

As soon as any man shall be found to be sick of the plague, he shall be shut up in his house. The house shall be shut up for a month.

The constable to see every shut up house be attended with watchmen. The watchmen shall get food for the people. This shall be paid for at public expense if they cannot afford it themselves. 99

SOURCE E From *Journal of the Plague Year* by Daniel Defoe 1722. Defoe was born in London in 1661. He tried to show what it was like during the plague by imagining conversations with people who were there at the time

66 *The story of the piper which amused people so much happened in John Hayward's parish. John Hayward went with the dead cart and bell to fetch dead bodies. He assured me that the story of the piper was true.*

People would give the piper food and drink and, in return, he would pipe to entertain them. One night he had too much to drink. As he lay fast asleep at a door, they lifted him up and threw him into the cart.

When the piper woke up, he called out, 'Hey, where am I?' 'You are in the dead cart, and we are going to bury you' says Hayward. 'But I ain't dead though' says the piper. This made them laugh, though John said they were frightened at first. They helped the poor fellow down, and he walked away. 99

SOURCE D From *The Plague and the Fire*, a book written by the historian James Leasor in 1962

66 *London depended on the farms around its wall for milk and food. Only the Lord Mayor's intelligent action saved the city from famine. Sir John Lawrence ordered his city officers to organise special routes for the country people who brought food in to the markets. They would not see and be frightened by the sights so familiar to Londoners: piles of bodies naked and dead on the stinking carts; mounds of corpses waiting on the edge of mass burial grounds.* 99

SOURCE F A statue of the 'Plague Piper'. It was made between 1665 and 1691

SOURCE G From the memoirs of Sir John Reresby. He left London in June 1665 to live in Yorkshire. He wrote his memoirs for his family between 1679 and 1689. They were not published outside the family until 1734

66 *1665: A great plague began this Summer at London. It was so violent that people would fall down dead in the streets.*

There is a story of a piper that, being dead drunk, fell asleep in the street. He was thrown into the cart amongst the bodies that were carried out of the town to be buried. The piper wakened as the cart was going, and took out his pipes and began to play.

Those that drove the cart, hearing a strange noise, ran away very frightened. They feared that they had take up the devil into their cart in the form of a dead man. 99

SOURCE H From *The Shutting Up of Infected Houses*, an anonymous leaflet written in 1665

   Infection may have killed thousands, but shutting up has killed its ten thousands. Think how careless most nurses are in attending the sick and how carefully they look for the opportunity to steal from their houses. It is worse than the Plague to be in the hands of those dirty, ugly women.

   There goes a set of spoons that will infect a hundred dishes. A man buys a fine child's coat that kills his son.

   There is a law against taking away infected goods from houses before forty days are passed. Most nurses do not wait even forty hours in case the new owners come and claim their property.

SOURCE I From *The Great Plague in London 1665* by the historian W.G. Bell. This book was written in 1924

   The Great Plague has left us the record of very few heroic actions. The plague brought to notice much that was evil in human nature.

   I am sure that the whole truth is not told. The best actions of men and women are left out. In the shut-up houses there must have been acts of courage and unselfishness. Of these my book tells nothing. They have not been preserved in letter and memoir. After two and a half centuries they are not likely now to be recovered.

SOURCE J From the writings of Roger L'Estrange in newsheets published during the plague of 1665

   20 July
Last week's Bill of Mortality records 1089 death. 867 deaths were in the out-parishes* and poverty and dirt destroyed half of them. Within the wall of the city only 56 died.

10 August
The Plague is very much increased, but in the road and open streets there is very little appearance of it. Most of those dead of the Plague are from ten of the out-parishes; and those too in the dirty parts of these parishes where the poor are crowded together and affect one another.

*out-parishes = the poorer parishes outside the centre of the city

SOURCE K From *The impact of the Plague in Tudor and Stuart England* by the historian Paul Slack, 1985

   The circulation of printed Bills of Mortality helped to encourage discussion of the plague. Most obvious from the London Bills was the concentration of the plague in poorer parishes.

   People had seen the plague as something sent by God which threatened everyone. Now they began to see it as a problem connected with the way people lived and as a threat to particular parts of London.

   By making the plague measurable, the Bills of Mortality weakened supernatural explanations. Attitudes were no longer dominated by religious faith or superstition.

SOURCE L The opening illustration for a book written by Dr Thompson in 1666. In the book he gives a detailed account of the dissection of the corpse of a plague victim

The Manner of Dissecting the PESTILENTIALL BODY.

Case study 2: Surgery after the Medical Renaissance – Richard Wiseman

Biography

1622 – born

1640 – became a surgeon in the Dutch navy

1643 – became a surgeon with the royalist forces in the English Civil War and then went into exile with Charles II

1657 – served in the Spanish navy

1660 – returned to England and became a royal surgeon when Charles II was restored to the throne

1672 – published *A Treatise on Wounds*

1676 – published *Several Chirurgical Treatises* (CHIRURGY was another word for surgery)

1676 – died

Where did Wiseman get his ideas from?

Having spent over 30 years as a surgeon in various countries, Richard Wiseman set about passing on his knowledge to younger surgeons. In the last years of his life he wrote two long books describing the surgical methods he had seen and used.

In his introductions he wrote:

SOURCE 1

66 *Know, reader, that in preparation [of these treatises] I have read all the eminent chirurgical authors, yet in the writing I was more conformed to my own judgement and experience than other men's authority.* 99

SOURCE 2

66 *... such men as have spent their whole time in a perpetual practice are the best instructors ... [I] spent my time in armies, navies and cities, not in universities, nor books ... we do not all spend our time talking in coffee houses and drolling over the accidents that befall one another in our profession.* 99

Wiseman had certainly read the works of Greek and Roman doctors. He frequently referred to Hippocrates and Galen and followed some of their ideas. For example, in choosing a diet for a patient he told his readers to note 'the CONSTITUTION of the patient, whether he be hot or cold, dry or moist, old or young, tough or tender and washy.'

He also used other methods and medicines that had changed little over the centuries, including many herbs.

SOURCE 3

66 *Many [herbs] are mentioned by the [ancient] authors ... the most common are Comfrey, Bugle, Mugwort, Plantain, Wild tansy, St Johnswort, Strawberry leaves ... some are to be boiled in water with white wine and honey ... their principal use is in wounds of the thorax and abdomen though they be of frequent use in all great wounds ...*

Turpentine for deep wounds which cannot be closed – one of the most powerful medicaments in all wounds. [It] preserves bruises from putrifying ... 99

Less usual was one recipe for oil which required the boiling of 'two puppies until the skin fall off the bones.'

Wiseman also knew and admired the work of more recent writers, including Paré. In *A Treatise on Wounds* he said that 'since Galen's time we have found little augmentation of knowledge, till some bold adventurers in these latter ages have made some fortunate essays at further discoveries'. However, Wiseman gave far more space in his books to describing his own cases – over 600 are mentioned – than he gave to modern or ancient medical writers.

What were his treatments like?

Wiseman's surgical operations were often rushed because they were done in the middle of battle, on land or at sea. He knew the best way to deal with wounds, writing that Paré 'proposes a more easy and sure way, passing the needle with a good strong thread through the skin … ' but, he continued, 'at sea your cauteries are at such times in readiness. Use them. They will secure your patient from immediate danger.'

During fighting at Weymouth in the Civil War, Wiseman treated a soldier shot in the heel. The bleeding was unstoppable. 'I applied my endeavours but after all I was put to the use of the actual cautery which I did successfully.'

Describing the treatment of wounds, Wiseman wrote:

SOURCE 4

66 *[for a stab wound] The weapon thus drawn out, cleanse the wound with rags or ought else and permit the wound to bleed accordingly … if there be hair growing about the wound shave it off, then wipe away the clotted blood with a sponge dipped in red wine, oxycrate or water.* 99

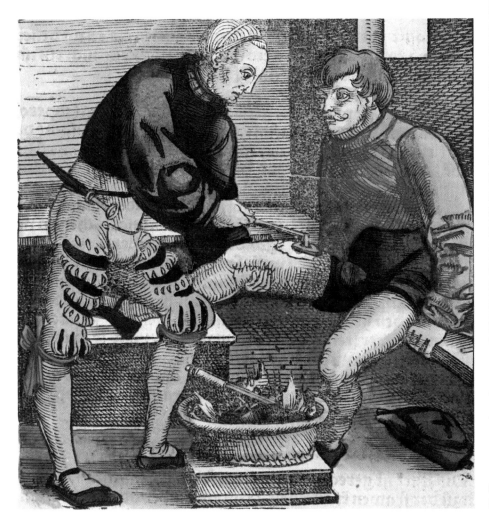

SOURCE 5

66 *[for a bullet wound] Having taken out the bullet dress it with oil as hot as the part will bear, not giving credit to any that shall persuade you to the contrary. On the second day [after the injury] consider the habit of the body … in these gunshot wounds it may be convenient for the body to be gently purged, thereby carrying off the bilious humour, which from their heat are most apt to ferment and flow into these wounds and cause pain and inflammation and ill symptoms …* 99

SOURCE 6

66 *[for a particularly large wound] The way to stop the FLUX of blood is by retaining the lips of the wound together by SUTURE or bandage and by applying such medicines as have a drying faculty … some of these mixed with a white of an egg … spread upon a double cloth and laid over the wound with compress and bandage … but if the artery bleed you must use the cautery … by it the vessel shrinks up at both ends, the flux [of blood] is immediately stopped and the part marvellously strengthened.* 99

1. What evidence is there in Sources 1–6 that Wiseman
a) was using new medical ideas
b) was using old ideas?

SOURCE 7 A surgeon cauterising a wound. Paré had warned about the dangers of cauterising wounds and of using boiling oil to help healing

Case study 3: Medicine in the home – James Woodforde

James Woodforde was a parson, born in 1740. He began to keep a diary in 1758 when he was a student at Oxford and continued it nearly every day until his death in 1803.

He spent his life amongst country people in villages in Somerset and Norfolk although he travelled many times to London to meet friends, see plays and visit the sights, such as the Tower of London. Source 1 gives extracts from his diary that deal with illness and medicine.

SOURCE 1

66 1776

June 4 … *My tooth pained me all night, got up a little after 5 this morning and sent for one Reeves a man who draws teeth in this parish, and about 7 he came and drew my tooth, but shockingly bad indeed, he broke away a great piece of my gum and broke one of the fangs of the tooth, it gave me exquisite pain all the day after, and my face was swelled prodigiously in the evening and much pain. Very bad and in much pain the whole day long. Paid the old man that drew it however. He is too old, I think, to draw teeth, can't see very well.*

November 3 … *This morning about 11 o'clock Dr Thorne came to my house and INOCULATED my servants Ben Legate and little Jack Warton against smallpox … Pray God my people and all others may do well, several houses have got the smallpox at present in Weston. O Lord send thy blessing of health on them all.*

November 22 … *John Bowles's wife … was inoculated by one Drake, formerly a sergeant in the Militia. He makes a deep INCISION in both arms and puts a plaister over, he gives no camomile but they take salts every morning … My neighbour Downing, father of the children lately inoculated, has got the smallpox in the natural way and likely to have it very bad – therefore I sent Harry Dunnell this evening to Dr Thorne's, to desire him to come tomorrow and see him, which he promised.*

1779

May 15 … *Bled my three horses this morning, two quarts each …*

May 22 … *My boy Jack had another touch of the AGUE about noon. I gave him a dram of gin at the beginning of the fit and pushed him headlong into one of my Ponds and ordered him to bed immediately and he was better after it and had nothing of the cold fit after, but was very hot …*

May 27 … *My maid Nanny was taken very ill this evening with a dizziness in the head and a desire to vomit but could not. Her straining to vomit brought on the hiccups which continued very violent till after she got to bed. I gave her a dose of rhubarb going to bed. Ben was also very ill and in the same complaint about noon, but he vomited and was soon better. I gave Ben a good dose of rhubarb also going to bed.*

1781

April 14 … *I got up very ill this morning about 8 o'clock, having had little sleep all the night, owing to the pain in my ear which was much worse in the night and broke, and a good deal of blood only came away. The pain continued still very bad all the morning tho' not quite so bad as before. It made me very uneasy about it. A throbbing pain in my ear continued till I went to bed. I put a roasted onion into my ear going to bed tonight.*

April 15 … *I thank God I had a tolerable night to sleep and was much better this morning for it …*

1784

March 9 … *Nancy [Woodforde's niece] very ill again this morning, kept her bed almost the whole day. I sent for Dr Thorne early, he came about 12 o'clock, says it is the fever which has been so long about these parts. Mr Thorne left a vomit for to be taking tonight and a rhubarb powder to take tomorrow. Nancy however ate some rabbit for dinner.*

March 11 … *Nancy taken very ill this morning about 3 o'clock, worse than ever. Mr Thorne came here about 11 and brought some quinine for her to take to begin at 12 o'clock and then every three hours to bed …*

March 12 … *Nancy a good deal better this morning, she taked quinine today every two hours till bed time. She complained of great lightness in her head and rather giddy …*

March 13 … *Nancy brave today … but the quinine has prevented [the fever's] return …*

1788

March 1 ... Ben returned about 4 o'clock this afternoon and he brought me a letter [saying that] Juliana was, it was much feared, in a decline, on account of her lately having had the measles and catching cold after, which has affected her lungs, she has been bled seven times ...

May 17 ... [Ben] brought me two letters ... which brought the disagreeable news of Juliana's death ...

1790

May 6 ... To 18 yards of black ribband, paid. Gave my brother half my black ribband. The ribband is designed to put round our necks to prevent sore throats.

September 24 ... Nancy was taken very ill this afternoon with a pain within her, blown up so as if poisoned, attended with a vomiting. I suppose it proceeded in great measure from what she ate at dinner ... some boiled beef rather fat and salt, a good deal of nice roast duck and a plenty of boiled damson pudding. After dinner by way of dessert she ate some greengage plums, some figs and raspberries and cream. I desired her to drink a good half pint glass of warm rum and water which she did and was soon a little better – for supper she had water-gruel with a couple of small tablespoonfuls of rum in it, and going to bed I gave her a good dose of rum and ginger. She was much better before she went to bed ...

September 25 ... Nancy thank God much better this morning – the rhubarb made her rise earlier than usual ...

1791

March 7 ... the smallpox spreads much in the parish. Abigail Roberts's husband was very bad in it in the natural way, who was supposed to have had it before and which he thought also. His children are inoculated by Johnny Reeve, as are also Richmond's children near me. It is a pity that all the poor in the parish were not inoculated also. I am entirely for it.

March 11 ... The stye on my right eyelid still swelled and inflamed very much. As it is commonly said that the eyelid being rubbed by the tail of a black cat would do it much good if not entirely cure it, and having a black cat, a little before dinner I made a trial of it, and very soon after dinner I found my eyelid much abated of the swelling and almost free from pain. I cannot therefore but conclude it to be of the greatest service to a stye on the eyelid. Any other cat's tail may have the above effect in all probability – but I did my eyelid with my own black tom cat's tail.

March 15 ... My right eye again, that is, its eyelid much inflamed again and rather painful. I put on a plaistor to it this morning, but in the afternoon took it off again as I perceived no good from it. I buried poor John Roberts this afternoon, aged about 35.

March 16 ... My eyelid is I think rather better than it was, I bathed it with warm milk and water last night. I took a little rhubarb going to bed tonight. My eyelid about noon rather worse owing perhaps to the warm milk and water, therefore just before dinner I washed it well with cold water and in the evening appeared much better for it ... Mr Custance gave me a Guinea to pay for the inoculation of Harry Dunnell's six children.

March 17 ... My eyelid much better today, washed it well with cold water this morning. Dr Thorne recommended the same to me when here. **99**

1. Which remedy did Woodforde use most often? (It appears five times.)
2. What different kinds of remedy did Thorne (Woodforde's doctor) use and recommend?
3. Woodforde records the deaths of two people in Source 1. What did they die of?
4. Which new method of preventing disease was being used in 1776?
5. Did Woodforde believe it was his cat's tail or his doctor which cured his eye problem?
6. Woodforde died less than 200 years ago. Are his remedies more like the ones we use today or the remedies Galen used almost 2000 years earlier?

7. How useful are Woodforde's diaries for finding out how illnesses were treated in the eighteenth century?

■ **ACTIVITY**

Over the coming weeks keep your own medical diary. Record not only what happens to you, but also what happens to your family or friends – just as Woodforde did. Note down illnesses, remedies, treatments and what effect the treatments had.

How would you treat Charles II?

On 2 February 1685 King Charles II was suddenly taken ill. Twelve doctors clustered around him, trying to save his life.

Your task is to take on the role of one of those doctors and suggest appropriate treatments. The questions below give you a series of choices to make. They are real choices based on actual treatments given to King Charles.

All the details were written up by Sir Charles Scarborough – one of the king's doctors.

SOURCE 1 Charles II

Instructions

1. For each decision choose the option or options that you think will be the most effective, but make sure you have good reasons for choosing them.
2. Record your choices and the reasons for them on your own record sheet.

   Remember: if your treatments fail and the king dies, the other doctors may try to blame you for his death! However, if the king lives, you will be richly rewarded. You may win a knighthood, a country house and a large pension!
Good luck!

February 2

At 8 o'clock in the morning the king collapses. For two hours his servants have known he is ill. As he is being shaved he gives a terrible shriek and falls unconscious. Immediately the king's physicians are called.

DECISION 1

Do you recommend to your fellow doctors:
a) opening a vein in the king's arm to bleed sixteen ounces of blood
b) calling in Mistress Holder, who treated the king's poisoned hand five years ago (see Source 3)
c) doing nothing
d) asking for an X-ray to be taken?

SOURCE 2 Sir Charles Scarborough (left). He is demonstrating the anatomy of the arm. Sir Charles Scarborough was one of the doctors who treated Charles II

SOURCE 3 John Aubrey, a scholar and gossip, writing in about 1680

  66 *His Majesty King Charles II had hurt his hand which he instructed his surgeons to make well. But they made it much worse, so that it swelled up and poisoned him up to the shoulder. He could not sleep and began to be feverish. Mrs Holder, wife of his Chaplain, among many other gifts has a strange wisdom in the curing of wounds. Mrs Holder was sent for at 11 o'clock at night. She made ready a* POULTICE *and applied it and gave his Majesty sudden ease. He slept well. Next day she dressed it and perfectly cured him, to the great grief of all the surgeons who envy and hate her.* 99

DECISION 2

Within an hour there is no improvement in the king's health. What should you do next:
a) bleed the king again
b) give more time for the first bleeding to work
c) purge the king by giving him pills that will empty his bowels
d) pray?

DECISION 3

Some of the king's servants do not think you are doing enough. They demand that you try another treatment. Do you:
a) give the king more pills to purge him some more
b) tell the servants that you are the expert and you know exactly what you are doing
c) place pigeons against the soles of the king's feet
d) shave the king's head and put burning tongs on his scalp to blister the skin?

February 3

The king can speak again but there is no other improvement. Everyone is growing more worried. Then the king has another attack.

DECISION 4

Should you begin the next stage of treatment by:
a) calling Mrs Holder to give the king a herbal remedy
b) bleeding the king again, this time opening two veins
c) giving the king some more of the Sacred Tincture which will keep his bowels empty
d) leaving the palace as swiftly as possible, saying that you have other patients to attend to?

February 4

The king is much better in the morning. The worst seems to be over but in the afternoon he has another attack.

DECISION 5

Should you:
a) continue bleeding the king
b) continue purging the king
c) prescribe the following medicine recommended by one of your colleagues: spirit of human skull, 40 drops, taken in an ounce and a half of Cordial Julep
d) abandon all treatments?

February 6

The king's health is worsening rapidly. The physicians are undecided about whether to use the remedy below.

> Every other hour – two scruples (two and a half grams) of BEZOAR STONE, a green stone found in the stomach of Persian goats. Bezoar is a much-famed remedy.

DECISION 6

What would you recommend? Should you use this remedy or not?

DECISION 7

The king is dead. Do you:
a) send the palace your bill for payment, knowing that you did your best
b) try to see the new king James II (Charles II's brother) so that you can blame the other doctors for Charles II's death
c) order a carriage and drive towards the coast as fast as you can?

How did you get on?

There is a score sheet on page 91. Use it to calculate your total score.

30 or more
If you scored 30 or more you would have been a very successful doctor in the 1680s.
20–29
If you scored 20–29 you have done well but need to be a little more ruthless in trying your remedies. Perhaps you are too kind to your patients?
10–19
If you scored 10–19 you clearly need a lot more training!
Less than 10
If you scored less than 10 you would have been a failure as a doctor in the 1680s. However, with your treatments the king might have lived!

How did the training of doctors change c.1350–c.1750?

THE LATE MIDDLE AGES were a period of increasing wealth in Europe. With this wealth came a new demand for doctors and an increased interest in developing the medical skills of doctors.

How were doctors trained in the late Middle Ages?

In AD900 the first university medical school in Europe had been set up. Others followed. Old manuscripts by Galen and other ancient writers were rediscovered and translated. By the late Middle Ages anyone who wanted to be a doctor had to train at one of the medical schools. (These trained doctors were usually known as physicians. PHYSIC means the art of healing.) Sources 1–5 show some of the skills and knowledge a medieval doctor would be taught at a medical school.

■ ACTIVITY

Imagine that you are a teacher in a medieval medical school. Use Sources 1–5 to help you list the topics you will teach to your students while they are training to be doctors.

Your course must sound interesting and relevant to your pupils, so you must be sure that it contains all the important topics.

Then write a prospectus for your course describing the most important topics on the list, and explaining why doctors need to study them.

SOURCE 1 A teacher presiding over dissection at a medical school. The oldest medical school in Europe was founded at Salerno around 900. By the 1200s Montpellier in France was the most famous but there were a number of others. At these schools students listened to lectures where the teacher read out passages from the works of Galen and other ancient writers. At Montpellier, after 1340, the students were allowed to study one corpse a year, but the dissection was done by the teacher's assistant, not by the student

Anathomia Mū dini Emēdata p doctozé meler̄ſtat

SOURCE 2 From the writings of Guy de Chauliac, a French doctor who lived c.1300–80

  Knowledge of anatomy is gained in two ways. One is by books. This is useful but it is not enough to discover all that can be learned by observation. The second way is by dissecting dead bodies, namely, of those who have been recently beheaded or hanged. By this we learn the anatomy of the internal organs, the muscles, skin, veins and sinews.

  Mondino of Bologna, who wrote about this, made dissections many times, and my master did the same, placing the dead body on the table and dealing with it in four lectures.

[In his books he made over 3200 references to other medical texts that he had consulted. The writer he mentioned most frequently was Galen (890 quotations), followed by the Arabic writers Avicenna and Rhazes. There were 120 references to Hippocrates.]

SOURCE 3 Adapted from codes of behaviour for doctors that developed throughout Europe in the period after AD1000

  A doctor should be willing to learn, be sober and modest, charming, hard-working and intelligent. Anyone wishing to become a good doctor must be able to study for long periods, so that his judgement and understanding improve by constant reading of different books. He should not be greedy. He should take care of the rich and poor quite impartially, for medicine is needed by all classes of people. If payment is offered, he should accept rather than refuse it. But if it is not offered, it should not be demanded. Whatever you hear in the course of your treatment, unless it is something that ought to be reported and judged, keep it secret.

A medieval doctor might believe in many of the explanations of disease on pages 48–49. A doctor would be trained to base his treatments on the theory of the four humours. He would examine the patient's urine and check its colour against a chart (such as Source 5) to help diagnose the illness. He may also have used ASTROLOGY to work out the position of the planets before deciding the best treatment. A table of the positions of the planets would be used by every doctor. The moon, in particular, was believed to have a great effect on the humours in the body and so the doctor had to know the moon's position before, for example, bleeding the patient.

Bleeding was one of the most common treatments because doctors believed wholeheartedly in the importance of keeping the body's humours in balance. One medical handbook claimed that blood-letting:

SOURCE 4

❝ ... *clears the mind, strengthens the memory, cleanses the guts, dries up the brain, warms the marrow, sharpens the hearing, curbs tears, ... promotes digestion, produces a musical voice, dispels sleepiness, drives away anxiety, feeds the bloods, rids it of poisonous matter and gives long life ... it cures pains, fevers and various sicknesses and makes urine clear and clean.* ❞

Given this list of effects it is not surprising that bleeding was common. Monastery records suggest that monks were bled between seven and twelve times a year. The bleeding continued until the patient was on the verge of unconsciousness which means that he had lost three or four pints of blood!

A range of techniques were used for bleeding. Sometimes the bleeding cup (as used by the Greeks, see Source 5 on page 18) was employed. LEECHES, which suck blood from human beings, were also used.

There were strict rules for blood-letting. One doctor in Paris had to show his skills by bleeding twenty people. He also paid for the meals and wine of his examiners. They still failed him!

SOURCE 5

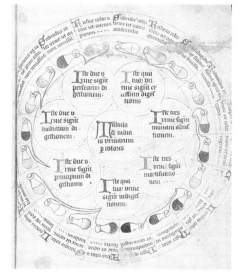

A urine chart. This was one of the basic tools which doctors used to diagnose illnesses. Wealthy families regularly sent urine samples to their doctors so that the doctors could look for signs of illness developing. The text around the outside of the chart describes the colour and the quality of the urine (whether it is cloudy or clear). The text in the middle groups the samples together according to what they tell the doctor about the patient's digestion. The best digestion is bottom left. Death (black urine) is bottom right

Could women become doctors in the Middle Ages?

Women were not allowed to go to universities, so although women still carried out much of the everyday medical care in towns and villages they could not train to become physicians. The effect was to devalue the skills of women healers. The Church, which oversaw the training of doctors, was particularly suspicious of the WISE WOMEN in villages. However, women continued to act as midwives, and they could still become surgeons.

SOURCE 6
Midwives attending a birth. Doctors did not get involved in childbirth in the Middle Ages. By the 1400s midwives in France and Germany had to gain licences, follow apprenticeships and keep to certain rules of behaviour

■ TASK

Some of the statements below are true and some are false.

Rewrite each statement, correcting it if necessary, and then explain what evidence on pages 82–83 proves that your new statement is correct. You may wish to add to the statements and make them longer.

Statements
a) Both men and women could become qualified doctors.
b) More illnesses were treated by women than by men.
c) Doctors were poorly trained and educated.
d) The ideas of Galen and Hippocrates had been forgotten.
e) It was important for doctors to understand astrology.

How were doctors and healers trained after the Medical Renaissance?

Licensed healers

Physician

Physicians were fully qualified doctors who had studied for fourteen years at university, seven of those studying medicine. They were all men.

They knew the work of Galen and many other ancient writers as well as that of Harvey, Vesalius and other more modern doctors.

For their work they charged large fees, especially in London. Even the fee of a country physician could be a month's wage for a labourer.

Surgeon

Surgeons or surgeonesses trained by watching and copying other surgeons in a long apprenticeship.

They were given licences by the local bishop, allowing them to treat patients and charge fees.

Despite their practical skills they were looked down on by physicians as second-class doctors.

Apothecary

An APOTHECARY sold and mixed medicines that had been prescribed by physicians.

Apothecaries were not supposed to treat the sick or prescribe medicines but many did so, especially for the poor, for a small fee.

There were many apothecaries in London and several in any town.

Midwife

Midwives were also licensed by the local bishop to supervise the last week of a pregnancy and deliver babies. However, if there were complications, the midwife handed her patient over to a physician.

Unlicensed healers

Family

The first person to treat nearly all sicknesses was the wife or mother of the patient.

Housewife-physician

Girls were expected to learn how to treat illnesses and common injuries.

Books were written especially to give advice on these subjects to ladies of the manor, and some read medical textbooks. Ladies treated people from their village and local farms as well as their own families and servants.

Wise woman

In every village and town there were wise women whom local people trusted because of their deep knowledge of herbs and other treatments, which had often been passed down through generations.

However, if a treatment went wrong then the wise woman could suddenly find herself accused of being a WITCH.

Travelling quack

At every fair and market there were tooth-pullers, herb-sellers and others who made their living as they travelled round the country. Some might do good because they had built up knowledge through experience. Many simply wanted to take the patients' money and run!

■ ACTIVITY

The illustrations above show you some of the healers who might be available in this period. Whom do you think each of the following would consult if they were ill:
a) a noble family   b) a rich lawyer
c) a farm labourer   d) a beggar?
Explain the reasons for your choice.

How did the status of women healers change?

In 1729 a surgeon in Fulham took on a new apprentice. Nothing surprising about that, you might think, but there was. The surgeon was a woman. Her name was Anne Saint and her apprentice was also a woman – Mary Webb.

In fact, a number of women surgeons can be found in the records of the sixteenth and seventeenth centuries. They came from families of craftsmen and churchmen, and often had fathers or brothers who were surgeons. A Mrs Cook was appointed as the surgeon-apothecary at Christ's Hospital, London, in the 1570s. As you can see from Sources 7 and 8, such women seem to have been very popular, especially among the poor, who probably made up the majority of their patients.

SOURCE 7 Records of the city of York, 1572. Male doctors had wished to stop Isabel Warwick treating the sick

❝ *[Isabel Warwick] has the skill in the science of surgery and has done good therein, it is therefore agreed that she, upon her good behaviour, shall use the same without obstruction by any of the surgeons of the city.* ❞

SOURCE 8 Epitaphs and memorials of several women healers

❝ *Margaret Colfe of Lewisham. Having been above 40 years a willing nurse, midwife, surgeon, and in part physician to all both rich and poor, without expecting reward. [Lewisham, 1643]*

Prudence Potter of Devon – her life was spent in the industrious and successful practice of physic, chirurgery and midwifery. [Devon, 1689]

Dorothy Burton – has excellent skill in chirurgery, sore eyes, aches etc., and has done many famous good cures upon divers poor folks, that were otherwise destitute of help. [1629]

Lady Halkett – she ministered every Wednesday to a multitude of poor infirm persons, besides what she daily sent to persons of all ranks who consulted her in their MALADIES. Next to the study of divinities, she seems to have taken most delight in those of Physic and surgery, in which she was no mean proficient. [1699] ❞

By the 1700s, however, women surgeons were disappearing, too. One reason for this was education. For centuries anyone who wished to become a physician had had to study at university, and women were not allowed to attend the universities. By the 1700s, surgery was going the same way. Many male surgeons were better educated and women, who were rarely allowed to learn Latin and Greek, were unable to match the men's education, however good their practical skills.

In the 1700s it also became fashionable among middle-class families to have a highly educated doctor. Some worried about what their friends would think if they continued to consult a woman, no matter how skilful she might be. The fashionable people were only interested in whether doctors had the right kinds of qualification.

SOURCE 9 From John Aubrey, *Brief Lives*, written around 1680. In this extract, Aubrey recalls Hobbes' comments on the fashion of having a learned doctor

❝ *Hobbes is regarded as one of the greatest philosophers to have lived. Mr Hobbes used to say that he had rather have the advice or take medicine from an experienced old woman, that had been at many sick people's bedsides, than from the learnedest but unexperienced physician.* ❞

A third reason why women lost their place to men was actually the result of an important invention. In about 1620 Peter Chamberlen invented obstetric forceps, used in the delivery of babies. With forceps a doctor could free a baby from the womb without killing it or its mother. However, anatomical knowledge was needed and it seemed that, as only men had studied anatomy at university, only men could use this life-saving invention. By 1700 men were rapidly taking over the task of delivering babies, something that had probably been the work of women since time began.

■ **TASK**

Copy these headings and write notes under them to show how each one helped exclude women from the medical professions.
■ Education
■ Fashion
■ Forceps

Did the Medical Renaissance change hospitals?

SOURCE 1 The Hotel Dieu in Paris. This is one of the few pictures of the inside of a medieval hospital. Hotel Dieu was not a typical hospital – the king's doctors worked there. It opened in 1452. The main hall measured 72 metres by 14 metres

IMAGINE THAT YOU are a patient standing at the gate of a medieval hospital. The first person you meet is the warden. He looks you up and down. Do you look respectable? How much money do you have? Why do you need help? Do you have an infectious or serious illness? He certainly will not let you into the hospital if you are infectious because you would spread sickness.

The warden decides you can be admitted. He opens the gate and you enter a courtyard. There are monks scurrying to a service but they pay you no attention. Their work is to pray for your soul, not look after your body. A servant leads you into the hall. It is so large it is like a church, but it is full of beds. At the end of the hall is a series of chapels where priests say mass every day. Patients can watch or join in. Above each bed is a lamp and there's a cutaway space in the wall for belongings. The servant helps you into bed alongside another patient. You are old and frail. You fall asleep.

Next day you awake. No need to worry about the doctor – there is no doctor. Doctors treat kings and nobles and wealthy merchants, not ordinary old folk in hospitals. You are cared for by the nuns and their helpers. They keep you warm, clean, rested and fed. Do you have any aches or pains? Do you feel queasy? They have some excellent herbal remedies, learned from the nuns who worked in the hospital before them. They also have books full of remedies in the monastery library.

All you have to do is rest and pray for the soul of the merchant who paid for the upkeep of your bed. Your prayers will speed his soul to heaven. Sleep, warmth, food and the nuns' herbal potions will make your old bones comfortable – that is what hospitals are for.

There were nearly 1200 places called hospitals in England and Wales but only about ten per cent of these actually cared for the sick. Some were very large. St Leonards in York had space for over 200 people. Others had only five or six beds.

SOURCE 2 From the rules of the hospital of St John, Bridgwater, 1219

No LEPERS, LUNATICS, or persons having the falling sickness or other contagious disease, and no pregnant women, or sucking infants, and no intolerable persons, even though they be poor and infirm, are to be admitted in the house; and if any such be admitted by mistake, they are to be expelled as soon as possible. And when the other poor and infirm persons have recovered they are to be let out without delay.

1. If you had the Black Death would you have been let into a hospital?
2. Why do you think hospitals made the rules described in Source 2?
3. Draw a spider diagram to show:
   a) who the *patients* were
   b) what *treatments* they received
   c) who *nursed* the patients in a medieval hospital.

Hospitals and the Medical Renaissance

Hospitals
Many medieval hospitals were part of monasteries. When Henry VIII closed the monasteries in the 1530s, many hospitals closed, too. However, others were taken over by town councils, especially the almshouses that looked after the elderly poor. In London the city council and charity helped to keep St Bartholomew's Hospital open. By the 1660s it had 12 wards and up to 300 patients. During the early 1700s many new hospitals were opened, paid for by local people, charities and town councils. Eleven new hospitals were founded in London and 46 in the rest of Britain.

Patients
In 1750 nearly all hospitals still looked after the poor. Anyone with any money paid for a doctor or nurse to look after them at home. Many hospitals still did not admit people with infectious diseases or long-term medical problems.

Hospitals and the Medical Renaissance

Treatments
Patients were kept clean and warm and were fed regularly. If they became sick they were given herbal remedies or bled. Simple surgery was carried out, such as setting fractured limbs or removing bladder stones, and sometimes desperate surgery was used, such as amputating a limb, if there was no other possible remedy. All treatments were free but patients were still expected to pray for their recovery.

Doctors and nurses
In the 1660s St Bartholomew's Hospital in London had three physicians and three surgeons, fifteen nursing sisters and a larger number of nursing helpers. The physicians had been trained at university but training carried on in the hospital. It was convenient for them to practise on the poor, not on wealthier patients. The nursing sisters were able to treat patients with herbal remedies but the nursing helpers did heavy, manual work – washing, cleaning and preparing food. They did not need special medical skills and so did not have any medical training. After the 1530s none of the nurses were nuns. Most nursing helpers were poorly paid.

4. Why did the number of hospitals change between 1350 and 1750?
5. Compare your spider diagram (Question 3 on page 86) with the one on this page. Take patients, treatments and doctors/nurses in turn. Explain the impact of the Medical Renaissance on them.
6. Do you think the Medical Renaissance led to great changes in hospitals? Explain your answer.

Why weren't people any healthier by 1750?

THIS PAGE SUMMARISES the key reasons why this news vendor is right. Let's start with those great medical discoveries. Why did they happen? You can find an important part of the answer in the boxing rings below!

1350

1750

Enquiry and challenges to tradition

Discoveries by:

Vesalius

Paré

Harvey

Social changes
- Better education
- The invention of printing
- Improved technology, e.g. better microscopes

Why didn't these discoveries make people healthier?

1. FURTHER VITAL DISCOVERIES WERE STILL TO BE MADE

Nobody understood what really caused disease, so none of these could really improve:

Treatments

Hospitals

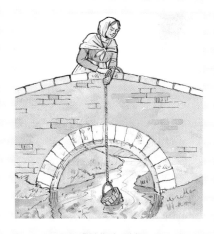
Public health

2. GOVERNMENTS WERE NOT TRYING HARD ENOUGH TO IMPROVE PUBLIC HEALTH

What was needed?

Clean water supplies

Sewers to take away waste

Plague! I must leave London – and leave the poor to die . . .

Why was there no action?
- Governments did not think it was their job to improve public health.
- Governments did not raise the money or labour force to carry out public health work.
- Without an understanding of the true causes of disease, governments did not realise it was important for them to take action to improve public health.

The health jigsaw: 1750

You should be familiar with this idea by now.

The jigsaw pieces represent the knowledge and developments needed by doctors to give people better health and longer life. This doctor in 1750 has some pieces of the jigsaw. The blank pieces are discoveries yet to be made.

1. What do you think should be shown on the blank pieces?
2. Look back to the similar picture on page 36. Does the doctor in 1750 have more in common with:
a) Galen
b) a medieval doctor
c) a doctor today?
   Explain your answer in a piece of extended writing.

How would you treat Charles II?: score sheet

Use this table to add up the points you have scored in the game on pages 80–81.
Mark them on your recording sheet.

DECISION 1
a) Exactly what the doctors did. Score 3 points.
b) Never! She has not been trained at a university. She's a woman. What can she know about medicine? Score 0 points.
c) This might have done Charles some good, but people may think that you don't know what to do and if the king dies they'll blame you for doing nothing! Score 0 points.
d) Score 0 points, but this is the least of your problems. You are about to be burned as a witch.

DECISION 2
a) Exactly what the doctors did! Score 2 points.
b) Do you believe in the theory of the humours or don't you? The more bleeding the better! Score 0 points.
c) Excellent idea, it will help balance the humours – score 3 points.
d) Very good idea. Pray for the king and yourself but don't let it interrupt the bleeding. Score 1 point.

DECISION 3
a) Good idea – score 2 points.
b) Yes, shout and scream at the servants by all means. You are the expert. However, this won't help the king. Have 1 point for showing that you're in charge.
c) This would be a good idea if the king had the plague but he has a different illness. Score 0 points.
d) Excellent, just what the doctors did in 1685. Score 3 points.

DECISION 4
a) No! You don't want that woman stealing the credit just when your treatments may work. Score 0 points.
b) Excellent again. Hippocrates and Galen would have been proud of you. Score 3 points.
c) Another good idea! Score 3 points.
d) This is the fastest way to execution. People will think you have secretly poisoned the king. Score 0 points.

DECISION 5
a) Score 3 points.
b) Score 3 points.
c) Score 3 points. (If you thought you should have chosen all three of A, B and C have a bonus point!)
d) Score 0 points. How will the king get better if you don't treat him?

DECISION 6
Yes – if you decided to use the bezoar stone score 3 points. It might work and at this stage anything is worth trying. Records show that the king's doctors used 58 different drugs in five days. No – score 0 points if you decided not to use bezoar.

DECISION 7
a) Score 3 points. You have spent five days trying to save the king with the best methods and medicines. Of course you deserve payment.
b) This is a tricky one. It might be a good idea but you don't want people to think that the doctors, including you, could have done more to save the king. Score 1 point. (After the king's death Charles Scarborough wrote an account of the treatment he and the other doctors used to prove that Charles had died of natural causes, not from poison or the mistakes of his doctors. This is how we know so much about the treatments used.)
c) Are you mad? You will be suspected of poisoning the king. Score 0 points.

MEDICINE AND HEALTH 1750–1900

Why was there so much progress in this period?

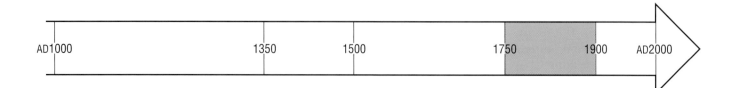

AD1000	1350	1500	1750	1900	AD2000	

OH NO, NOT AGAIN! You've seen this kind of 'progress' claim before on page 44 and on page 88. However, in Chapter 2 you saw that 400 years of medical progress did very little to improve the health of ordinary people.

In this story of medicine and health you are now coming to a period which is often talked about as a time of great progress. Between 1750 and 1900:

■ scientists and doctors made giant steps forward in understanding the true causes of disease
■ they discovered ways of preventing some of the killer diseases
■ there were enormous improvements in public health. Many towns improved sewers and fresh water supplies.

In Chapter 3 you will investigate why historians regard this period as a time of such great progress in medicine and health, and you will discover some of the factors which helped bring about this progress.

You will also look at whether, in this period, medical progress at last began to affect the health of ordinary people. Is the news vendor right or is it just wishful thinking?

■ **TASK**

1. Make a list of the reasons why there was a medical revolution in the period 1750–1900.
2. Why hadn't this happened earlier?

Changing Britain 1750–1900

IN THIS PERIOD there were great changes in medicine. Source 1 shows the key reasons why changes took place.

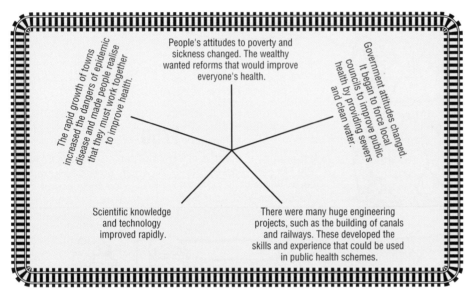

SOURCE 1 Factors leading to change in medicine, 1750–1900

People's attitudes to poverty and sickness changed. The wealthy wanted reforms that would improve everyone's health.

The rapid growth of towns increased the dangers of epidemic disease and made people realise that they must work together to improve health.

Government attitudes changed. It began to force local councils to improve public health by providing sewers and clean water.

Scientific knowledge and technology improved rapidly.

There were many huge engineering projects, such as the building of canals and railways. These developed the skills and experience that could be used in public health schemes.

SOURCE 2 The beginning of the Industrial Revolution – *Coalbrookdale by Night*, painted by Philippe Jacques de Loutherbourg in 1801. Coalbrookdale, in Shropshire, was the home of the iron industry, and the new factories and their dramatic fires attracted artists keen to paint scenes like this, which no one had ever seen before. To many of them this was a vision of hell on earth

SOURCE 3 *Over London by Rail*, an engraving of terraced houses in London by Gustav Doré, 1872. Industrial towns were full of grim terraces. Houses were crammed together close to factories and workshops because, until the later 1800s, people had to walk to work – there was no transport. When these houses were built, between 1750 and 1850, there were no laws about providing sewers, fresh water or toilets in houses. People collected water from pipes in the streets. Refuse piled up in gutters

SOURCE 4 This illustration was published in the *Illustrated London News* in 1897. It shows the technological changes that had taken place since Queen Victoria had become queen sixty years earlier, in 1837

1. Think back to history classes in Years 8 and 9.
a) Which industries grew rapidly during the Industrial Revolution?
b) In which parts of the country did towns grow rapidly?
2. Look at Sources 2 and 3. Why were living and working conditions dangerous to health?
3. How would unemployment and poverty affect the health of the people?
4. In 1665 Charles II and his councillors did nothing to protect the people from the plague. By 1900 governments were working hard to save people from disease. Using these sources, explain why you think the attitudes of governments had changed by 1900.
5. Look at Source 4.
a) What had been the main changes in power and energy?
b) What does this tell you about the pace of developments in science and technology?
c) Why do you think developments in science and technology led to great improvements in medicine?

Smallpox: how did Jenner make his breakthrough?

THE GREATEST MEDICAL triumph before 1850 was the discovery of a way to prevent smallpox, which had previously been one of the biggest killer diseases.

The first method of prevention – inoculation

Epidemics of smallpox broke out in Britain every few years. Many died from it. The horror of smallpox was not just the danger of death but the physical scars it caused. For many, especially the poor, smallpox also left a family isolated. Tradesmen and friends were frightened away. When someone had the disease their house, belongings and goods had to be disinfected, and the damage that this caused was not paid for. Sufferers feared they would lose their jobs. To avoid financial ruin people often tried to prevent others finding out that a family member had smallpox.

In the eighteenth century a method of avoiding smallpox was introduced to Britain from China where it had been used for centuries. Chinese doctors had noticed that people who had suffered a mild form of smallpox often survived during later epidemics. They developed a method of inoculation which involved spreading matter from a smallpox scab onto an open cut in the skin. This gave people a mild dose of the disease and protected them from the full force of a severe attack.

This method of inoculation gradually spread through Asia, helped by the growing trade between China and the rest of Asia. It was observed in Turkey by Lady Mary Wortley Montague. She had only just survived an attack of smallpox and was keen that her children should not suffer the same disfiguring disease. In 1721 she had her children inoculated and they survived the next smallpox epidemic. Lady Montague was an influential woman; she had many friends who were doctors. They saw the potential of preventing smallpox and of making money from inoculation. As you saw in Source 12 on pages 78–79, inoculation became common. Whenever smallpox epidemics raged during the eighteenth century, some doctors made a fortune from mass inoculation (see Source 2).

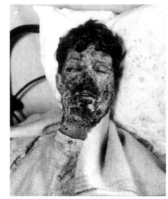

SOURCE 1 A patient with severe smallpox scabs

In Maidstone mass inoculations were carried out by Daniel Sutton during an epidemic in 1766. Source 3 shows their impact. This information was recorded by Reverend John Howlett who was a supporter of mass inoculation.

1. Draw a graph to show the figures in Source 3.
2. Mark on the graph the date when mass inoculations were carried out in Maidstone.
3. How effective was inoculation in your opinion?

Date	Total deaths	Deaths from smallpox	
		Total	As % of all deaths
1740–51	1594	260	16.3
1752–63	1616	202	12.5
1764–75	1798	76	4.2
1776–87	1992	122	6.1
1788–99	2308	31	1.3

SOURCE 3 Deaths from smallpox in Maidstone, 1740–99

There seems little doubt that inoculation reduced the likelihood of dying from smallpox but inoculation itself involved some risk. Some people died of the mild dose that they were given. Others became carriers of the disease and it is probable that they spread smallpox to people with whom they came into contact. Therefore some people refused the treatment.

As you can see from Source 2, doctors also charged a substantial fee for their work, so the very poor could not afford inoculation.

4. What factors led to inoculation being introduced to Britain in 1721?
5. Why did inoculation not totally solve the problem of smallpox?
6. If you had lived in Maidstone in the 1700s would you have paid to be inoculated?

The second method of prevention – Edward Jenner and vaccination

Edward Jenner was a doctor in Gloucestershire. When Jenner offered inoculation against smallpox he was puzzled to find that many people refused. He discovered from the local farmers that people believed that they would not catch smallpox if they had already had a mild disease called cowpox. They did not think they needed Jenner's inoculations. Jenner examined this idea and discovered that dairy maids, who often caught cowpox, did seem less likely than other people to catch smallpox. He wondered whether he could use cowpox as a method of preventing smallpox.

> **SOURCE 4** Extracts from Dr Jenner's casebook, published in *An enquiry into the causes and effects of Variola Vaccinae, known by the name of cowpox*, 1798
>
> 66 *Case 16*
> *Sarah Nelmes, a dairy maid near this place, was infected with cowpox from her master's cows in May 1796. A large sore and the usual symptoms were produced.*
> *Case 17* James Phipps
> *I selected a healthy boy, about eight years old. The matter was taken from the [cowpox] sore on the hand of Sarah Nelmes and it was inserted on 14 May 1796 into the boy by two cuts each about half an inch long. On the seventh day he complained of uneasiness, on the ninth he became a little chilly, lost his appetite and had a slight headache and spent the night with some degree of restlessness, but on the following day he was perfectly well.*
>
> *In order to ascertain that the boy was secure from the CONTAGION of the smallpox, he was inoculated with smallpox matter, but no disease followed. Several months later he was again inoculated with smallpox matter but again no disease followed.* 99

Jenner tried the same experiment with 23 different cases and recorded his observations. Only then did he conclude 'that the cowpox protects the human constitution from the infection of the smallpox'.

Jenner wrote up his findings and submitted them to the Royal Society for publication in 1798. However, as you will see from page 98, there was much opposition to Jenner's ideas and the Society rejected his work.

Jenner therefore published his findings himself (see Source 4). He called the technique vaccination because the Latin word for cow is *vacca*. His book was widely read and distributed. Parliament thought Jenner's work was very significant and he was given a grant of £30,000 to open a vaccination clinic in London.

By 1803 doctors were using the technique in America. Thomas Jefferson, President of the United States, championed it. He believed Jenner had made the complete eradication of smallpox a possibility. In 1805 Napoleon had all his soldiers vaccinated, and by 1812 Arabic and Turkish translations of Jenner's work were being sold in central Asia. In 1852, more than 50 years after Jenner's discovery, the British government made vaccination compulsory. You can see the results in Source 5.

7. What do Jenner's methods tell you about the way doctors were trained by 1800?
8. How were:
a) scientific investigation
b) government action
c) improved communications
   important in the discovery and development of vaccination?

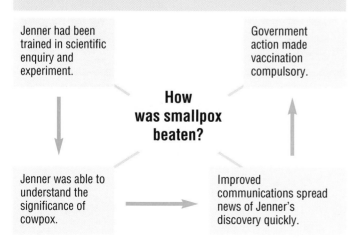

How was smallpox beaten?

Jenner had been trained in scientific enquiry and experiment.

Government action made vaccination compulsory.

Jenner was able to understand the significance of cowpox.

Improved communications spread news of Jenner's discovery quickly.

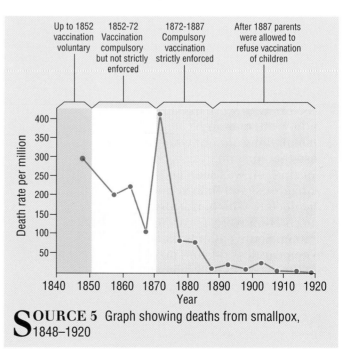

SOURCE 5 Graph showing deaths from smallpox, 1848–1920

Why was there opposition to vaccination?

You might think that vaccination sounds like a good idea. Many people agreed, and Jenner's methods were widely copied. However, you will also be aware from your study of the history of medicine that new ideas have often been opposed. The Royal Society refused to publish Jenner's research because of opposition to his ideas. After Jenner had published his findings, more than 100 leading London doctors signed a declaration of confidence in his research and announced their support for vaccination. Despite this, opposition still continued.

There were many reasons why people were against vaccination.

- Some people simply did not like anything new. What's more, this particular idea sounded very odd.
- Others did not accept the evidence that Jenner had recorded. Sceptics thought it was unbelievable that a disease that comes from cows could protect people against a human disease such as smallpox. Jenner still could not offer any explanation as to why vaccination worked so he was unable to answer the criticisms satisfactorily.
- Doctors who were making money out of doing inoculations did not want to lose that income.
- Vaccination was seen as dangerous, and indeed not all the doctors who performed vaccination were as careful as Jenner. Some patients died when careless doctors mixed up the vaccines and infected them with smallpox instead of cowpox. Other doctors used infected needles and killed their patients that way.

SOURCE 6 *The cowpock – or – the Wonderful Effects of the New Inoculation* by James Gillray

SOURCE 7 *The curse of humankind* by George Cruikshank, 1808

Added to all these problems was the fact that vaccination was not free. Some people, particularly the poor, were not vaccinated, and had to run the serious risk of catching smallpox – 40,000 people died in a dreadful epidemic in the late 1830s.

The greatest opposition to vaccination came after the government made it compulsory in the 1850s. Never before had any government forced a medical treatment on the entire population. There was outrage against this attack on personal liberty. Compulsory vaccination was seen by some as an attempt by doctors and the medical profession to take over all health care. Opposition to it was particularly strong among herbalists. In 1887 the opposition succeeded in allowing parents to refuse to have their children vaccinated.

9. Look at Sources 6 and 7. Which of the cartoons was inspired by the Anti-vaccine Society in 1802, when Jenner, with the aid of a government grant, opened his vaccination clinic in St Pancras, London?
10. Which cartoon was in favour of the use of Jenner's new vaccine?
11. Why was there so much opposition to vaccination in the nineteenth century?

■ ACTIVITY 1

Divide into pairs. One person in each pair list the arguments for vaccination. The other list arguments against vaccination. Now present your case to your partner as persuasively as you can.

How important was Jenner's work?

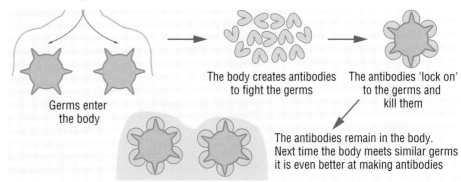

SOURCE 8 How immunity works

We now know why Jenner's vaccination worked: cowpox is almost the same VIRUS as smallpox, so when the body reacts to cowpox it also becomes IMMUNE to the very similar disease of smallpox.

Jenner did not realise this; he did not even know that smallpox was caused by a virus. There were no powerful microscopes which would have enabled him to examine smallpox matter and see what it contained. He could not explain how or why his method worked. It was simply the result of careful observation and experiment.

Jenner's vaccination undoubtedly saved many lives, and he is now considered significant for other reasons as well. Jenner was the first immuniser. He made deliberate use of the knowledge that recovering from a mild form of a disease gives human beings protection (or IMMUNITY) against a more severe form. This was the basis of the science of immunology which was to be pursued with such success by Pasteur and others half a century later – a story which you will follow up on pages 100–105.

12. Why couldn't Jenner explain why vaccination worked?
13. If doctors could prevent smallpox, why could they not prevent other diseases?
14. How do you think the ideas of Jenner might prove useful to other doctors searching for the causes of disease?

■ ACTIVITY 2

Source 9 is to be used to illustrate an encyclopaedia entry about Jenner. Write the text for the encyclopaedia entry to go with it. Describe what the statue shows, then explain:

■ who Jenner was
■ how he developed vaccination
■ why his work was important.

SOURCE 9 A nineteenth-century statue of Jenner injecting the arm of James Phipps

How did scientists discover the causes of disease?

IN THE 1860s understanding of disease reached a turning point. Scientists proved that germs cause disease. Over the next six pages you are going to investigate why this breakthrough occurred in the 1860s, and why it was important for the future development of medicine.

How did people explain disease in the 1800s?

For centuries common sense had told people that there was a connection between dirt and disease, but they had not been able to explain what the link was. In the early 1800s the popular explanation was miasma or bad air. Poisonous fumes (called miasma) were given off from rubbish and decaying matter. The fumes were swept from one place to another by the wind.

This was not a new theory. During the Great Plague of 1665 people had carried strong-smelling herbs with them to overcome the fumes which they thought spread the plague. In the nineteenth century, bad air seemed a better theory than ever. The growing towns were full of refuse which gave off terrible smells – no wonder the towns were so full of disease! Florence Nightingale believed in this theory. That is why she wanted hospitals to be well-ventilated, clean and airy (see pages 130–31).

This idea may have been wrong, but it was closer to the truth than the theory of the four humours, and measures based on it often worked. Clearing away rubbish did help to prevent disease.

1. The miasma theory of disease was mistaken. Why do you think people believed it?

To see how scientists finally explained the link between germs and disease you need to look back 150 years to the 1600s.

Step 1: the discovery of micro-organisms
In the late 1600s a Dutch clockmaker called Anthony van Leeuwenhoek made some of the earliest microscopes. His first microscopes had only one lens, and the image was distorted and fuzzy, but Leeuwenhoek patiently used them to study everything from water drops to peppercorns. To his amazement, almost everything he looked at contained tiny organisms which he called animalcules. He found them in food, drops of water, human excreta, animal intestines. He even found them in the waste material he scraped from between his own teeth. He described his findings in a series of 200 papers to the Royal Society in London.

Step 2: improved microscopes
Leeuwenhoek's discovery interested other scientists, but at that time microscopes were not good enough for his idea to be pursued further. However, by the early 1800s purer glass was being produced and the science of optics was better understood. In 1830 Joseph Lister, a British scientist, developed a microscope that magnified 1000 times without distortion. With these improved microscopes scientists could observe in detail the behaviour of micro-organisms.

Step 3: Louis Pasteur's germ theory
In the 1850s Louis Pasteur, a French scientist, became interested in micro-organisms when he was asked to help a brewing company find out why their vats of alcohol were going bad. Pasteur discovered that a particular micro-organism was growing vigorously in the liquid. He developed a theory that these germs (called germs because the micro-organism is germinating or growing) were the cause of the problem.

Pasteur solved the brewer's problem, showing him how to kill these harmful germs by boiling the liquid. As a result, Pasteur became well known in France and he was called in by other industries who had similar problems. He found that micro-organisms seemed to be responsible not only for beer, wine and vinegar fermentation going bad but also for milk turning sour.

Pasteur was an ambitious man who was keen to spread his theories further. In 1860 he got that opportunity when the French Academy of Science organised a competition for scientists to prove or disprove SPONTANEOUS GENERATION, an old theory about what causes decay (see Source 1).

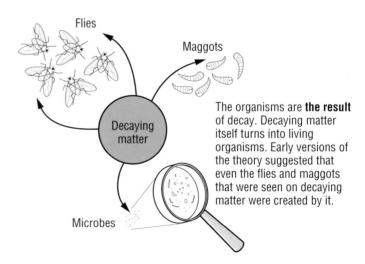

The organisms are **the result** of decay. Decaying matter itself turns into living organisms. Early versions of the theory suggested that even the flies and maggots that were seen on decaying matter were created by it.

SOURCE 1 The old theory: spontaneous generation

Step 4: the battle between germ theory and spontaneous generation

The miasma theory of disease made scientists very interested in decaying matter. They had long been aware that decaying matter was full of flies and maggots. Now through their microscopes they also saw micro-organisms. The question was, where did these things come from? There were two theories (see Sources 1 and 2).

The competition found Pasteur up against another leading French scientist – Pouchet. Pasteur devised a series of ingenious experiments to prove that his theories were correct (see Source 3). They succeeded triumphantly, and in 1861 Pasteur published his GERM THEORY.

Louis Pasteur

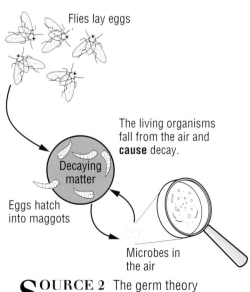

Flies lay eggs

The living organisms fall from the air and **cause** decay.

Decaying matter

Eggs hatch into maggots

Microbes in the air

SOURCE 2 The germ theory

THEORY	EXPERIMENT
The air contains living micro-organisms	He took sterile flasks out into the streets of Paris, opened them briefly, then sealed them again. Bacteria grew in them.
Microbes are not evenly distributed in the air	He repeated the experiment in various places around France including high mountains. The number of bacteria varied.
Microbes in the air cause decay	He filled two flasks; one with stale air and the other with ordinary air. In the first there was no decay; in the second decay proceeded as normal.
Microbes can be killed by heating	He heated a material in a flask to make it sterile. He drove the air out, then sealed the flask. It remained sterile even 100 years later.

SOURCE 3 Pasteur's theories and experiments

Step 5: linking micro-organisms to disease

Pasteur had proved the power of micro-organisms to make beer go bad. In his germ theory he also said:

'If wine and beer are changed by germs, then the same can and must happen sometimes in men and animals.'

He speculated: could disease be caused by the same process as wine going sour or material decaying? Harmful germs get into a body, grow rapidly and cause the disease.

He soon had an opportunity to put this to the test. The French silk industry was being ruined because of a disease which was affecting their silkworms. Pasteur was called in to investigate. Here again he found that a particular micro-organism seemed to be causing the silkworms' disease.

Step 6: proving the link between bacteria and human disease

Pasteur was a scientist, not a doctor. He carried out his early experiments with beer, wine and silkworms. It was a German doctor, Robert Koch, who took up the challenge of applying Pasteur's ideas to human diseases. As you can see from page 102, Koch conducted a series of painstaking experiments which proved once and for all that specific micro-organisms cause specific human diseases.

■ TASK

1. Draw a flow chart to show steps 1–6 above.
2. Explain how each step was important.
3. For each step indicate what factors helped scientists make that step.

How important was Robert Koch?

Robert Koch was born in Germany in 1843. As a doctor he became interested in Pasteur's germ theory. He bought a microscope and from 1875–78 he methodically studied anthrax, a disease which affects both animals and humans.

Koch's meticulous research so impressed people that the German government gave him a full-time job and a talented team of bacteriologists to continue his research. His methods were followed by other scientists in their search for the causes of disease.

This imaginary interview is how he might explain the importance of his work.

Question: Which experiment first started your research?
Answer: Some scientists thought they had found the bacteria that cause anthrax. I wasn't happy. I wanted to prove it, beyond a shadow of a doubt.

Q: So – describe this famous experiment.
A: I took some organs from sheep that had died of anthrax. In the organs I found the BACTERIUM which everyone said caused anthrax. I extracted it, grew it, studied it, and then injected a mouse with it. After a time the mouse developed anthrax.

Q: So you proved it?
A: Not so fast! There is a lot more yet. I took some blood from the infected mouse. Again I isolated out the anthrax bacterium. Again I grew it on a medium, to check it was still the same. I injected it into a new mouse and it developed anthrax too. I repeated this process over and over again through twenty generations of mice. They all caught anthrax, and at the end I still had the same bacterium as at the beginning. Then, and only then, did I pronounce that this was the bacterium which causes anthrax.

Q: So why was that a useful experiment?
A: Because it provided a method which everyone could follow. Using my methods they have already identified the causes of typhoid, tuberculosis, the dreaded cholera, tetanus and so on. [You can see the list in Source 5.] I am confident more will follow.

Q: Is your anthrax experiment the only thing which makes you famous?
A: No. That was only the beginning. My next step was to make a better medium for growing and observing bacteria. If you want to find out about bacteria you have to be able to see them! Some of my rivals such as Pasteur were still using liquids.

I perfected a solid medium, then a better way of growing bacteria, and finally a way of staining them so they could be observed more easily.

Q: Staining – what's that?
A: I was looking for the bacteria that cause blood poisoning. I couldn't see them although I knew they must be there. My solution was to stain them purple so I could see them.

Q: What advice would you give to someone wanting to find out more about medicine?
A: Be scientific. Be systematic. Record everything. Repeat everything. You will only avoid false conclusions if you try everything out again and again. Check your results: don't believe them the first time.

SOURCE 4 A contemporary cartoon. Koch is shown slaying the tuberculosis bacillus

2. What answer do you think Koch would have given to these questions:
a) What is your greatest achievement?
b) How will your research help people find cures for disease?
c) What was the most important factor in your success?

Did germ theory help scientists cure diseases?

There was no doubting the importance of Koch's achievements. They inspired other scientists to search for the causes of many diseases.

> **SOURCE 5** Using Koch's methods, the causes of these diseases were identified very quickly. The starred ones were discovered by Koch and his team
>
> | | |
> |---|---|
> | 1880 TYPHUS | 1886 Pneumonia |
> | 1882 TUBERCULOSIS* | 1887 MENINGITIS |
> | 1883 CHOLERA* | 1894 Plague |
> | 1884 TETANUS | 1898 Dysentery |

Koch's success spurred Louis Pasteur into action again. Pasteur was nationalistic and ambitious. France and Germany were deadly rivals at this time. France had lost a bitter war to Germany in 1870–71. Pasteur was already a world-famous scientist but it greatly troubled him that Koch and Germany seemed to be getting ahead of France in the battle to explain disease. For the rest of his life, despite a severe stroke which paralysed the left side of his body, Pasteur applied himself to what he considered the greatest challenge of all – finding cures for disease.

Pasteur knew he could not compete with Koch's work on his own. By this time he was powerful enough to be able to raise money from the French government and he gathered around him a team of doctors and vets to help with the research.

A new vaccination: chicken cholera

Pasteur had thought a lot about Jenner's work on smallpox. He was sure that smallpox was not the only disease that could be prevented by vaccination, but as he did not know how vaccination worked he had to continue his search by trial and error.

In 1879 Pasteur was researching chicken cholera, a disease that was troubling French farmers at the time. As you can see from Source 6 below, this led to an amazing discovery. Old germs IMMUNISED the chickens against the disease. Clearly, exposure to the air had weakened the germs. Pasteur called this method vaccination to show his debt to Jenner.

Pasteur was now more confident of his method and in 1882 he turned his attention to rabies. This disease is passed to humans from a bite by an infected dog. It is not a common disease in humans, but it causes certain death and the patient suffers terribly in the process. After two years of careful research Pasteur developed a rabies vaccine which worked. Soon people from all over Europe were flocking to Paris to be treated by Pasteur.

3. Did Pasteur's method of vaccination work in the same way as Jenner's method? Explain how.
4. Jenner's vaccination did not lead to other discoveries but Pasteur's did. Why?

SOURCE 6 How an effective vaccine against chicken cholera was discovered

■ TASK

1. Work in pairs to study the achievements of Pasteur and Koch. Copy and complete the chart below to show the reasons for their success.

These are some of the extra factors you might consider to go in place of the question marks:

- ■ individual genius
- ■ role of chance
- ■ the support of governments
- ■ warfare
- ■ links with industry
- ■ improved communications
- ■ improved technology.

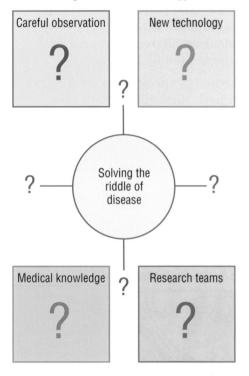

2. Use your chart to write an essay: 'Why were the causes of disease finally discovered in the 1860s and 1870s?'

The first cures

Pasteur's vaccinations could only prevent disease, but as you can see from Source 7 the first cures were soon to follow.

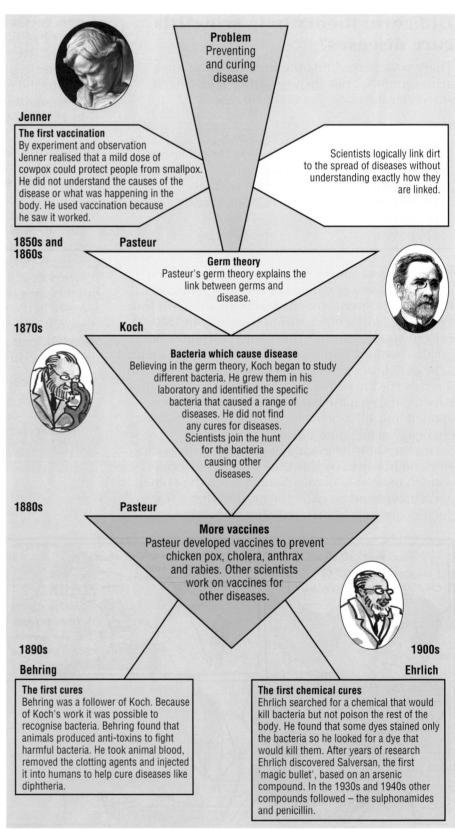

Problem
Preventing and curing disease

Jenner
The first vaccination
By experiment and observation Jenner realised that a mild dose of cowpox could protect people from smallpox. He did not understand the causes of the disease or what was happening in the body. He used vaccination because he saw it worked.

Scientists logically link dirt to the spread of diseases without understanding exactly how they are linked.

1850s and 1860s
Pasteur
Germ theory
Pasteur's germ theory explains the link between germs and disease.

1870s
Koch
Bacteria which cause disease
Believing in the germ theory, Koch began to study different bacteria. He grew them in his laboratory and identified the specific bacteria that caused a range of diseases. He did not find any cures for diseases. Scientists join the hunt for the bacteria causing other diseases.

1880s
Pasteur
More vaccines
Pasteur developed vaccines to prevent chicken pox, cholera, anthrax and rabies. Other scientists work on vaccines for other diseases.

1890s
Behring
The first cures
Behring was a follower of Koch. Because of Koch's work it was possible to recognise bacteria. Behring found that animals produced anti-toxins to fight harmful bacteria. He took animal blood, removed the clotting agents and injected it into humans to help cure diseases like diphtheria.

1900s
Ehrlich
The first chemical cures
Ehrlich searched for a chemical that would kill bacteria but not poison the rest of the body. He found that some dyes stained only the bacteria so he looked for a dye that would kill them. After years of research Ehrlich discovered Salversan, the first 'magic bullet', based on an arsenic compound. In the 1930s and 1940s other compounds followed – the sulphonamides and penicillin.

SOURCE 7 How scientists discovered cures for disease

Key individual: Louis Pasteur – was his germ theory the greatest breakthrough in the history of medicine?

Why was Pasteur so important?

Louis Pasteur
(1822–95)

Pasteur proved that bacteria (germs) make milk, beer and other products go bad and that they also cause disease in silkworms.

This led to Pasteur's germ theory which he published in 1861. He suggested that germs caused human diseases. This put an end to old ideas about the causes of disease, such as bad air (miasma) and the theory of the four humours.

Later in his career (1849–82) Pasteur developed vaccination to prevent diseases such as rabies.

Pasteur's scientific method of careful experiments which tested his theories inspired other scientists and doctors.

Pasteur's work led other scientists, such as Robert Koch, to make vital new discoveries which proved that germs cause human diseases.

■ ACTIVITY

Write an obituary of Pasteur, explaining why he was so important in the history of medicine. You should write about 300 words.

But remember, Pasteur's germ theory was only a theory. He did not *prove* that germs cause human diseases. I did that and, with my research team, identified the particular germs that cause individual diseases. Perhaps these pages should really be about me?

Robert Koch (1843–1910)

Why were sewers and water supply improved in the nineteenth century?

FOR HUNDREDS OF years people had known that there was a link between dirt and disease although no one was sure exactly what the connection was. During the late eighteenth century and the first half of the nineteenth century, conditions in many British towns became worse than ever. The population was growing so rapidly that towns could not cope with the need to house people and provide them with water and facilities to remove their sewage. In these conditions, the killer diseases spread with terrifying ease and speed. The conditions were so bad that many people's health may even have been worse than the health of people living in earlier centuries.

A COURT FOR KING CHOLERA

SOURCE 1 A drawing of London made in the 1840s. Similar conditions could be found in other growing towns in Britain and Europe

1. Look at Source 1. List as many threats to health as possible.
2. Why do you think people let the towns get like this?

The battle over public health

Some people thought that the government should force local councils to clean up their towns. However, there were also many who believed that the government should keep out of people's lives – this attitude is called LAISSEZ-FAIRE. They believed the government should allow each local area to control its own affairs. This usually meant letting the local ratepayers make all the decisions. They certainly did not want the government to force them to pay for improvements to their towns. Such people were nicknamed 'the Dirty Party' by their opponents.

This battle between local authorities and the government played a central part in the story of public health in nineteenth-century Britain.

The debate rumbled on inconclusively until …

Cholera!

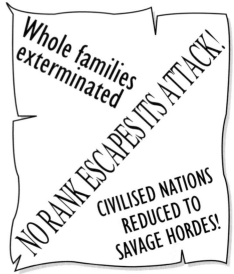

Whole families exterminated

NO RANK ESCAPES ITS ATTACK!

CIVILISED NATIONS REDUCED TO SAVAGE HORDES!

These newspaper headlines are talking about cholera. They reflect the fear that struck the country when cholera reached Britain for the first time in the early 1830s. There were other diseases which killed far more people, but cholera was the most frightening because it was a 'shock disease' that struck quickly. Sufferers were suddenly gripped by diarrhoea and vomiting. More than 500 millilitres of fluid could be lost each hour in the diarrhoea and, if not replaced, caused death in only a few hours. It was a swift, painful and unpleasant death, hence the fear it inspired.

SOURCE 2 *Methodist* magazine, 1832

    66 To see the number of our fellow creatures, in a good state of health, in the full possession of their wonted strength, and in the midst of their years, suddenly seized with the most violent spasms, and in a few hours cast into the tomb, is calculated to shake the firmest nerves, and to inspire dread in the strongest heart. 99

NOTICE!!!

We are credibly informed by a correspondent that the much-admired

JAPANESE CHEROOTS

are highly recommended by the faculty abroad as being a sure preventive of that raging disorder the

Cholera Morbus;

they have been recently imported into this Country, and are found to be of that mild and fragrant nature that they may be used by

The Fair Sex

without producing nausea. Their confirmed anti-contagious virtues and delicate fragrance have already procured them a very high and just estimation.

Vide Morning Herald, Nov. 12, 1831.

ARLISS, Printer, Addle Street, Wood Street, Cheapside

SOURCE 3 A cigar advertisement, 1831

When cholera struck for the first time in 1831, many ideas were put forward to explain its causes. Sources 4–8 are some of them.

3. Copy and complete this table using Sources 4–8 to help you.

What people believed caused the Black Death in the 1300s	Was this cause used as an explanation of cholera?	Evidence
A punishment from God		
Movements of the planets		
Earthquakes		
Children's misbehaviour		
Dirt in the streets		
Poisons in the air		

4. Add other explanations for cholera given by Sources 4–8.
5. Why were some medieval explanations for disease still being used?

SOURCE 4 Edinburgh Board of Health, 1833

66 *Experience proves that notorious drunkards were amongst the victims ... the intemperate, the old and the infirm, and poor ... half starved children ... worn out prostitutes.* 99

SOURCE 5 Bishop Blomfield, 1832

66 *Cholera is a sign to increase the comforts and improve the moral character of the masses.* 99

SOURCE 6 Dr Southwood Smith, 1841

66 *Cholera was due not to want of food and great misery ... but to EFFLUVIAL poisons [bad air that carried disease].* 99

SOURCE 7 William Farr, a doctor and Superintendent of the Statistical Department of the Registrar General

66 *Although elevation of habitation ... does not shut out the cause of cholera, it reduces its effect to insignificance.* 99

SOURCE 8 Thomas Wakely, a doctor writing in the medical journal *The Lancet*, 1831

66 *We can only suppose the existence of a poison which progresses independently of the wind, of the soil, of all conditions of the air, and of the barrier of the sea; in short, one that makes mankind the chief agent of its dissemination.* 99

Discovering the causes of cholera – the work of John Snow

Cholera is actually spread by infected water. The faeces of a sufferer contain the cholera germ and if they get into the water supply the disease spreads rapidly. Many people studied the 1832 epidemic and, after careful observation of the disease, deduced that there was a link between cholera and water supply. Of course, as Source 9 shows, people at the time (thirteen years before Pasteur) did not understand that germs caused cholera.

SOURCE 9 Part of a letter from a Mr Perkins to the government's Board of Health in 1848

66 ... my impression is that [the miasma] chemically infects exposed water, and the poorer classes using such water are consequently the greatest sufferers. 99

Cholera returned regularly throughout the century. The next major epidemics were in 1848 and 1854.

In 1854 Dr John Snow made a breakthrough in proving that there was a link between cholera and water supply. Snow, a London doctor, used meticulous research, observation, and house-to-house interviews to build up a detailed picture of a limited cholera epidemic which hit one particular area of central London. Sources 10 and 11 come from his published reports on the outbreak.

6. Read Source 10. What methods did Snow use to investigate the epidemic?
7. How does Snow explain the many deaths in Broad Street?
8. How does Snow explain that there were no deaths in the brewery?
9. Which parts of Snow's evidence do you think would be the most important in convincing doubters about the link between water supply and cholera?

■ ACTIVITY

Write a letter from John Snow to the public health officials for London advising them what to do to help prevent further outbreaks of cholera.

SOURCE 10 Extract from Snow's account *On the Mode of Communication of Cholera*, 1854

66 *The most terrible outbreak of cholera which ever occurred in this kingdom is probably that which took place in Broad Street, and the adjoining streets, a few weeks ago. Within two hundred and fifty yards of the spot where Cambridge Street joins Broad Street, there were upwards of five hundred fatal attacks of cholera in ten days. The mortality in this limited area probably equals any that was ever caused in this country, even by the plague; and it was much more sudden, as the greater number of cases terminated within a few hours. The mortality would undoubtedly have been much greater had it not been for the flight of the population ...*

... On proceeding to the spot, I found that nearly all the deaths had taken place within a short distance of the [water] pump. There were only ten deaths in houses situated decidedly nearer to another street pump. In five of these cases the families of the deceased persons informed me that they always sent to the pump in Broad Street, as they preferred the water to that of the pump that was nearer. In three other cases, the deceased were children who went to the school near the pump in Broad Street ...

... There is a Brewery in Broad Street, near to the pump, and on perceiving that no brewer's men were registered as having died of cholera, I called on Mr Huggins, the proprietor. He informed me that there were above seventy workmen employed in the brewery, and that none of them had suffered from the cholera – at least in a severe form – only two having been indisposed, and that not seriously, at the time the disease prevailed. The men were allowed to drink a certain quantity of malt liquor, and Mr Huggins believes they do not drink water at all; he is quite certain that the workmen never obtained water from the pump in the street. There is a deep well in the brewery, in addition to the New River water ...

... As there had been deaths from cholera just before the great outbreak not far from this pump-well, and in a situation elevated a few feet above it, the evacuations [excreta] from the patients might of course be amongst the impurities finding their way into the water ... 99

SOURCE 11 Map of the Broad Street area

A widow living in the suburbs, in an area otherwise clear of cholera, died of the disease. It was later discovered that she had a bottle of water from Broad Street sent to her every day because she liked it.

535 people lived in this workhouse. They got their water from another source. Only five died.

70 people worked at this brewery. It had its own water supply and gave its workers free beer to drink. No one died.

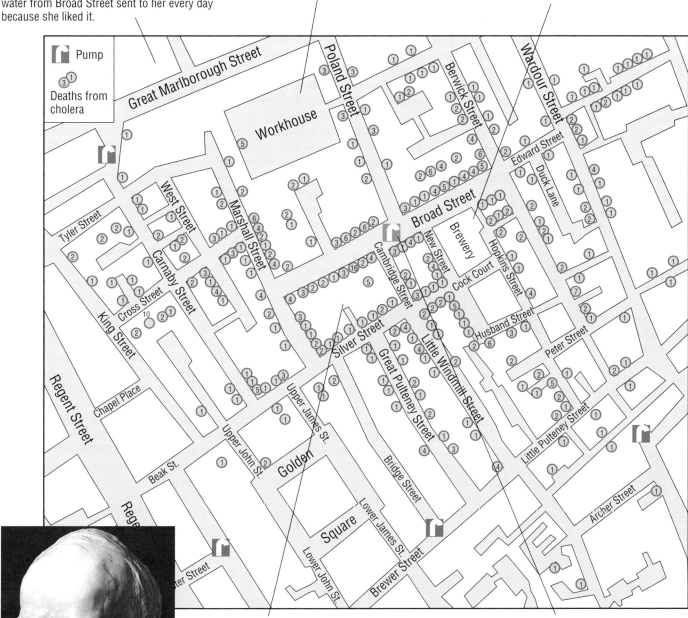

200 people worked in a factory here. They got their water from the Broad Street pump. Eighteen died.

After collecting his evidence Snow was allowed to remove the handle of the water pump in Broad Street. There were no more deaths. It later came to light that a cesspool, one metre away from the pump, had a cracked lining allowing the contents to seep into the drinking water.

SOURCE 12 Plaster-cast bust of John Snow. Snow died in 1858, aged only 45, three years before the publication of Pasteur's germ theory which helped explain the results Snow had recorded

Edwin Chadwick and public health reforms

Cholera was a very frightening disease but it was far from being the only danger to health. Conditions in the countryside were often as bad as in the towns.

Bad water supplies, inadequate drains, damp houses, and indifference to rubbish all helped spread disease. Diarrhoea, typhus and the dreaded typhoid and cholera sometimes ravaged cottages as severely as they did the slums of the city.

SOURCE 13 *Punch* cartoon, 1861. Mr Punch (to landlord): 'Your stable arrangements are excellent. Suppose you try something of the sort here?'

SOURCE 14 From *The Times*, 1850, describing the village of Wark, Northumberland

66 *The very picture of slovenliness and neglect. Wretched houses piled here and there without order – filth of every kind scattered about or heaped up against the walls – horses, cows, and pigs lodged under the same roof as their owners and entering the same door – in many cases a pigsty beneath the only window of the dwellings – 300 people, 60 horses and 50 cows, besides hosts of pigs and poultry – such is the village of Wark.* 99

Edwin Chadwick

SOURCE 15 Edwin Chadwick as represented by the *Pictorial Times* in 1846

In the 1830s a civil servant called Edwin Chadwick was employed by the POOR LAW COMMISSION. The Commission supervised the help that was given to the poor out of the local taxes, which were called rates. Chadwick was asked to report on the living conditions and the health of the poor in both town and country areas. Chadwick's report concluded that much poverty was due to ill health caused by the foul conditions in which people lived, and that the best way of reducing the cost to the ratepayer of looking after the poor was to improve their health. His recommendations on how to do this are described in Source 17.

SOURCE 16 Average age of death in Liverpool (urban) and Rutland (rural area) in 1840. These statistics were gathered by Chadwick for his report. He used them to show the contrasts in life expectancy in different places and for different social classes

SOURCE 17 From Edwin Chadwick's *Report on the Sanitary Conditions of the Labouring Population* which he wrote in 1842

66 *First – That the various forms of epidemic disease amongst the labouring classes are caused by atmospheric impurities produced by decaying animal and vegetable substances, by damp and filth, and close and overcrowded dwellings. The annual loss of life from filth and bad ventilation are greater than the loss from death or wounds in any war in which the country has been engaged in modern times.*

Second – That the most important measures and most practical are drainage, the removal of all refuse from the streets and the roads and the improvement of the supplies of water. The expense of public drainage and supplies of water would save money by cutting the existing charge resulting from sickness and mortality.

Third – For the prevention of disease it would be a good economy to appoint a district MEDICAL OFFICER *with special qualifications.* 99

Why was there opposition to public health reforms?

Chadwick's recommendations posed a problem for the government. It knew it should put them into action, but such matters were usually handled by the local ratepayers. They were the ones who were responsible for the care of the poor in their area. Local ratepayers were trying to reduce the cost of looking after the poor, not increase it.

The government knew that any attempt to force local councils to follow the recommendations would be unacceptable. Local businessmen and politicians would certainly not accept being told by the government to pay for public health reforms.

For the next 30 years a struggle went on between towns and central government as to how to solve these problems.

Following Chadwick's report the government at first did nothing. Then, in 1848, faced by the second major epidemic of cholera, Parliament reluctantly approved the Public Health Act of 1848. This set up a system, run by the government's Board of Health, to encourage (but not force) local authorities to improve conditions in their area. The Act allowed local authorities to make improvements if they wanted to and if they had the support of their ratepayers. It enabled them to borrow money to pay for the improvements. Sources 18 and 19 comment on the effectiveness of these voluntary measures.

SOURCE 18 Report on discussions in Leeds in the 1840s by James Smith

66 *A proposal was made for the complete sewerage of the streets. I was present for nearly six hours of this debate. The chief theme of the speakers in opposition related to the means of saving the pockets of the ratepayers with very little regard to the sanitary results.* 99

The cost of improving public health was indeed very high. Eleven million pounds was borrowed by local councils between 1848 and 1872 but, not surprisingly, only a few local authorities took any new measures. By 1872 only 50 councils had appointed Medical Officers of Health, although this had been one of Chadwick's main proposals. Six years later the government's Board of Health was disbanded, to the great delight of its critics.

SOURCE 19 Published in *The Times*, 1 August 1854

66 *The Board of Health has fallen. We prefer to take our chance with cholera than be bullied into health. Everywhere the board's inspectors were bullying, insulting and expensive. They entered houses and factories insisting on changes revolting to the habits or pride of the masters and occupants. There is nothing a man hates so much as being cleaned against his will, or having his floors swept, his walls whitewashed, his pet dung heaps cleared away, all at the command of a sort of sanitary bumbailiff. Mr Chadwick set to work everywhere, washing and splashing, and Master John Bull was scrubbed and rubbed till the tears came to his eyes and his fists clenched themselves with worry and pain.* 99

10. Why did Chadwick want improvements in public health?
11. Why was there little progress in public health in the 1850s?

■ **ACTIVITY**

You are a local councillor who has decided to oppose new public health schemes in your town. Write a speech that you will deliver to your fellow councillors explaining your views and trying to win their support.

Why was public health finally improved?

Through the 1850s progress continued very slowly. Councils could ignore public health if they wished, and many did. The decisive change came with the 1875 Public Health Act which finally forced local authorities to provide clean water, proper drainage and sewers, and to appoint Medical Officers of Health. Why did the government pass this Act?

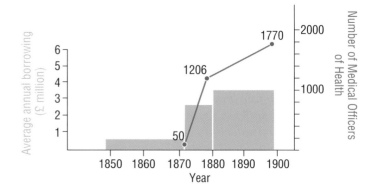

SOURCE 20 Number of Medical Officers of Health and average amount borrowed by councils for public health improvements, 1850–1900

■ TASK 1

1. Make your own copy of Source 21 and draw arrows to show how these different causes are connected to each other.

2. Add other causes if you think there are things we have missed out. Show how they are connected to the other causes.

3. Now use your completed diagram to help you write an essay explaining why you agree or disagree with this statement: 'It was impossible to make any real improvements in public health in Britain before 1861.'

Scientific developments
Pasteur's germ theory had finally proved the link between dirt and disease.

New voters
In 1867 working-class men had been given the vote. This meant that MPs were more likely to take notice of the needs of the people in their towns who were the main victims of poor public health.

The weakening of *laissez-faire*
As a result of all these changes the government saw it could no longer leave important public health measures to individuals or councils. The government realised that it was in everyone's interest to force towns to clean up.

Statistics
From 1837 the government collected statistics on births, marriages and deaths. William Farr used these to compile an accurate picture of where the death rate was highest and what people died of. He was able to prove, beyond any shadow of a doubt, a link between unhealthy living conditions and high death rates. He also published details of which were the most unhealthy towns, which shamed some of them into action.

HM REGISTRY OF BIRTHS DEATHS & MARRIAGES

The 1875 Public Health Act
This laid down in detail all the duties that were expected of a local council. All towns were forced to perform these tasks. They included the provision of clean water, proper drainage and sewerage, and the appointment of a Medical Officer of Health.

Education
Education was improving. In 1870 the government made every local authority set up schools. Health education was taught in many schools. Improved literacy made it possible for people to read pamphlets from Medical Officers giving advice about drainage, ventilation, diet, personal cleanliness, care of children and care of the sick.

Cholera
In 1865 cholera came back again. With the link between the disease and dirty water proved once and for all by John Snow, and then explained by Pasteur's germ theory, ratepayers were finally prepared to take action to clean up their towns.

Some cities led the way
Look at Leeds – a major industrial town – for example. Until 1866 very little action had been taken (see Source 18). Then in 1866 the town appointed its first Medical Officer of Health. In the same year a pressure group was formed to force the council to act. It was backed by the local newspaper who publicly blamed the council for 2000 unnecessary deaths in Leeds each year. In 1870 a local firm got a court order to prevent sewage being pumped into the river from which it drew its own water. In 1874 Leeds had its first sewage purification works. In other towns, throughout the country, similar changes were taking place, and towns began to compete with each other to be the cleanest.

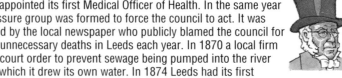

SOURCE 21 Factors leading to the 1875 Public Health Act being passed

Public health is more than sewers and water!

The improved water supply and better sewers were only one part of a range of measures taken by the government and local councils which had an effect on people's health. Source 22 summarises some of the other measures.

A never-ending story?

The last few pages might have given you the impression that all public health problems were solved in the 1870s. This was far from the case. Improvements in medicine and health always take a long time. When Charles Booth investigated the East End of London in 1889 he found many people living in appalling conditions of poverty and ill health. From 1881 INFANT MORTALITY actually started to go up again after a decade of progress. The struggle to improve the living conditions and therefore the health of ordinary people continued into the twentieth century and to the present day. You will pick up the story again on page 162.

S OURCE 23 Written by the Reverend Samuel Barnet, 1889

66 *The mother among the poor, in her joy that a son is born into the world, cannot look forward to his life. What is it to her that science has proved stronger than disease? The rich man's family may grow up unbroken around the hearth ... The children of the poor must die, and the family circle is broken by death which carries off the weakly ... What is it to the poor that it has been proved how cleanliness is the secret of health? They cannot have the latest sanitary appliances. They cannot take baths ... or have constant change of clothing; they cannot secure that the streets shall be swept, or, as the inhabitants of Belgrave Square, protect themselves from the neighbourhood of the tallow-factory.* 99

■ TASK 2

Research
Working in groups, research one or more of the measures shown in Source 22. You might also want to research other topics which we have not included.

S OURCE 22 Public health measures

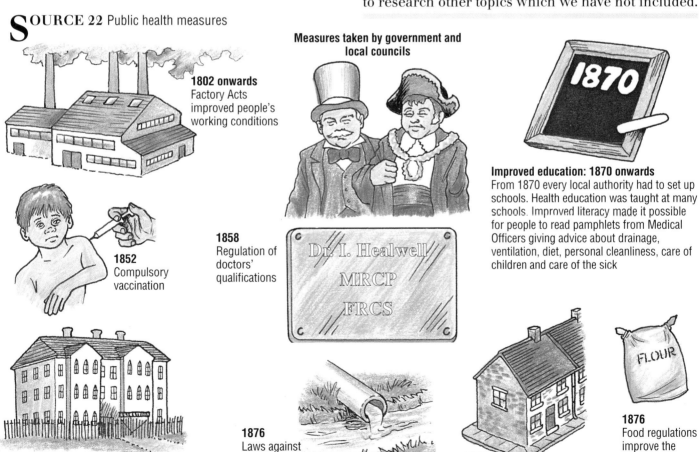

Measures taken by government and local councils

1802 onwards
Factory Acts improved people's working conditions

1852
Compulsory vaccination

1858
Regulation of doctors' qualifications

Dr. I. Healwell
MRCP
FRCS

Improved education: 1870 onwards
From 1870 every local authority had to set up schools. Health education was taught at many schools. Improved literacy made it possible for people to read pamphlets from Medical Officers giving advice about drainage, ventilation, diet, personal cleanliness, care of children and care of the sick

1889
Isolation hospitals for infectious diseases

1876
Laws against pollution of rivers

1876
Building regulations

1876
Food regulations improve the quality of food sold in shops

FLOUR

Key individual: Edwin Chadwick – did he save more lives than anyone else?

The government asked me to investigate how the poor lived and why there was so much sickness among the poor. All this sickness meant that richer people were paying higher and higher taxes to help the poor. If the poor were healthier they would be able to work. They would no longer need handouts and so taxes would be lower.

This is what my report said when I completed it in 1842. It was called *Report on the Sanitary Conditions of the Labouring Population*.

AND HERE'S MY SOLUTION!

1. The poor live in dirty, overcrowded conditions.

2. This causes a huge amount of illness.

3. Many people are too sick to work and so become poorer still.

4. Therefore other people have to pay higher taxes to help the poor.

We can cut taxes and save money in the long run by:

3. providing clean water supplies

1. improving drainage and sewers

4. appointing medical officers in each area to check these reforms.

2. removing refuse from streets and houses

That may save money in the long run but I'll be paying even higher taxes in the next couple of years to pay for all your reforms, Mr Interfering Chadwick!

Six years later, in 1848, the government did pass a Public Health Act. Here's what it said.

Local councils are ENCOURAGED to make public health reforms. However they do not have to make reforms.

My friends and I liked the 1848 Act. We did not want to pay for public health reforms. We resented the government telling us we had to be healthier!

However, that wasn't the end of the story. Cholera came back in 1854 and 1865. At last, in 1875, the government passed another Public Health Act. This time it FORCED local councils to provide clean water, proper drains and sewers and to appoint a Medical Officer of Health. After that great changes were made and people began to be healthier and live longer. The great epidemics of cholera and other diseases died out. That saved many, many lives.

■ TASK

1. Why were governments slow to make the changes Chadwick wanted?
2. Would Chadwick have had more chance of persuading politicians to reform public health in the 1840s if Pasteur had already published his germ theory by then, instead of twenty years later? Explain your answer.
3. Explain how each of these factors helped to improve public health:
a) Pasteur's germ theory
b) John Snow's work on cholera
c) changing government attitudes (politicians believed that governments ought to help people live better lives)
d) extension of the vote (in 1867 most men in towns were given the vote for the first time).
4. Which of these reasons do you think was most important in improving public health? Don't forget Chadwick's own work.

How did surgery improve in the nineteenth century?

Why was surgery so dangerous in the early 1800s?

Surgery in the early 1800s was dangerous and painful. Surgeons had to work quickly. At the Battle of Borodino in 1812 Napoleon's surgeon, Dubois, amputated 200 limbs in 24 hours. There was no way of completely relieving the pain suffered by the patient, nor was it possible to replace blood by TRANSFUSION, although blood vessels could be tied with ligatures to stop the bleeding.

Sometimes operations went dreadfully wrong. Robert Liston was a famous London surgeon who once amputated a leg in two-and-a-half minutes but worked so fast that he accidentally cut off his patient's testicles as well. During another high-speed amputation Liston amputated the fingers of his assistant and slashed the coat of a spectator who, fearing that he had been stabbed, dropped dead with fright. Worse was to follow. Both the assistant and the patient died of infection caught during the operation or in the hospital ward.

Infection was the greatest danger to patients after an operation. Germs might enter the wound and cause blood poisoning. Almost half of all patients who had leg amputations died from blood poisoning. One famous surgeon, James Simpson, said that 'the man laid out on the operating tables of our hospitals has more chances of death than the English soldier on the fields of Waterloo'.

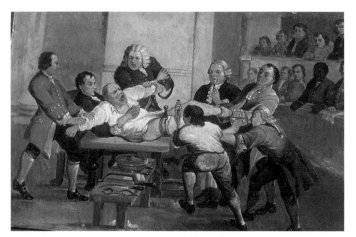

SOURCE 1 An operation around 1800

1. Look carefully at Source 1 and then make a list of all the possible sources of infection.
2. What evidence is there in Sources 1–3 that surgeons had copied the ideas of Ambroise Paré (page 60)?

SOURCE 2 The novelist Fanny Burney's account of her MASTECTOMY operation in 1811. She survived and lived for many years afterwards

… when the dreadful steel was plunged into the breast – cutting through veins – arteries – flesh – nerves – I needed no injunctions not to restrain my cries. I began a scream that lasted unintermittingly during the whole time of the incision – I almost marvel that it does not ring in my ears still! so excruciating was the agony. When the wound was made, & the instrument was withdrawn, the pain seemed undiminished, for the air that suddenly rushed into those delicate parts felt like a mass of minute but sharp & forked poignards [daggers], that were tearing at the edges of the wound, but when I felt again the instrument … I thought I must have expired, I attempted no more to open my eyes – they felt so firmly closed, that the eyelids seemed indented to the cheeks …

SOURCE 3 An account by Professor James Syme of his amputation of a leg at the hip joint. Syme was Clinical Surgeon at Edinburgh Royal Infirmary from 1833 to 1869

I introduced a narrow knife about a foot long … I cut along the bone, which started, with a loud report, from its socket. Finally I passed the knife around the head of the bone, cutting the remaining portion of the ligament, and this completed the operation, which certainly did not occupy at the most more than one minute.

[My assistant] relaxed [the torniquet so] that we might estimate the size and number of the bleeding vessels. It seemed at first sight as if the vessels which supplied so many jets of arterial blood could never all be closed … a single instant was sufficient to convince us that the patient's safety required all our [speed], and in the course of a few minutes HAEMORRHAGE was effectually restrained by the application of ten or twelve ligatures.

3. Use Sources 1–3 to explain in your own words why:
a) pain
b) bleeding
c) infection
   made surgery so dangerous.
4. From what you already know about nineteenth-century medicine, which of these problems do you expect to be solved first?

The problem of pain

Look up the following references which show how surgeons dealt with the problem of pain in earlier periods: Source 3 on page 24; Source 5 on page 53. Such herbal remedies had some effect but in the early 1880s there were still only three operations which surgeons could carry out with some success: the amputation of limbs, trephining, and the removal of superficial TUMOURS. All were carried out as swiftly as possible to reduce the pain suffered by the patient. Surgeons were used to ignoring the pain of their patients.

However, medical knowledge was advancing rapidly and some surgeons felt that if the patient could be 'knocked out', it would give them more time to operate and to improve their techniques. During the same period chemistry was developing and scientists were finding that certain chemicals could have an effect on the human body. In 1799 Sir Humphry Davy discovered that laughing gas reduced the sensation of pain: 'It seems capable of destroying pain and might probably be used in surgical operations'. Forty years later dentists used it to ease the pain of tooth extractions and other surgeons were experimenting with different substances. Source 4 describes the first successful operation using ether.

> **S**OURCE 4 An account of an operation to remove a neck tumour using ether as an anaesthetic by John Collins Warren, senior surgeon at Massachusetts General Hospital in 1846
>
> 66 *The patient was arranged for the operation in a sitting posture, and everything was made ready … The patient was then made to inhale a fluid from a tube with a glass globe. After four or five minutes he appeared to be asleep, and was thought by Dr Morton to be in a condition for the operation. I made an incision between two or three inches long in the direction of the tumour, and to my great surprise without any starting, crying, or other indication of pain.* 99

A year later, ether was used by J. R. Liston in London to anaesthetise a patient during a leg amputation. However, ether had severe drawbacks as an anaesthetic. It irritated the lungs, causing the patient to cough during the operation. It was also unstable and produced inflammable vapour. Soon other surgeons were searching for a better alternative.

Why was there opposition to anaesthetics?

James Simpson was Professor of Midwifery at Edinburgh University. One evening in 1847 he invited several colleagues to his home. They sat around the table experimenting with different chemicals. Simpson wrote later 'I poured some of the [CHLOROFORM] fluid into tumblers in front of my assistants, Dr Keith and Dr Duncan, and myself. Before sitting down to supper we all inhaled the fluid, and were all "under the table" in a minute or two, to my wife's consternation and alarm.'

SOURCE 5 Simpson and friends recovering from the effects of chloroform. A drawing made in 1857

Simpson realised that in chloroform he had discovered a very effective anaesthetic. He soon started using it to help relieve women's labour pains during childbirth. He wrote articles about his discovery and other surgeons started to use it in their operations.

However, with painless operations now a real possibility, it may surprise you that the first reaction of many surgeons was intense opposition to the use of anaesthetics.

Some put forward medical arguments. Chloroform was a new and untested gas. No one knew for sure if there would be long-term side effects on the bodies or minds of patients. They did not know what dose to give to different patients. The first death from the use of chloroform (see Source 8) scared surgeons and gave opponents of anaesthetics powerful evidence of their danger.

There were also moral and religious arguments, as you can see from Source 6. Some people were particularly opposed to the idea of easing the pain of childbirth – believing that this would be unnatural.

What's more, anaesthetics did not necessarily make surgery safer. With a patient asleep the doctor could attempt more complex operations, thus carrying infections deeper into the body and causing more loss of blood. The number of people dying from surgery may even have increased after the discovery of anaesthetics!

SOURCE 6 Letters to the medical journal *The Lancet* in 1849 and 1853

66 *The infliction [of pain] has been invented by the Almighty God. Pain may even be considered a blessing of the Gospel, and being blessed admits to being made either well or ill.* 99

66 *It is a most unnatural practice. The pain and sorrow of labour exert a most powerful and useful influence upon the religious and moral character of women and upon all their future relations in life.* 99

SOURCE 7 Army Chief of Medical Staff, 1854

66 *... the smart use of the knife is a powerful stimulant and it is much better to hear a man bawl lustily than to see him sink silently into the grave.* 99

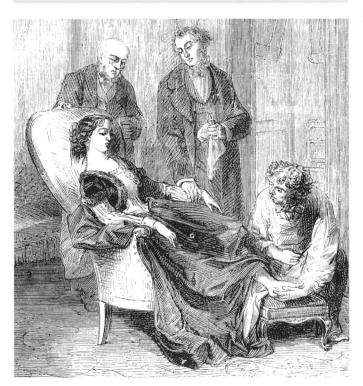

SOURCE 8 In 1848 Hannah Greener died whilst being given chloroform during an operation to remove her toenail

Why were anaesthetics accepted?

James Simpson presented a powerful case for anaesthetics. He brought the example of Ambroise Paré to his defence.

SOURCE 9 James Simpson speaking to a meeting of doctors in Edinburgh in 1847

66 *Before the sixteenth century surgeons had no way of stemming the flow of blood after amputation of a limb other than by scorching with a red hot iron or boiling pitch. The great suggestion of Ambroise Paré, to shut up the bleeding vessels by tying them, was a vast improvement. It saved the sufferings of the patient while adding to their safety. But the practice was new, and like all innovations in medical practice, it was at first and for long, bitterly decried ... attacked ... suppressed.*

We look back with sorrow on the opponents of Paré. Our successors in years to come will look back with similar feelings. They will marvel at the idea of humane men confessing that they prefer operating on their patients in a waking instead of an anaesthetic state, and that the fearful agonies that they inflict should be endured quietly. All pain is destructive and even fatal in its effects. 99

The struggle continued for ten years, with anaesthetics gradually winning wider acceptance. The final breakthrough came when Queen Victoria accepted the use of chloroform during the delivery of her eighth child in 1857. She publicly praised 'that blessed chloroform'. With the support of the queen, opposition to anaesthetics was doomed. From now on they became a standard part of surgical practice.

■ TASK

Explain how the following factors played a role in either encouraging or opposing the development of anaesthetics:

■ attitudes and beliefs
■ war
■ individual genius
■ Queen Victoria
■ chance
■ government.

SOURCE 10 Written by Margaret Matthewson of Shetland. She was from a poor family and she worked as a servant. In 1877 she went to Edinburgh for a shoulder operation by Professor Cheyne. The operation would not have been possible before the days of anaesthetics. She survived the operation although she died one year later from a recurrence of the problem. She wrote this account while convalescing

❝ *The big theatre door was open and we went in. Professor Cheyne bowed and smiled. There were a lot of people sitting in the gallery and four people sitting around the table.*

Doctor Cheyne came and laid a towel saturated with chloroform over my face and said 'Now breathe away.' I then felt the Professor's hand laid gently on my arm as if to let me know that he was near … I felt myself go weaker and weaker and every nerve and joint relaxing and breaking up as it were, a very solemn moment thus staring death in the face, and I believed I never should awaken to look on the things of time any more but was indeed entering eternity.

[Finding he needed more time to complete the operation, the surgeon gave her an extra large dose of chloroform. After the operation she took seventy minutes to regain consciousness.]

I was conscious of no more until I awoke in a bed in a strange ward. My first thought was 'My arm! Is it off or not?' I at once sat up to feel for it. I found it bandaged to my waist and breathed a sigh of thankfulness.

I felt very sick and kept on vomiting … at intervals for several hours … I doubt it will be sometime ere I get over this horrid chloroform taste and its effects. ❞

■ ACTIVITY

Source 2 on page 116 and Source 10 above describe surgery before and after the development of anaesthetics. Imagine James Simpson wants to use these two sources to show how valuable the development of anaesthetics has been to patients and surgeons. Use Sources 2 and 10 to write an extra paragraph for his speech in Source 9.

How did germ theory affect surgery?

With the introduction of anaesthetics, surgery certainly became less painful, but it was not safer. Until the acceptance of germ theory in the 1860s, surgeons did not take any precautions to protect open wounds from infection. They reused bandages, thus spreading gangrene and skin infections from patient to patient. Doctors did not wash their hands before an operation, nor did they STERILISE their equipment, and some of them operated wearing old pus-stained clothes.

Ignaz Semmelweiss

Semmelweiss was a Hungarian doctor working in Austria. He was very concerned by the deaths of apparently healthy women after childbirth. Some doctors regarded this as inevitable, but Semmelweiss observed that women whose babies were delivered by midwives were much less likely to die from infection than women who were delivered by medical students. He believed the reason for this was that the medical students came straight to the delivery rooms after they had been dissecting dead bodies. If they simply washed their hands, he thought, they would reduce the risk of infection to women.

SOURCE 11 A notice placed by Dr Ignaz Semmelweiss at the entrance of the maternity ward in the General Hospital in Vienna, 15 May 1847

From today, 15 May 1847, any doctor or student coming from the postmortem room must, before entering the maternity wards, wash his hands thoroughly in the basin of chlorinated water placed at the entrance. This order applies to everyone, without exception.

Semmelweiss pursued his crusade with great passion. He even called doctors who did not wash their hands murderers. However, at the time, he was regarded as a crank and a fanatic, and was said to be mentally unstable. It would be many years before the sensible measures he was suggesting would be adopted by others.

5. Could Semmelweiss have known about Pasteur's germ theory in 1847?
6. Why do you think Semmelweiss faced opposition to such a simple measure?
7. Who did more to help women in childbirth: James Simpson or Ignaz Semmelweiss?

Joseph Lister

Joseph Lister was one of the outstanding surgeons of the nineteenth century. He had researched gangrene and infection, and had a keen interest in the application of science to medicine. His father had been the pioneer of the improved microscope. Lister's reading of the work of Pasteur on germ theory, published in 1861, led to his own discoveries.

SOURCE 12 From an article in *The Lancet*, 1869, by Joseph Lister, Professor of Surgery, Glasgow University

66 *When it had been shown by the researches of Pasteur that the septic property of the atmosphere depended on minute organisms suspended in it, it occurred to me that decomposition in the injured part [following an operation] might be avoided by applying as a dressing some material capable of destroying the life of the floating particles.* 99

Lister had seen carbolic spray used to treat sewage. After experiments he found that a thin mist of carbolic acid sprayed over the wound during surgery limited infection. By following this with careful bandaging the wound would heal and not develop gangrene.

SOURCE 13 Operation with carbolic spray. One assistant is using chloroform to anaesthetise the patient, another is mopping up blood with a sponge

SOURCE 14 Joseph Lister, *On the New Method of Treating Compound Fracture*, 1867

66 *James, aged 11 years, was admitted to the Glasgow INFIRMARY on August 2, 1865, with compound fracture of the left leg caused by the wheel of an empty cart passing over the limb a little below the middle. The wound, an inch and a half long and three quarters of an inch broad, was over the line of the fracture.*

A piece of lint dipped in carbolic acid was laid on the wound, and splints padded with cotton wool were applied. It was left undisturbed for four days and, when examined, it showed no sign of suppuration. For the next four days the wound was dressed with lint soaked with a solution of water and carbolic acid and olive oil which further prevented irritation to the skin. No pus was present, there seemed no danger of SUPPURATION, and at the end of six weeks I found the bones united, and I discarded the splints. The sore was entirely healed … 99

SOURCE 15 From Lister's own record of amputations

	Total amputations	Died	% who died
1864–66 (without antiseptics)	35	16	45.7
1867–70 (with antiseptics)	40	6	15.0

■ ACTIVITY 1

You are a journalist who has been asked to report on Lister's antiseptic surgery. Describe in detail the measures he has taken to reduce the risk of infection. Explain why he has taken each of these measures. You could include a comparison of Source 1 on page 116 and Source 13.

Why was there opposition to antiseptics?

You already know that new medical techniques often meet with great opposition. Antiseptics were no exception.

To start with, many surgeons opposed Lister's methods, and he was seen as a fanatic. His carbolic spray, which soaked the operating theatre, seemed very extreme. It cracked the surgeon's skin and made everything smell. The new precautions caused extra work, and made operations more expensive and less pleasant for the surgeons.

Surgeons were still convinced that speed was essential in an operation and because of the problem of bleeding it often was. It seemed that Lister's antiseptic methods just slowed operations down.

Pasteur's ideas had spread very slowly. Even trained surgeons found it difficult to accept that there were tiny micro-organisms all around which could cause disease.

One surgeon regularly joked with his assistants that they should shut the door of the operating theatre in case one of 'Mr Lister's MICROBES' flew in.

For many centuries surgeons had lived with the idea that a lot of their patients would die. When Lister said he had achieved such good results, their first reaction was one of disbelief. For many the next reaction was to feel defensive.

When some surgeons did try copying Lister's methods they did not achieve the same results. This was usually because they were less systematic, but that didn't stop them criticising Lister. Others argued that antiseptics actually prevented the body's own defence mechanisms from operating effectively.

Lister was not a showman like Pasteur. He did not give impressive public displays. Indeed, he appeared to be cold, arrogant and aloof and was sometimes critical of other surgeons.

Lister was always changing his techniques. He did this because he wanted to find a substance that would work equally as well as carbolic spray, but without the corrosion that it caused. His critics simply said he was changing his methods because they did not work.

SOURCE 16 Opposition to the use of antiseptics

■ ACTIVITY 2

Work in pairs. Role play an argument between Lister and one of his critics. Use the text and sources above to help you.

How did Lister change surgery?

Despite opposition, Lister's methods marked a turning point in surgery. In 1877 he moved to London to train young surgeons under his own supervision. In 1878 Koch found the bacterium which caused SEPTICAEMIA. This gave a great boost to Lister's ideas. By the late 1890s his antiseptic methods (which killed germs on the wound) developed into aseptic surgery, which meant removing all possible germs from the operating theatre. To ensure absolute cleanliness, various measures were introduced.

■ Operating theatres and hospitals were rigorously cleaned.
■ From 1887 all instruments were steam-sterilised.
■ In 1894, sterilised rubber gloves were used for the first time. For however well surgeons' hands were scrubbed, they could still hold bacteria in the folds of skin and under the nails.

In 1892 Lister and Pasteur were together given an award at the Sorbonne University in Paris for their contribution to the fight against disease.

With some of the basic problems of surgery now solved, surgeons attempted more ambitious operations. The first successful operation to remove an infected appendix came in the 1880s. The first heart operation was carried out in 1896 when surgeons repaired a heart damaged by a stab wound.

■ TASK

Draw a timeline from 1850–1900. Above the line mark important dates in the work of Pasteur and Koch (see pages 100–105). Below it mark important dates in the development of safer surgery. Then use it to write answers to these questions.

1. How was Lister's work linked to Pasteur's germ theory?
2. What other factors helped lead to improvements in surgery?

But what about bleeding?

The third great problem of surgery was bleeding. Lister also made a contribution here. He improved on Paré's ligatures by using sterilised catgut which did not pose such a great risk of infection.

Other surgeons experimented with blood transfusion, but despite their many attempts it often failed. The blood clotted, and even when it was successful many patients mysteriously died. The explanation for that would not be found for another twenty years – a development which we return to on page 152.

K ey individual: Joseph Lister – did he revolutionise surgery?

JOSEPH LISTER WAS one of the most important individuals in the history of surgery. This page summarises the reasons why he was so important. You might even owe your life to him!

■ TASK

1. How did Lister's background help to make him successful?
2. What was Lister's great discovery?
3. How was his work helped by the discoveries of Pasteur and Koch?
4. What were the short-term and long-term benefits of Lister's work?

What was Lister's background?

■ His father was a medical pioneer who developed improved microscopes.
■ He had the best medical training. He learned to challenge and question existing ideas and he did research into infected wounds.
■ He became Professor of Surgery in Glasgow and later in London.

What did Lister do?

■ He tackled the problem of patients dying after surgery. Even after successful operations, patients often died because their wounds became infected.
■ Lister had read Pasteur's work on bacteria. He worked out that bacteria might be causing the infections and so used carbolic spray to kill these bacteria. This was antiseptic surgery.
■ The percentage of his patients who died after operations fell from 46 per cent to 15 per cent.

Why was Lister's work important?

In the short term
■ More of his patients survived.
■ His ideas spread and were used by other doctors, although at first many doctors did not believe in Lister's discovery.

In the long term
■ Other doctors built on his ideas. Hospitals and operating theatres became much cleaner places. All medical instruments were sterilised effectively.
■ Longer and more complicated operations became possible as the danger of infection was reduced.

Was everything about medicine changing?

So far in this chapter you have been learning about a series of great breakthroughs:

JENNER'S DISCOVERY OF A VACCINATION AGAINST SMALLPOX

PASTEUR'S GERM THEORY and KOCH'S RESEARCH PROVING THE CAUSES OF DISEASE

IMPROVEMENTS IN PUBLIC HEALTH – CLEAN WATER, BETTER DRAINAGE AND SEWERS – LED BY PIONEERS SUCH AS CHADWICK

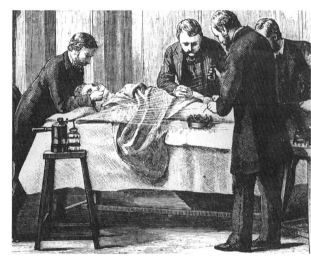

THE REVOLUTION IN SURGERY – SIMPSON'S ANAESTHETICS AND LISTER'S ANTISEPTICS

BUT was everything changing in medicine?

If you were an ordinary person

Who could you go to see if you were ill?

What kinds of cures and treatments would you use?

Were all the doctors and hospitals using the new ideas?

Pages 124–29 explore these questions and help you to decide whether the Medical Revolution affected everybody.
    You can start on the next page by playing a game – if you dare!

123

■ ACTIVITY

You have seen this kind of exercise before, on pages 32–33 when you looked at medicine in ancient Rome. This time you are in nineteenth-century Britain, and it is your child who is ill.

1. Get into pairs. You will each need a counter to move around the game board.
2. Choose one of the **families** from Box A.
3. Your child has a terrible cough and a high temperature. Choose one of the **healers** from Box B.
4. On the board opposite start by putting your counter on the number your healer instruction tells you to.
5. Take turns following the instructions in your square. At each turn note down what happens.
6. If your child dies or recovers before your partner's, try the game again using a different healer.
7. When you have finished the game, discuss with your partner whether the different healers, treatments and remedies were helpful. You will find out more about them on pages 126–27.

Box B: Healers

Visit a doctor – go to square 1.

Use a patent remedy – go to square 21.

Treat the child yourself at home – go to square 7.

Go to a chemist – go to square 8.

Go to a herbalist – go to square 4.

Box A: Families

Mr and Mrs Grace are very well off. They inherited land and money from their parents.

Mr Gilbert is a clerk in a shipping office, working ten hours a day. He does not want his wife to work as that would not be 'respectable'. They have just enough money to live on, provided there are no unexpected bills.

Mrs Williams earns a few pennies doing laundry. Her husband works at the docks, provided an 'ill wind' does not keep the ships out of port. If there are no ships he earns nothing.

WILL YOUR CHILD SURVIVE?

1
Your choice of doctor depends on how much money you have. Graces go to 11. Gilberts go to 20. Williamses go to 27.

2
Your sister says you must keep the child wrapped up warm at home with the window closed. If you agree, go to 14. If not, go to 7.

3
Buy Morrison's Vegetable Universal Compound, pills that cure everything by purging the patient. Go to 14.

4
At the herbalist the Williamses cannot afford the prices. Choose another healer. The Graces and Gilberts decide to try a herbal cure. The herbalist recommends treacle, tincture of lobelia and aniseed water. If you agree, go to 29.

5
The dispensary gives free medicine to working people who don't have much money. You try the medicine. Go to 25.

6
The Williamses discover they cannot afford any more pills. Go to 22. The Graces and Gilberts buy some more. Go to 25.

7
You are given lots of advice. If you listen to your friend, go to 26. If you listen to your sister, go to 2. If you listen to your brother, go to 18.

8
The chemist mixes you a remedy made from sodium tartrate, Ipecacuhana wine and laudanum. The Williamses cannot afford this mixture. Choose another healer. If the Graces and Gilberts choose this remedy, go to 15. If they do not, choose another healer.

9
On your way home you meet a man selling Dr Drummond's Herbal Tonic which he says cures any disease or disability. If you buy some, go to 16. If not, choose another healer.

10
There is still no improvement. The doctor suggests you take the child to the seaside to drink seawater. It can be very effective. If you agree, go to 19. If you disagree, go to 22.

11
Your physician is very confident. He has seen plenty of these cases. He recommends bleeding the child, followed by purging. If you agree, go to 24. If not, choose another healer.

12
The bleeding and purging bring no improvement. The doctor recommends another medicine to help your child vomit to clear out her system. You can't afford the medicine so he sends you to 5.

13
You take the child home, but you have no work so it is hard to feed her. Go to 17.

14
The treatment has no immediate effect. You could try some more and go to 6 or, if not, go to 22.

15
The remedy is not working. The chemist suggests doubling the dose. The Gilberts cannot afford more. Choose another healer. The Graces can afford another dose. If you choose this, go to 23. If not, choose another healer.

16
Dr Drummond's Herbal Tonic cures almost everything but not your child's fever. Choose another healer.

17
The doctor says the child is no better. He says he will try bleeding her, but he is not hopeful. Go to 30.

18
Your brother says the best remedy is to skin and roast a mouse and then get the child to eat it whole. If you agree, go to 28. If not, go back to 7.

19
The journey is too much for the weak child. She dies. When the physician's bill arrives you pay it. He did everything he could.

20
Your doctor recommends bleeding the child and then regular doses of purging. If you agree, go to 12. If you disagree, go to 22.

21
At the shop there are many patent medicines to choose from. Choose 3 or 31.

22
It is time to choose another healer or go to 9.

23
Your child recovers. Perhaps there was something in the remedy or perhaps it was because your child had clean bedding, plenty of food and fresh water.

24
The bleeding and purging have not helped. Your doctor bleeds the child again and also makes her vomit. Go to 10.

25
There is still no improvement. Choose another healer or go to 30.

26
Your friend says that the best remedy is for the child to ride a donkey seven times in a circle or be passed under it seven times. If you agree, go to 14. If not, go back to 7 or choose another healer.

27
The doctor for the poor thinks it is best to bleed the child but says she is too weak through lack of food. He recommends you take her home to rest and to feed her and then bring her back. If you agree, go to 13. If not, choose another healer.

28
Your child dies. Your brother says there was nothing wrong with his suggestion. You should have listened to him sooner.

29
The fever falls briefly then returns. If you decide to go back to the herbalist, go to 32. If not, choose another healer.

30
Your child grows weaker and dies. You do not blame the doctor or the medicines. They were the best you could get.

31
Buy Holloway's pills and ointment which cure everything by purging the patient. Go to 14.

32
The herbalist recommends a mixture of dropwort and comfrey. The Gilberts cannot afford another treatment and choose another healer. The Graces buy the mixture and go to 23.

Were home remedies changing?

Domestic medicine

Many illnesses were still treated at home, as they had been throughout the centuries. Home care had changed little and mainly involved providing comfort, food and warmth – so long as the family could afford them.

Home carers also used treatments such as herbal remedies which they had learnt from their ancestors or which had been published in early medical books. The approach to treatment at home was dominated by common sense and useful information passed from generation to generation.

Domestic medicine of this sort rarely provided a cure but it gave the patient a sense of security and control over their own treatment. However, one useful development was the introduction of thermometers which helped home carers to make simple diagnoses.

> ## SOURCE 1 Traditional home remedies
>
> 66 *For influenza* **either** *mix ginger into a drink of tea* **or** *mix half a pound of treacle with half a pint of vinegar and three teaspoonfuls of laudanum. Take three times a day.* 99
>
> 66 *To cure tuberculosis breathe into a freshly-made hole in the turf or try the breath of stallions and cows.* 99
>
> 66 *To cure epilepsy take the skull of a young woman, pound it into small bits, mix with treacle and take in small doses.* 99
>
> 66 *To cure smallpox apply cool boiled turnips to the feet or make a drink out of ground ivy.* 99

Patent medicines

By 1800 people were supplementing their traditional family remedies with visits to 'quack' doctors or shops where they could buy 'patent' medicines or 'cure alls'. These made little or no contribution to the improvement of health but were cheaper than prescriptions from doctors.

Another reason why people bought patent medicines or visited 'quacks' was that qualified doctors could not cure many illnesses. In the 1850s James Ward set up in Leeds as a 'cancer curer' using herbal remedies. He was criticised by local doctors but challenged them to a contest, each to treat twenty patients. The winner was to be the one who had most surviving patients. No doctor took up his challenge. Even though they thought Ward's remedies were useless, they knew that their own more scientific methods were no better.

Patent medicines in the nineteenth century were big business. Between 1850 and 1900 sales of patent medicines increased by 400 per cent. They did not come under any government control until the 1880s. That meant that false claims could be made without any fear of prosecution. There was also no control over the manufacturing standards or the ingredients in the medicines – some of which were positively dangerous. Thomas Holloway's pills contained ginger, soap and aloes, a very powerful purgative, until a court case against him in the 1860s. Afterwards they contained milder ingredients – lard, wax and turpentine – but they still claimed to cure all illnesses. Deaths and illnesses resulting from overdoses and addiction were common if some patent medicines were taken regularly.

James Morrison started manufacturing his Vegetable Universal Medicines in 1825. They were made of lard, wax, turpentine, soap and ginger. They had no active ingredient yet the pills were supposed to cure everything from fever, scarlatina, tuberculosis, smallpox and measles to the effects of old age. By 1834 Morrison was selling over one million boxes of pills a year throughout Europe and the British empire.

SOURCE 2 A pedlar selling patent medicines in a London street in 1877

SOURCE 3 From F.B. Smith, *The People's Health*, 1971

66 The man who came to see Dr Strachan of Clackmannan, Scotland in 1861 was one of many poor patients who were suffering from leg ULCERS. *We now know that this, with typhus, is a classic indication of poor diet and hygiene. The doctor recorded that his patient 'had been at many doctors, and had tried all the Holloway's ointments and other infallible remedies'. [Holloway's ointments were 'cure all' medicines advertised and sold widely.]*

The doctor examined him and 'with great difficulty ... got him a larger allowance from the poor's funds, and some of his friends assisted him ... As soon as the man's system got into good condition the ulcers began to heal and ... the poor man was restored and fitted for his work'.

When the man next met Dr Strachan he informed the doctor that he was getting on very well. 'Well doctor, I tell you what it was that cured my legs, and it will be useful to other folk. It was just moose wels [spider's webs]. Jenny Donald advised me to try them, and they cured my legs at once.' 99

Improved medicines

In the late 1800s there was some progress in the production of medicines. In the 1880s the government introduced laws to control the making of patent medicines. By 1900 many of the harmful ingredients were removed from the 'cure all' pills.

The rapidly-developing chemical industry also discovered the first really effective chemical drugs in the 1880s – the painkillers aspirin and antipyrin. As scientific research into drugs developed so did the interest of manufacturers. By 1900 companies like Boots, Wellcome and Beecham had formed the basis of the pharmaceutical industry which we know today.

1. What evidence is there in Source 1 that home remedies were not changing?
2. What cured the patient in Source 3?
3. What sort of treatment did the patient think had cured him?
4. Was the doctor able to cure the patient's illness?
5. Why do you think people bought 'cure all' products in the nineteenth century?
6. Why did medicines improve in the late 1800s?
7. Why do you think home remedies were slow to change in the 1800s?

A DRESSMAKER'S DILEMMA

"At the age of sixteen," said Miss Moore, "I was dressmaking in the village. One afternoon, mother and I were taking a walk across the fields; suddenly I fell to the ground, and lay there some time. With great difficulty I reached home. I was immediately put to bed, and two doctors were summoned, both of whom were of opinion that my fainting was due to anaemia and neuralgia. I was like a mad thing at times: the pain drove me almost frantic."

"You look robust and healthy enough now."

"Yes, and I feel well and strong too. But for nearly four years, I was racked with pain in my head, neck, and shoulders. People thought I should die, and death to me would have been a happy release. My heart was also disordered for I had palpitation, and dreaded going upstairs. But now" (she concluded), "I can run up with anyone, and can do a day's sewing with perfect ease."

"To what do you attribute so great a change?"

"To nothing else than Dr. Williams' Pink Pills for Pale People."

MOTHERS
OUGHT

TO

KNOW

THIS.

If your Daughters have Pale Faces, Weakness, Palpitation, Bloodlessness, NICHOLL'S MAYHATINE BLOOD PILLS quickly bring the rosy colour to the pallid cheeks, and change a delicate, undeveloped irregular girl into a strong, well-developed woman. They are tasteless, make rich, red blood; invaluable to Ladies as a Strengthening Regulator. All Chemists, or post free 3 doz., 1s. 1½d.; 9 doz., 2s. 9d.; 18 doz., 4s 6d.

I. W. NICHOLL, Phar. Chemist, **25 High St., BELFAST.** Thousands of Testimonials.

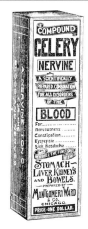

SOURCE 4 Advertisements for patent medicines

Could hospitals and doctors help the sick?

Doctors

If you had an infectious disease such as whooping cough (the disease in the activity on pages 124–25), doctors and other healers could have done little to help you for most of the nineteenth century. Many of their methods, such as bleeding and purging, were similar to remedies which had been used a thousand years earlier. Nevertheless, some important changes were under way.

From the 1750s ordinary people were able to call on the services of a local doctor or general practitioner. Doctors usually trained through an apprenticeship. They attended medical lectures and walked the wards of a hospital as the pupil of a respected surgeon or physician. They learned to use new devices such as the stethoscope, which was invented in 1816. (The modern-style stethoscope was developed in 1860.) They were aware of the most effective drugs and herbal remedies for common ailments. In addition to this, doctors acted as 'male midwives'.

The majority of local doctors were well respected because they worked hard. They usually had standard charges but these were often waived if a patient was too poor to pay. At the beginning of the 1800s doctors had good incomes, mainly from their wealthy patients but also from contracts with the local parish for the care, midwifery and vaccination of the poor.

From the 1860s the training of doctors had to keep up with new discoveries. Over the next 50 years training became much more scientific because of:

- the discoveries of Pasteur and Koch about germ theory
- the development of anaesthetics
- the development of antiseptic and aseptic surgery.

But all these doctors were men. Couldn't women become doctors?

Find out the answer on page 132.

Training
- Attended lectures on medicine
- Followed surgeons and physicians around hospital wards, learning from experienced doctors

Work
- Treated private patients
- Treated the poor in the workhouse
- Delivered babies
- Carried out vaccinations
- Made up medicines

Equipment
- Thermometers
- Stethoscopes

Payments
- Wealthy patients paid them for their treatment
- The local parish council paid them for treating the poor
- People paid for medicines

SOURCE 5 Doctors in the mid-nineteenth century – a summary

Hospitals

Death rates from infection were high, because wards were not cleaned often enough or effectively enough.

Cramped, stuffy wards helped infections to spread quickly.

Nursing staff were not trained.

Nurses were often criticised for being dirty or drunk.

There were few toilets and the sewerage system was poor, so infections spread easily.

SOURCE 6 Dangers to health posed by hospital wards in the early 1800s

This is what hospital wards were like in the days before Pasteur and Lister. Nobody knew that germs existed and no one understood the importance of antiseptics. For many people, hospitals were the places they went to to die – if not from the disease they had when they went in, then from another disease they caught on the wards. Anyone who had the money paid for nurses and doctors to visit them at home. Even operations were carried out at home because this seemed a healthier place than a hospital ward.

But I changed all that. I wanted to train to be a nurse but there were no training schools in Britain for nurses in 1850. However, there was a school for nurses in Germany so I went there to train. On the next two pages you can find out how I changed hospitals and nursing.

Why was Florence Nightingale able to improve hospitals?

FLORENCE NIGHTINGALE was born in 1820. Her parents were wealthy and did not expect her to get a job. They expected her to marry a rich man and have children. However, Florence Nightingale believed that God wanted her to be a nurse.

New hospitals had opened in many towns during the eighteenth century but conditions in many of them were poor. There was no planned training for nurses and many people thought nursing was a job only for uneducated women who could do nothing else. This was one of the reasons why people feared going into hospital, where diseases spread quickly and there was a high death rate. Anyone who could afford it paid to be nursed and even operated on at home. In 1851 more nurses worked in private homes than in hospitals.

In 1851 Florence Nightingale went to Germany to work in a hospital for three months. There she learned about how nurses were trained and how they could help to make patients healthy. When she returned to England, she worked in a hospital for sick 'gentlewomen', but her life really changed in 1854 when war broke out in the Crimea between Russia and Britain.

'The Lady with the Lamp'

The Crimean War was the first war in which war reporters could send back reports to newspapers using the new telegraph system. This meant that news from the war arrived almost instantly instead of weeks later. As a result, British people were horrified to hear that half the wounded British soldiers were dying in army hospitals because of dirt and lack of good nursing. Something had to be done! That was why a government minister asked Florence Nightingale to lead a group of trained nurses to the Crimea to solve this problem.

When she reached the Crimea, she reorganised the army hospitals. New wards were built, and scrubbed regularly to keep them clean. Sheets and towels were boiled regularly, and good food was given to the wounded. The results were amazing. In six months the death rate among the wounded fell from 42 per cent to 2 per cent! The newspapers in Britain reported her work and she became famous as 'The Lady with the Lamp'.

Developments in nursing training

After two years she returned to Britain. Using the £50,000 that had been raised for the Nightingale Fund, she set about improving conditions in hospitals in Britain and improving the training of nurses. First she published a book on improving army hospitals. In it she used statistics and charts to prove her arguments. She was a pioneer of using statistics in medicine to show what changes were needed.

In 1859 Florence Nightingale published *Notes for Nursing*, setting out her ideas for nurses and hospitals. She stressed the importance of 'the proper use of fresh air, light, warmth, cleanliness, quiet and the proper selection and administration of diet'. In 1860 she also set up the first training school for nurses, using the money raised while she was in the Crimea. Her aim was to train matrons, who would, in turn, train the ordinary ward nurses.

Florence Nightingale's work in training nurses came at a key time in the development of medicine because of the many important changes taking place. Between 1860 and 1900 hospitals and especially surgery were changing rapidly, following Pasteur's germ theory and the development of anaesthetics and antiseptics. Nurses needed new skills to make the most of these changes and the new training schools ensured that nurses developed these skills. For example, nurses needed to understand Lister's work on antiseptics if they were to make sure that conditions in operating theatres were germ-free. In turn, the more advanced medicine also led to increased demand for trained nurses. The improvements in hospitals gradually put an end to the tradition of people being nursed and operated on in their own homes, for fear of catching diseases in hospitals.

SOURCE 1 Hospital ward, Scutari, in the Crimea, in 1856: Florence Nightingale at work

Another result of these changes was that attitudes to nurses changed. Now that nurses were trained and not just fetching and carrying like domestic servants, people respected them much more. Nursing also became a respectable job for young women to do. It was vital that there were more nurses because the number of patients in hospitals was rising rapidly at that time, as you can see in Source 2.

	1861	**1921**
Number of patients	About 65,000	228,500
Hospital beds per thousand people	3.2	6.1

SOURCE 2 Number of patients and provision of hospital beds, 1861 and 1921

Problems in 1860	Solutions in 1920
Unhygienic surgery and dressings	Aseptic surgery and dressings
Untrained nurses	Trained nurses
Cramped, stuffy wards	Spacious, light, well-ventilated wards
Poor sanitation, toilets and sewerage	Good sanitation
Lack of cleanliness	Cleanliness

SOURCE 3 A summary of changes in hospitals between 1860 and 1920

■ TASK

1. Florence Nightingale played a key role in improving hospitals and nursing, but she was helped by other factors. Give at least one example of how each of these factors contributed to the improvements:
   a) communications
   b) science and technology
   c) changing attitudes
   d) war
   e) improvements in medical knowledge.
2. Which reasons were most important in helping Florence Nightingale improve
   a) the role of nurses b) the conditions in hospitals?
3. Why was the period from 1850 to 1920 so important in the history of nursing and hospitals?
4. It is 1907. Florence Nightingale has been awarded the Order of Merit, an award for great service to Britain and its people. Write the speech to be given by the Prime Minister at the ceremony, explaining what Florence Nightingale achieved and why her work is so important.
5. Do your own research to find out who Mary Seacole was and whether she also deserved the Order of Merit.

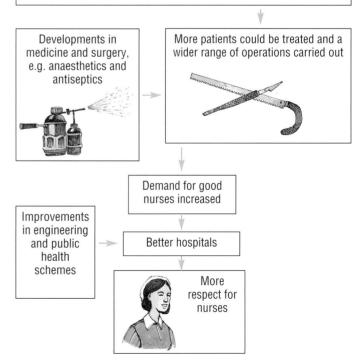

SOURCE 4 Why were there so many changes in hospitals and nursing?

Was the role of women in medicine changing?

THE SIMPLE ANSWER to that question is yes – but very, very slowly. Six hundred years of change had steadily reduced the status of women in medicine.

In the Middle Ages the Church allowed only men to train as physicians. In the 1600s the Church also took over the licensing of all healers. It did not give licences to wise women or village healers because they were often suspected of being witches.

As you saw on page 85, by the 1700s surgeons also had to have a university degree. As women could not go to university they were effectively barred from becoming surgeons.

In the 1700s male doctors became fashionable, and began to take over the traditional role of midwives among wealthy families because they were the only ones trained to use the new forceps.

Finally, in 1852, the government introduced the Medical Registration Act which required all doctors to belong to one of the Colleges of Physicians, Surgeons or Apothecaries. All of these were closed to women!

Of course, women still played the major role as healers in the home, and as nurses, but the days when they could become doctors were long over.

In the 1850s women began to fight back. However, the problems for ambitious women began long before they reached the age when they might want to study medicine. Schools for girls were a rarity before the 1860s – certainly ones that taught anything other than reading, writing, cooking and dressmaking. Science? That was a subject for boys! Even those girls lucky enough to be educated at a good school found that their days of learning were over when they reached their mid-teens because women were not allowed to attend universities. Most men could not see any sense in educating women when their most important roles were as obedient wives, dutiful mothers and efficient housekeepers.

Despite these obstacles a handful of women fought for the right to become doctors. Elizabeth Blackwell was the first woman to qualify as a doctor in the United States in 1849. She visited England ten years later, inspiring Elizabeth Garrett to follow in her footsteps. Elizabeth Garrett was the first woman to qualify in Britain as a doctor but she had to overcome immense difficulties, first to get training, and then to be allowed to practise as a doctor.

■ ACTIVITY 1

Boxes A–D tell the story in four stages of the fight by women to become doctors. Boxes E–H explain the different ways in which men tried to block women's progress. Match up the boxes in pairs, showing how men tried to push back each advance by women.

Box A
During the 1860s Elizabeth Garrett worked as a nurse and then attended lectures at the Middlesex Hospital.

Box C
In 1874 six women, led by Sophia Jex-Blake, completed the medical course at Edinburgh University.

Box E
The Colleges of Surgeons and Physicians refused to allow women members which therefore stopped Garrett from working as a doctor. She had to take the College of Apothecaries to court before it accepted her as a member. After that it too changed its rules so that women could not become members.

Box G
For five years after 1876 the Royal College of Surgeons refused to allow anyone to take exams in midwifery, as a way of preventing women from learning alongside men.

Box B
Elizabeth Garrett passed all the exams to qualify as a doctor. The final step before she could work as a doctor was to become a member of one of the Colleges of Surgeons, Physicians or Apothecaries.

Box D
In 1876 a law was passed opening all medical qualifications to women.

Box F
Male students at the hospital protested that Elizabeth Garrett should not be allowed to attend lectures.

Box H
Edinburgh University said that it could only give medical degrees to men. The women had to complete their degrees in Dublin, or Zurich in Switzerland.

SOURCE 1 Letter from Elizabeth Garrett to a friend, 1859. Her father did help her later

❝ I have just concluded a satisfactory talk with father on the medical subject. He does not like it, I think. He said the whole idea was disgusting and he could not entertain it for a moment. I asked what there was to make doctoring more disgusting than nursing, which women were also doing and which ladies had done publicly in the Crimea. He could not tell me … I think he will probably come round in time. I mean to renew the subject pretty often. ❞

SOURCE 2 Thomas Huxley, a leading scientist, 1851

❝ In every excellent characteristic, whether mental or physical, the average woman is inferior to the average man. ❞

SOURCE 3 The views of the novelist W.M. Thackeray in the 1850s on what an ideal woman should be like

❝ An exquisite slave: a humble, flattering, tea-making, pianoforte-playing being, who laughs at our jokes, however old they may be; coaxes us and fondly lies to us throughout life. ❞

SOURCE 4 A statement made by students at Middlesex Hospital, London, in 1861, in protest at Elizabeth Garrett attending lectures

❝ We consider that the mixture of sexes in the same class is likely to lead to results of an unpleasant character.

Lecturers are likely to feel some restraint through the presence of females in giving that explicit enunciation of some facts which is necessary.

The presence of young females as spectators in the operating theatre is an outrage on our natural instincts and feelings and calculated to destroy those sentiments of respect and admiration with which the sex is regarded by all right-thinking men. Such feelings are a mark of civilisation and refinement. ❞

SOURCE 5 Elizabeth Garrett, the first woman to qualify as a doctor in Britain

1. Were men or women doing more to care for the sick around 1860?
2. Read Source 1. Why did many men accept women as nurses but not as doctors?
3. What does Source 3 suggest are the qualities of an ideal woman?
4. Why was it nearly impossible for women to become doctors?
5. Explain how each of these factors helped limit or increase the role of women in medicine:

   ■ attitudes and beliefs
   ■ governments
   ■ technology
   ■ education
   ■ individuals.

■ **ACTIVITY 2**

Write a reply from Elizabeth Garrett to the medical students who wrote the letter in Source 4. Try not to be too rude! It might make them worse.

Key individuals: Florence Nightingale and Elizabeth Garrett Anderson

The problem

In the 1850s hospital wards were dirty and unhealthy. The death rate was high. Nurses were given no training and had a bad reputation.

Florence Nightingale
(1820–1910)

The solutions

1. In the Crimea

Working with a team of nurses, Florence Nightingale transformed army hospitals. The death rate fell from 42 per cent to just 2 per cent. This provided powerful evidence of the success of her methods.

The results

By 1901 hospital wards were clean, death rates were low and there were 68,000 trained nurses. They enjoyed a high reputation.

2. In Britain

In 1859 Nightingale published *Notes for Nursing* and opened the first training school for nurses. She advised on hospital design, stressing the importance of cleanliness and fresh air.

The problem

There was widespread opposition to women in medicine in the 1870s. Women were unable to qualify as doctors.

Elizabeth Garrett (1836–1917). After her marriage, she was known as Elizabeth Garrett Anderson

The fight

1. Elizabeth Garrett attended lectures at Middlesex Hospital. Male students protested but could not stop her.

2. She passed all her exams to qualify as a doctor. Now the Colleges of Surgeons, Physicians or Apothecaries had to decide whether to accept her as a qualified doctor. They refused.

The result

Women were now allowed to train and qualify as doctors. However, progress was slow. The first real increase in the number of women doctors came when there was a sudden demand for more doctors during the First World War.

3. She took the College of Apothecaries to court to force them to accept her. In 1876 a new law was passed opening all medical qualifications to women.

Exam practice: the role of Florence Nightingale

Pages 136–39 give you a typical Paper 2 exam. In Paper 2 you are being tested on your ability to use sources in context. In other words, you need to use your knowledge to understand and evaluate sources.

Look through the sources and the questions below to see how they relate to each other.

Study Sources A–L and then answer Questions 1–8 below.

1. Study Sources A and B. What impression of nurses are these sources trying to give? Explain your answer, using the sources. **(5)**
2. Study Sources B and C, and use your own knowledge. Do you think that Mrs Prig was typical of nurses at the time? Explain your answer using Sources B and C, and your own knowledge. **(7)**
3. Study Source D. What can you work out from this source about Florence Nightingale's character? Explain your answer, using the source. **(6)**
4. Study Sources E and F. How useful are Sources E and F for a historian enquiring into the problems Florence Nightingale faced in the Crimea? Explain your answer, using the sources. **(8)**

5. Study Sources E and G. Use the evidence of these sources to explain why Florence Nightingale's work in the Crimea became so well known in England at the time. **(8)**
6. Study Sources H and I, and use your own knowledge. What evidence is there in Source I to show that Louise Pringle was a 'Nightingale' nurse? Explain your answer using these sources and your own knowledge. **(7)**
7. Study Sources I, J and K. How far does the evidence of Sources J and K challenge Louise Pringle's criticisms of Mrs Porter (Source I)? Explain your answer, using the sources. **(8)**
8. Study Sources H and L, and use your own knowledge. Do you think the author of Source H has exaggerated Florence Nightingale's importance to the history of nursing in the nineteenth century? Explain your answer, using your own knowledge and any information from the sources you find helpful. **(11)**

(Total: 60 marks)

SOURCE A A cartoon of a nurse drawn in 1840

SOURCE B An extract from *Martin Chuzzlewit*, a novel by Charles Dickens, published in 1844. In this extract, the nurse, Betsy Prig, is handing her patient over to the care of another nurse, Sarah Gamp. Charles Dickens wrote in his introduction to this novel that 'Mrs Betsy Prig is an accurate description of a hospital nurse'.

❝ *'How are we?' asked Mrs Gamp.*
Mrs Prig said, 'He's as cross as two sticks. He wouldn't have been washed if he'd had his own way.'
'She put soap in my mouth' said the unfortunate patient, feebly.
'Couldn't you keep it shut then?' said Mrs Prig.
Mrs Prig seized the patient by the chin and began to scrape his unhappy head with the hair brush. The brush was the hardest possible instrument and his eye-lids were red with the pain.
Then Mrs Gamp and Mrs Prig put on his coat.
'I don't think it's quite right' said the poor invalid. 'There's a bottle in my pocket. Why have you made me sit on a bottle?'
'Oh' cried Mrs Gamp, 'he's got my gin bottle. I put it in his coat when it hung behind the door.' ❞

SOURCE C From *A History of Nursing*, by Patricia Donahue, 1995. This drawing of Rahere ward in St Bartholomew's Hospital was made in 1844. Many books label this drawing wrongly. They say it shows a 'Gamp' style nurse, simply because she is wearing the usual clothes worn by her class at that time. Although hospitals, including this one, had many nurses who were uncaring gin-drinkers, it is recorded that the sister of Rahere ward at the time of this picture was: 'very watchful. She could report correctly the progress of a case; and from her wages she saved all she could and left it in her will to the hospital.'

SOURCE D Extracts from two private letters from Florence Nightingale in Scutari to Sidney Herbert, Secretary of State at War

66 *(i) 25 November 1854*
When we came, there was no soap or basins or towels in the wards. The consequence of all this are fever, cholera, gangrene, lice . . . Two or three hundred arm-slings, stump-pillows and other medical appliances are being weekly manufactured and given out by us. No arrangement seems to have been made to do this before.

(ii) 10 December 1854
To land 25 casks of sugar from the boats it took four oxen and three men six hours. It needed two passes and two requisitions.* There are no pack horses. The quarter-master in charge of supplies apologised for seizing the cart. I received his apology with a smile and a kind word, because he was only doing his duty. All carts are required for military use.
What we have achieved:

■ *A great deal more cleaning of wards – mops, scrubbing brushes given out by ourselves*
■ *the supervision and stirring up of the whole organisation generally*
■ *repair of the wards for 800 wounded ...* 99

*requisitions = the army forms which had to be filled in

SOURCE E An extract from *The Times* newspaper, 16 October 1855

66 *On Wednesday Mr Bracebridge* gave a lecture in Coventry describing his experiences of British hospitals in the Crimea. He described the difficulties Miss Nightingale and her party faced when they arrived in the Crimea. When they arrived at Scutari, there was no kitchen, coal or candles. They soon set to work, however, to make the place comfortable. In two days they had made a great change to the look of the inside of the building.*

At first they were despised by the doctors for their lack of medical knowledge. But two or three days later, after 600 wounded were brought down, they dressed the wounds of 300 of them. The doctors began to think they might be of some use.

Without The Times *Fund, so many things which were needed urgently would never have been obtained.*
(Cheers from the audience) 99

*Mr and Mrs Bracebridge were Florence Nightingale's friends and went out to the Crimea to work with her. They returned to England in 1855.

SOURCE F From a letter written in November 1855 by Dr John Hall to the Director of the Army Medical Service. Dr Hall was Chief of the Medical Staff in the Crimea

66 *Such nonsense was uttered by Mr. Bracebridge and reported with approval in* The Times. *He talked about Miss Nightingale putting hospitals containing three or four thousand patients in order in a couple of days helped by* The Times *Fund. I despise the man for such exaggerations and I pity the ignorant multitude who are taken in by these fairy tales.* 99

SOURCE H From a history of the Edinburgh Royal Infirmary in the 1870s. It was written by a historian, Martin Goldman, in 1987

66 *Florence Nightingale was one of those great individuals who single-handedly changed history. Before her, nursing was a generally despised profession. Florence Nightingale changed that.*

Many of the nurses in the Edinburgh Royal Infirmary in the 1870s were 'Nightingales'. Either they were nurses trained directly by Florence Nightingale at St Thomas' Hospital, London or they were trained in Edinburgh by Nightingale-trained Nurses.

Although 'the Nightingales' had arrived, there were plenty of the old type still around. The most celebrated of these was Mrs Porter. She had become a hospital legend. 99

SOURCE I From the diary of Miss Louise Pringle. Miss Pringle had trained at the Nightingale School. She went to Edinburgh in 1872 to set up a school to train nurses according to Florence Nightingale's methods

66 *7 November*
Left St Thomas' at 9 a.m. Had a pleasant journey. Dined from the basket Miss Nightingale provided. It was packed with good things.

8 November
One head nurse, Mrs Porter, looked quite a dear old lady but her wards were not well kept. She has been 27 years here.

21 November
At half past eleven at night we began a round of the wards. We found in nearly all the wards a riot of laughing and talking going on among the nurses and patients. Nurse Porter's wards were the noisiest; the old lady herself was very loud. Our own wards presented a pleasing contrast and we appreciated even more than ever before the St Thomas' system. The patients were asleep and the night nurse was quietly in charge. 99

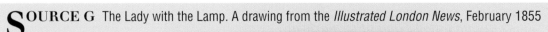

SOURCE G The Lady with the Lamp. A drawing from the *Illustrated London News*, February 1855

KEY INDIVIDUALS: FLORENCE NIGHTINGALE AND ELIZABETH GARRETT ANDERSON

SOURCE J A doctor, F. Caird, who had worked at the hospital in the 1870s remembers Nurse Porter. This extract is from a book published in 1927

66 *The worthy nurse, Mrs Porter, made her nightly round, candle stick in hand and carrying a tray of refreshments. Thorough and good-hearted, many were the kindnesses she showed to poor patients. Many would find on the morning they left the hospital, a small sum of money under their candlestick to help them on their way home.* 99

SOURCE K A poem about Nurse Porter written by William Henley when he was a patient in the hospital for some months in 1873. His poems were published in 1898

66 *These thirty years has she been nursing here,*
Some of them under Syme*, her hero still,
Much she is worth and even more is made of her.
Patients and students hold her very dear.
The doctors love her, tease her, use her skill.
They say 'the chief' himself [Joseph Lister] is half-afraid of her. 99

*James Syme was a leading surgeon. He died in 1870.

SOURCE L A map to show the spread of the Nightingale system of nursing education. The dates show approximately the year of the first nursing school in each country

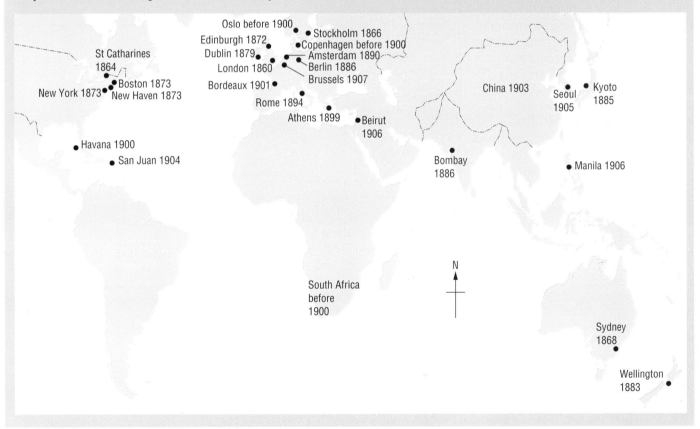

Medicine from 1750–1900 – a summary

Galen's ideas are questioned

For more than 1500 years Galen's ideas had dominated medicine. In the sixteenth and seventeenth centuries, however, the advances in anatomy and science which you studied in Chapter 2 had led some people to begin to challenge Galen's authority.

Between 1600 and 1900 what we now think of as modern science began to develop. Instead of looking at ancient books for ideas, scientists now used their own detailed observation, experiment and measurement to build up an accurate picture of the natural world. During this scientific revolution old explanations were questioned – Galen's included – and if they were found to be inaccurate they were abandoned. Gradually the works of Galen and other ancient writers became less and less important.

... but some of Galen's treatments live on!

In the history of medicine you will find that treatments and ideas about disease do not always change at the same pace. People sometimes continue to use treatments long after the ideas on which they are based have been abandoned. This is either because the treatments work, or because there are no alternatives. In the nineteenth century some of Galen's treatments continued to be used, as you can see from Source 2.

SOURCE 2 Doctor applying leeches to bleed a patient in the late 1700s

SOURCE 1 Why had doctors stopped reading Galen in the nineteenth century?

New understanding of the body
In the 1500s Vesalius (page 58) had begun a revolution in the understanding of the human body. He showed that Galen's descriptions were incomplete and, sometimes, even wrong. He encouraged all doctors to do their own dissections on human corpses rather than relying on Galen's work.

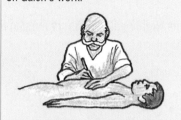

Old ideas were challenged
Scientists gradually discovered that many ancient ideas about the natural world – particularly the Greek theory of the four elements which had formed the basis for the theory of the four humours – were wrong. For example, they discovered that air itself is made up of different gases.

The microscope
The invention of the microscope helped further to undermine Galen's work. For example, it proved that Harvey's ideas were right (pages 62–63).

From the 1600s doctors and scientists increasingly used microscopes to investigate medical details which Galen could not possibly have discovered. Galen was simply irrelevant to such work.

New explanations for disease
It was difficult to disprove the theory of the four humours by experiment, but by the nineteenth century scientists did not accept it as an explanation of disease – it simply did not fit in with their new understanding of the natural world. They developed their own explanations of disease based on careful observation and research.

The most popular theory in the early 1800s was that 'bad air' caused disease, but by 1860 scientists had found a much more accurate explanation.

Training of doctors
These new ideas and techniques were being spread through better training for doctors. It became part of their training to carry out dissections, to use microscopes and to think scientifically. Galen's books were no longer important. The Catholic Church, which had been such a strong supporter of Galen in the Middle Ages, was no longer in control of medical training.

How did changes in the nineteenth century affect medicine and health?

The medical revolution was linked to the other great revolution of 1750–1900. New industries appeared; workers flocked to the factory towns and the population grew very quickly.

Britain led the way, but similar changes were also taking place in other countries at the same time. Many of these changes had a major impact on medicine and health as you can see from Source 3.

■ **TASK**

Look at Sources 1 and 3. Choose three changes which you think are particularly important in influencing medicine and health in the period 1750–1900. Explain your choice.

SOURCE 3 How did life in the nineteenth century affect medicine and health?

Urbanisation
The growth of towns created many health problems. Poor housing and infected water supplies made killer diseases spread more rapidly than ever before.

Changing political attitudes
In 1800 Parliament believed it should not interfere in people's lives. If people were unhealthy that was their business! By 1900 Parliament was making laws to improve people's health in a way that would have been unthinkable in earlier centuries: for example, forcing towns to install sewers.

Scientific medicine
Science helped medicine. Scientists discovered the links between micro-organisms and disease. Chemists researching the properties of different substances found, for example, a gas which could be used as an anaesthetic and a dye which killed bacteria.

Technology
Developments in steel produced a thin syringe needle that did not break; improvements in glass-making led to better microscope lenses and the first thermometer.

Engineers gained experience of big projects when they built the canal and railway systems. They were able to use this experience in the building of water pipes and sewage systems throughout the country.

Improved communications
Communications were revolutionised in this period.

Faster trains allowed scientists and doctors to gather at conferences and learn from each others' ideas. By 1900 you could get from London to Edinburgh in nine hours and from London to Paris in less than a day.

There were more newspapers and improved education meant more people could read. News could be reported more quickly because of the invention of the telegraph. For example, details of important scientific experiments carried out in France were reported in British newspapers the next day.

Entrepreneurs
Medicine became big business. Some entrepreneurs made millions of pounds from almost useless remedies. However, others put money into scientific research to find drugs which would help to cure disease.

War
Major wars during the period affected developments in health. For example, the Crimean War in the nineteenth century led to improvements in the standards of nursing and hospitals.

Was there a medical revolution?

■ TASK

This chart shows three areas of progress in
nineteenth-century medicine. Make your own copy
of the chart and then:

1. Explain what you consider to be the most
   important progress in each area. Support your
   explanation with evidence from pages 92–141.
2. For each area explain whether changes worked
   through to affect the health of ordinary people.
   Again support your explanation with evidence
   from pages 92–141.
3. Use your annotated chart to write an essay
   explaining which of the areas you think saw the
   most important changes. Give reasons for your
   choice and evidence to support it.

■ ACTIVITY 1

There is no jigsaw picture on this page as there was
at the end of the previous chapters. Instead, you are
going to produce one. Look back at the pictures on
pages 36 and 90. Then either:

a) draw your own '1900 version' showing all the
   new ideas and information which were available
   to doctors in 1900
   or
b) describe in words what you would put in the
   picture for 1900.

■ ACTIVITY 2

1. Divide into teams. Each team takes the role of
   one of the key individuals shown on the page
   opposite.
2. Your team's task is to give a three-minute
   presentation to your class, explaining why you
   deserve to be described as the most important
   individual in the history of medicine between
   1750 and 1900. Use the criteria here to help you.
3. After all the presentations, take a class vote on
   who you think was the most important
   individual. Or you could organise this as a cup
   draw with quarter finals, semi-finals and a grand
   final debate!

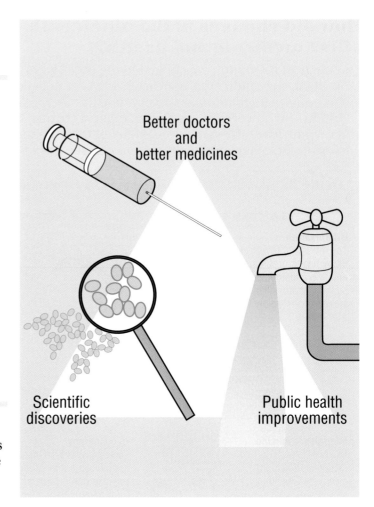

Better doctors
and
better medicines

Scientific
discoveries

Public health
improvements

In your own lifetime, did
you help many people to
live healthier lives?

Did you help many people
to live healthier lives in the
long run?

Who
was the most
important?

Were others able to build
on your work and make
further discoveries?

Edward Jenner

Edwin Chadwick

Louis Pasteur

Robert Koch

Joseph Lister

James Simpson

Elizabeth Garrett

Florence Nightingale

MEDICINE AND HEALTH SINCE 1900

Why have medicine and health improved so rapidly since 1900?

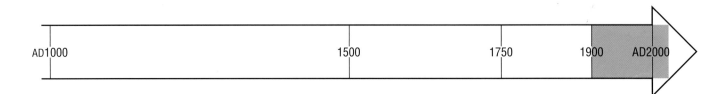

AT THE END of the nineteenth century one writer summed up the achievements of the century as follows: 'The authorities in the great provincial cities have been pushing their activities into the dark places of the earth; slum areas are broken up, sanitary regulations have been enforced, the policeman and the inspector are at every corner. A series of factory acts, building acts, public health acts have continually attacked the worst of the evils ... the forces of progress are against these older social diseases, which must eventually disappear ... '

However, despite all the important changes that took place in the 1800s, at the end of the century there was still a great deal of ill-health and misery.

- Life expectancy in 1900 remained below 50 years of age.
- In 1899, 163 out of every 1000 babies born died before their first birthday.

- Doctors and surgeons were often unable to cure their patients. There were no antibiotics to fight internal infection.
- In surgery, anaesthetics and antiseptics had taken much of the pain and danger out of operations, but problems of bleeding and infection remained. Appendix operations, for example, were still considered dangerous.
- The majority of families could not afford to go to a doctor.
- Many people were still living in unhealthy housing.

There was still much to discover, but since 1900 there have been greater improvements and more rapid changes in medicine and health than ever before. The chart below shows you the main reasons for this rapid improvement.

Communications and education
Ideas were able to spread rapidly. More doctors were trained. Advertising campaigns were used to promote public health.

Earlier discoveries
Doctors were able to build on the key scientific discoveries and methods of people such as Pasteur.

Technology/Science
Rapid advances allowed doctors to make new discoveries (e.g. DNA) and develop new techniques (e.g. keyhole surgery).

Why have medicine and health improved so rapidly?

War
The two world wars encouraged government spending, research and experiment, as doctors tried to find better ways to treat casualties.

Government and attitudes
Governments realised that people needed help and that medicines and treatment should be free for all.

Money
Governments spent far more on research and care. So did companies hoping to make money from medicine.

SOURCE 1 The reasons for the rapid advances in medicine since 1900

How did methods of treatment change during the twentieth century?

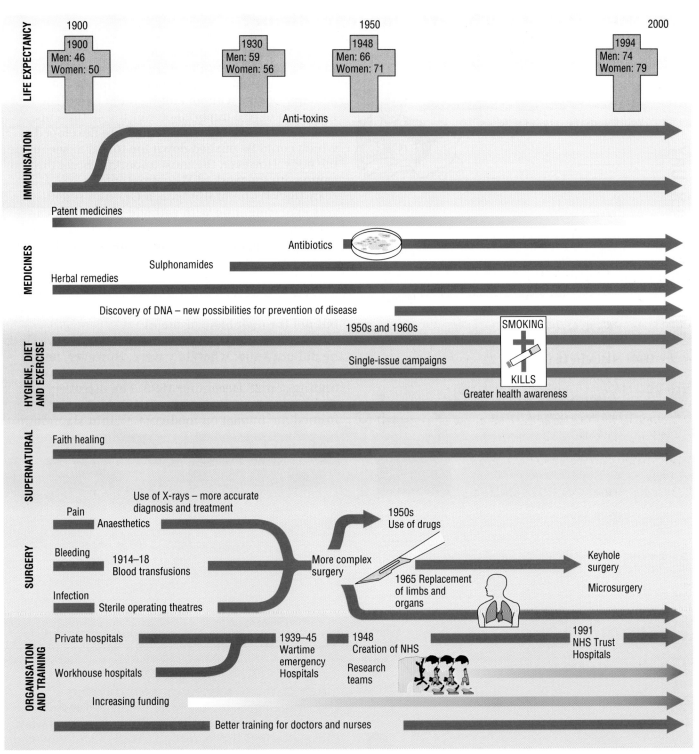

SOURCE 1 Changing methods of treatment in the twentieth century

■ **ACTIVITY**

Which of these developments do you think did the most to increase life expectancy?

The impact of science

Case study 1: How did X-rays change medicine?

NINETEENTH CENTURY

In the nineteenth century doctors could not see inside the bodies of their patients. To try to find a tumour, the doctor would hit the patient's chest, listening for any sound of 'dullness'.

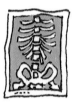

1895
Röntgen published his findings.
1896
Hospitals all over the world were using X-ray machines. The US army used X-rays to find bullets in their wounded soldiers during the Spanish–American War.

1900 TWENTIETH CENTURY
1900
X-rays were being used to treat lumps and bumps, ulcers and tumours.
1914–18
Mobile X-ray units were developed by Marie Curie for use close to the battlefields of the First World War.

1918–39
The harmful effects of gamma radiation were realised. Measured doses started to be used.

In the second half of the twentieth century safer methods of radiography were used.

DANGER: DO NOT ENTER

In the late twentieth century different types of deep scan, such as PET scans and CAT scans, were introduced. These give a more accurate picture of the inside of the body.

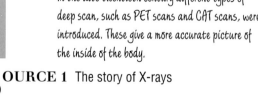

SOURCE 1 The story of X-rays

NINETEENTH CENTURY (vertical label)

TWENTIETH CENTURY (vertical label)

Stage 1: Röntgen and X-rays

In the mid-nineteenth century doctors could, for the first time, get information about the insides of patients' bodies without cutting them open. The first invention of real importance was the stethoscope, and then a series of instruments were developed which could be pushed down the throat to see inside the body. However, the most important breakthrough came with the work of Wilhelm Röntgen.

In 1895 Wilhelm Röntgen, a German scientist, was experimenting with cathode rays which cause splashes of light in a glass tube. He had covered the tube with black paper but was amazed to find the rays were still lighting up the other side of the room. They were passing through the paper! He investigated further and found that they could also pass through wood, rubber and even human flesh, but not through bone or metal.

Röntgen called these mysterious rays X-rays since he did not know what they were. However, he did understand their importance. He published his findings on 28 December 1895. The discovery caused great public excitement, and it had an immediate impact on medicine. Within six months hospitals had installed X-ray machines.

SOURCE 2 A portable X-ray machine

Stage 2: Marie Curie and radiotherapy

One of the key scientists who pioneered mobile X-ray machines during the First World War was Marie Curie. Marie Curie grew up in Poland and moved to Paris as a student. There she worked with Pierre Curie, whom she later married. They began their research, developing Röntgen's work on X-rays, with very little money. They worked in an old dissecting room that they described as 'a cross between a stable and a potato cellar'. However, as their work developed successfully, they were given better facilities at the University of Paris.

Marie Curie's greatest discovery came when she and her husband noticed that their skin was being burned by the material they were handling during their research. This led to the discovery of radium, which began to be used in radiography to diagnose cancers and in radiotherapy to remove cancerous growths from patients. This was the beginning of modern treatments of cancer and is still the basis of treatments used today.

By now the Curies' work had become so sophisticated and difficult that they needed to build up a team of research scientists who could share ideas and skills. One of these scientists was the Curies' daughter Irene. As a result of their work, the Curies developed a greater understanding of atoms and their power and this led to the splitting of the nucleus of an atom by other scientists in the 1940s.

Marie Curie was awarded two Nobel prizes for her work on X-ray radiography and radium treatment. She is the only woman to win two Nobel prizes. She was a woman of enormous energy, patience and determination, but her work cost her her life. She died of leukaemia from handling radioactive materials.

SOURCE 3 Marie Curie and her daughter, Irene, photographed in 1920

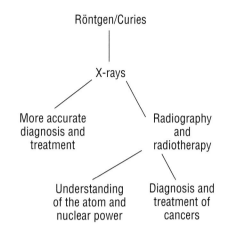

Röntgen/Curies

X-rays

More accurate diagnosis and treatment

Radiography and radiotherapy

Understanding of the atom and nuclear power

Diagnosis and treatment of cancers

SOURCE 4 The consequences of the work of Röntgen and the Curies

Why were so few women involved in scientific research in the nineteenth and early twentieth centuries?

At the beginning of the nineteenth century few women were involved in scientific research, and when they were it was usually with other members of their families. Many of the important institutions did not allow women to be members. Universities did not allow women to use their laboratories or take degrees. Many men believed women were too weak to be involved in advanced education; some even believed women had smaller brains!

Attitudes started to change very gradually at the end of the nineteenth century and by the end of the First World War women began to be accepted. Women became more involved in scientific research in the twentieth century but it was a long, slow process and it was not until the last quarter of the twentieth century that woman had equal access to a scientific education and job opportunities.

SOURCE 5 *Radium* by Imp: cartoon of Pierre and Marie Curie, published after the discovery of radium

1. Who is holding the radium?
2. What impression does this give of who was mainly responsible for its discovery?
3. What role is implied by the position of Marie in the cartoon?
4. Of what value is this cartoon to the historian?
5. Write a historically accurate caption and explanation of this cartoon for publication in a school textbook.

■ TASK

1. Why did the discoveries of
   a) Röntgen
   b) Marie Curie
   lead to better treatments and better health?
2. How did the following factors help to develop these discoveries:
   a) individuals' skills and intelligence
   b) finance
   c) war?

Case study 2: unravelling the secrets of DNA – the greatest development in medical history?

DNA stands for deoxyribonucleic acid. This is not a science book so you do not need to remember its full name – you can just talk and write about DNA. Just as important, while you're doing history, you will not need to explain **how** DNA works or understand a list of scientific terms such as CHROMOSOMES and proteins. All the science you need to know is in Source 1.

In history you are interested in:

- **Causes**: What factors led to the understanding of DNA?
- **Significance**: Why are these discoveries described as 'a breakthrough in the history of medicine'?

What is DNA?
- Inside every CELL of your body are several identical strings of DNA.
- A tiny part of your DNA looks like this:
- You can think of DNA as a long list of instructions like a computer program that operate every cell of your body. There are more than 3000 million letters of code in your body's program – an amazing number!
- These instructions are grouped together into sets of instructions called GENES.
- Each gene has a different function. For example – some decide your eye colour or how much hair you have. Some decide whether you will develop a disease or disability.
- Everybody's DNA carries slightly different instructions – which is why human beings are all different.

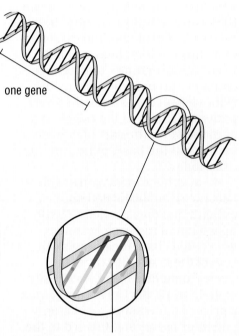

one gene

A base 'pair' which joins the two parts of the double helix

How were the DNA discoveries made?
DNA wasn't 'discovered' in one brilliant experiment. It took a series of discoveries over a long period to unravel the secrets of DNA gradually.

SOURCE 1

Turning Point 1 – Discovering the structure of DNA
In the early twentieth century scientists knew DNA existed, and knew it carried genetic information. However they did not know **how** it did this. The first step in understanding how it worked was to identify the structure of DNA.

Many scientists had tried and failed to work out this structure. But in 1953 two scientists working at the Cavendish Laboratory in Cambridge finally succeeded. Crick and Watson (see Source 2) discovered that the structure of DNA was a double helix, or a pair of interlocking spirals, joined by 'bases' (in pairs) which were like rungs of a ladder (see Source 1). They also proved that this DNA blueprint for life was present in every cell and could make an exact copy of itself and so could pass on information from one generation to the next.

This was the vital launch pad for further discoveries over the next fifty years.

Turning Point 2 – Mapping the human genome
The complete set of genes of a living organism is called a genome. In 1990 the Human Genome Project set out to identify the role of each of the 100,000 genes in a human DNA molecule and compile a complete map of human DNA.

This was a very complex operation. Research teams in eighteen countries took part, led by the USA, Britain, Japan, France and Canada. Each team worked on a different part of human DNA. Without large teams, this work simply could not be done.

Money came from two sources: governments and large drug companies (who hoped to profit from developing drugs based on understanding DNA).

Computerisation was vital both in analysing and recording the data. Without computers the Human Genome Project would have been impossible. The information carried in human DNA would fill 80,000 books the size of this one. But the electronic equivalent can fit on 5 CD-ROMs and can be passed around the world in minutes via the internet.

Why was the structure of DNA discovered in 1953?

Important developments in medicine are usually caused by a combination of different factors. Here are the factors that led to the discovery of the structure of DNA.

The role of key individuals
Born in 1916, Crick originally trained as a physicist at London University. Then he changed the direction of his research to molecular biology and genetics.

Watson, an American born in 1928, went to Chicago University aged only 15 where he started his research into DNA. He was only 24 when he made this discovery.

They were both experts in their own areas, but were quite prepared to go outside their fields to get at the answers they needed. This adventurousness was unusual.

Teamwork
Francis Crick and James Watson had different, complementary skills: Watson knew more about genetics; Crick knew more about biophysics. They also inspired each other. One of their biographers describes them as: 'fun-loving, ambitious, impatient and mercilessly candid'. Crick says they were not held back by politeness – if one of them was heading off in the wrong direction the other told him so. This saved time and energy and kept them on track.

Although Crick and Watson did individual research they also involved Maurice Wilkins and Rosalind Franklin from London and other colleagues in Cambridge. This brought together a team with a wide range of skills and knowledge.

Earlier research and discoveries
Not all the important discoveries were made in the 1950s. For hundreds of years scientists knew that some illnesses can be inherited. During the nineteenth century Mendel showed that characteristics could pass from one generation to the next. Scientists using improved microscopes also discovered how cells in the body were made up. Crick, Watson and others were able to build on this earlier work.

Technological and scientific developments
At each stage of work on DNA, scientists made use of the latest developments. They built on new knowledge in other types of science, for example, genetics and biochemistry. They also used new technologies such as X-ray photography.

Money
This kind of detailed scientific research is very expensive, uses complex equipment, employs highly skilled people and takes a lot of time. Money came from two sources – governments and industry.

SOURCE 2 (From left to right) Watson, Crick, Wilkins and Franklin: the four scientists who helped discover the structure of DNA

ACTIVITY

1. You are going to draw a factors chart like the one on page 64.
a) Put 'Discovering the structure of DNA' in the centre and draw five boxes around the outside.
b) In each box summarise one of the factors described on the left.
c) Are any of the five factors connected? Draw lines between the factors that are connected.
d) For each line, explain why there is a connection. For example, 'Money and teamwork are connected because …'
2. Which factor (or factors) do you think was the most important in discovering the structure of DNA?
3. Now do a similar chart for the Human Genome Project – using the information on the opposite page.
4. Which factor (or factors) do you think was the most important in the Human Genome Project?

■ The Nobel Prize and a forgotten heroine?
Maurice Wilkins worked at King's College, London and was an expert in X-ray photography. He was joined by Rosalind Franklin in 1951. She developed a technique to photograph a single strand of DNA and was the first person to take X-ray photographs of DNA. However, she was not able to describe the structure of DNA herself. She stopped working with Wilkins because they did not get on well together.

Their photographic techniques helped Crick and Watson analyse and describe DNA. The breakthrough – the discovery of the structure of DNA – was so important that nine years later, in 1962, Crick, Watson and Wilkins were awarded the Nobel Prize for medicine.

Franklin was not awarded the prize. Some people wondered why and thought that perhaps it was because she was a woman or because she had argued with Wilkins. But the explanation is that she died of cancer, aged 37, in 1958, four years before the Nobel award, and Nobel Prizes are never awarded posthumously (after death).

Why are the DNA discoveries seen as 'a breakthrough'?

Some people regard the DNA discoveries described on pages 148–49 as an even more important breakthrough than Pasteur's germ theory.

Think back to the 1830s or 1840s (see pages 106–111). The biggest medical problem of the time was infectious disease. People lived in fear of diseases such as diphtheria, whooping cough, polio or tuberculosis. When an epidemic struck, the disease could spread quickly through the population killing tens of thousands of people. No one really understood the causes of these diseases and so there was no reliable way to prevent them or to cure people once they caught them.

Then Louis Pasteur showed that germs (bacteria) caused these diseases. Pasteur's germ theory was the *greatest breakthrough in medical history* – at the time! If scientists knew what caused disease they could then find ways of preventing diseases and curing them. Pasteur, Koch and others developed vaccines to prevent these diseases (as you can see in the chart on page 104. Within a hundred years many of the most feared infectious diseases had been eliminated in the developed countries such as the UK. In the UK the average life expectancy went up from around 45 to around 65 in a hundred years.

Germ theory was a great breakthrough but it does not explain all diseases or solve all medical problems. In fact, germ theory does not help explain, prevent or cure the most feared and damaging diseases of the twentieth century such as cancer or heart disease. It does not explain inherited conditions like Down's syndrome or diabetes which can be passed from parent to child. Today, the most feared medical problems are not the illnesses caused by germs that get into the body but conditions caused by changes in the body itself.

So the discovery of DNA may turn out to be an *even more important* breakthrough than Pasteur's germ theory because it may help scientists and doctors to prevent or cure these illnesses.

Thanks to Pasteur we know that bacteria cause disease. Now we can develop vaccines that stop people catching these infectious diseases.

If only we could stop people developing other kinds of illnesses!

Now we understand DNA, we can deal with genes that cause inherited illnesses!

But how long will it take? And which illnesses? Is it really that simple?

Looking to the future

There are lots of 'mays' and 'mights' on these pages. This is because we are still at the beginning of the DNA revolution. Every day new discoveries are being made. We do not know where these discoveries will lead. Remember – when Pasteur developed his germ theory scientists did not know exactly what it would lead to. It took a hundred years for the full impact to be clear. We cannot say for sure what these DNA discoveries will lead to – even in five years' time let alone fifty or a hundred!

However at this point we can see patterns or directions.

Gene therapy – using genes from healthy people to cure the sick. Research has shown that some diseases and disabilities, such as cystic fibrosis, Huntington's chorea, sickle-cell anaemia and muscular dystrophy are caused by a single abnormal gene. Gene therapy would take normal genes from a donor and put them into the DNA of someone suffering from one of these illnesses. This is possible, in theory, but not yet in practice.

Customised drugs – creating drugs to cure one person's particular health problem. Drug treatments of the future could be designed to deal with a particular gene in a particular person. These 'custom drugs' would be less haphazard than at present where the same drug is given to millions of different people regardless of their genetic make-up.

UNDERSTANDING DNA COULD LEAD TO...

GENETIC ENGINEERING – creating new varieties of plants and animals. Genetic modification of plants is already happening. For example, a gene from a drought-resistant wheat can be added to the DNA of a high-yielding wheat to make a new variety of wheat that produces lots of grain even in dry conditions. Similar techniques are being used to produce more perfect animals. In theory the same techniques could be used to produce more perfect human beings – with parents being able to 'design' their children: not only their gender, but also their appearance, and intellectual ability. At the moment, this is more science fiction than science fact and scientists are sceptical about whether this could come about.

Genetic screening or testing – identifying the illnesses people could suffer from and preventing them. If doctors know the exact gene responsible for medical conditions they can test or screen patients as part of preventive medicine. For example, they can spot who is likely to get cancer and help them to avoid activities that might trigger the cancer to start. This is already done to check unborn babies for possible conditions such as Down's syndrome.

■ ACTIVITY

1. '*The discovery of DNA is a bigger breakthrough than germ theory.*' Work in pairs to prepare a speech either supporting or opposing this statement. Use the information on pages 148–51 and your knowledge of earlier developments in medicine.

■ DISCUSSION

Genetic research raises some very controversial questions. That is why the Human Genome Project has set aside 5% of its budget to deal with the ethical, legal and social issues involved. Here are some ethical questions for a class discussion – you can probably add many more to the list yourself.

2. Who should have access to someone's genetic information?
a) Should you be told about your own genetic make-up? How would you deal with knowing you were likely to develop a certain disease?

b) DNA 'fingerprinting' is very useful in crime detection, rape cases and paternity suits. Should everyone be forced to provide a DNA sample to be held on a central register in order to help the police solve crimes?
3. Who profits and who pays?
a) Drug companies have poured massive amounts of money into the research that has led to these discoveries. Should they now be allowed to make big profits from that information?
b) Gene therapy will be expensive. Who should have access to genetic treatments? Who should pay?
c) Some companies are trying to patent the genes they have discovered and made. Should this be allowed?

How and why has surgery become more 'hi-tech'?

What medical progress was made during the first part of the twentieth century?

Modern surgery is able to deal with injuries and illness in three ways.

- The body can be cut open, repaired and diseased tissue removed.
- Doctors can help repair the body by using drugs and medicines.
- Limbs and organs can be replaced.

This HI-TECH SURGERY has been made possible by a number of key discoveries and improvements since the 1890s.

Improvement 1: X-rays

The ability to X-ray the body helped doctors to diagnose illness and disease (see pages 146–47). It was the First World War that really confirmed the importance of the X-ray in surgery. More machines were quickly manufactured to meet the new demands and they were soon installed in major hospitals all along the Western Front. X-rays immediately improved the success rate of surgeons in removing deeply lodged bullets and shrapnel which would otherwise have caused fatal infections.

Whilst X-rays were being used it was noticed that they could also destroy diseased skin. As early as 1902 some doctors were directing X-rays onto tumours and lumps and finding that sometimes the diseased tissue was destroyed. As the century progressed doctors became better at directing and controlling some of the more harmful effects of X-rays. Today radiotherapy is still used to treat cancer.

Improvement 2: Blood transfusion

Blood transfusion had been regularly tried in the 1800s but, mysteriously, it had sometimes worked and sometimes failed. Then in 1901 scientists discovered that there were different blood groups. They realised that transfusion only worked if the donor's blood group matched the receiver's.

This discovery finally made transfusion practical. However, in the years before the First World War it was still performed with on-the-spot donors because doctors had no way of storing blood properly – it just coagulated (changed into clots or semi-solid mass).

During the First World War vast amounts of blood were needed. This made the use of on-the-spot donors very difficult. Many soldiers bled to death in the trenches before blood could be got to them. The search began for a better method of storage and transfusion.

This led doctors to the discovery that the liquid part of the blood (the plasma) could be separated from the tiny cells in the blood (corpuscles). The cells could be bottled, packed in ice and stored where they were needed. The cells only had to be diluted with a warm saline solution and usable blood was ready. This discovery helped save many lives both in the trenches and on the operating table.

SOURCE 2 An early demonstration of the technique of blood transfusion

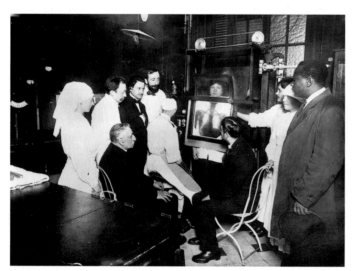

SOURCE 1 X-raying a patient in the 1920s

152

Improvement 3: Fighting infection

In Britain aseptic surgery was practised in all hospitals and success rates in operations were much higher than they had been 30 years earlier. However, on the battlefield and under the pressure of enormous numbers of operations, it was often difficult to prevent the infection of wounds. This was made worse by the presence of bacteria which lodged in clothing. When soldiers were wounded, fragments of clothing would enter the wound and the bacteria would cause GAS GANGRENE.

> **SOURCE 3** A medical description of gas gangrene during the First World War
>
> *After forty-eight hours the edges of the wound begin to swell up and turn … making a gape. The cut surface takes on a curious half-jellied, half-mummified look; then the whole wound limb begins to swell up and distend in the most extraordinary fashion, turning as it does so, first an ashy white and then a greenish colour. This is because the tissues are being literally blown out with gas, and on pressing the fingers down on this balloon-like swelling, a distinct crackling or tiny bubbling sensation can be felt.*

By trial and error, surgeons arrived at the answer to this problem. They cut away infected tissue and soaked the wound with a saline solution. This was a practical advance made possible by experiment on the large number of casualties during wartime.

However, this was only a limited improvement and surgeons were all too well aware of their helplessness against serious infection. It was not until the development of penicillin (see pages 158–61) that the problem of infection was really beaten.

Practice makes perfect!

Faced by hundreds of thousands of casualties surgeons learned fast. They:

- developed new techniques to repair broken bones
- improved methods of grafting skin which later formed the basis for plastic surgery
- improved surgery of the eye, ear, nose and throat
- successfully attempted brain surgery.

The developments in skin-grafting techniques opened up new possibilities for plastic surgery. In the First World War Harold Gillies set up a plastic surgery unit and treated over 2000 men injured in the Battle of the Somme. In the Second World War

Archibald McIndoe (who had been Gillies' assistant) developed better techniques, partly because he had to treat thousands of airmen burned by aviation fuel.

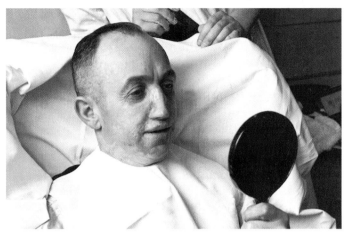

SOURCE 4 A patient examines his reconstructed nose and skin graft

Many surgeons who learned these and other skills in battlefield hospitals set up as specialists back at home after the war. There were similar developments in the other countries involved in the war.

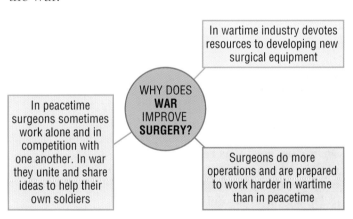

SOURCE 5 Chart summarising the views of Heneage Ogilvey, a British surgeon, about the relationship between war and surgery

1. What evidence is there on pages 152–53 to support the views in Source 5?

■ TASK

'War helped more than it hindered developments in medicine.'

Explain whether you agree with this statement.

Why has surgery developed even more rapidly in recent years?

During the 1930s and the years of the Second World War the medical breakthroughs of the early 1900s were improved. The Second World War also had a great impact through measures that prevented illness and disease, for example, improved diet; public health campaigns; immunisation and the emergency hospital service (see page 166).

Improved anaesthetics

Until the 1930s anaesthetics were still breathed in by the patient. This worked, but it was difficult to control the dosage and operations had to be hurried. In the 1930s Helmuth Wesse discovered new anaesthetics and developed a method of injecting them directly into the blood stream. This allowed dosage to be more precisely controlled and operations could now last longer.

Antibiotics

With the discovery and mass production of penicillin during the Second World War (see pages 158–61) the risk of infection during surgery was reduced. This increased the success rate of complex operations considerably.

Developments such as these helped lead to rapid progress, especially in transplant and replacement surgery. There were many other factors at work as well, as you can see on page 155.

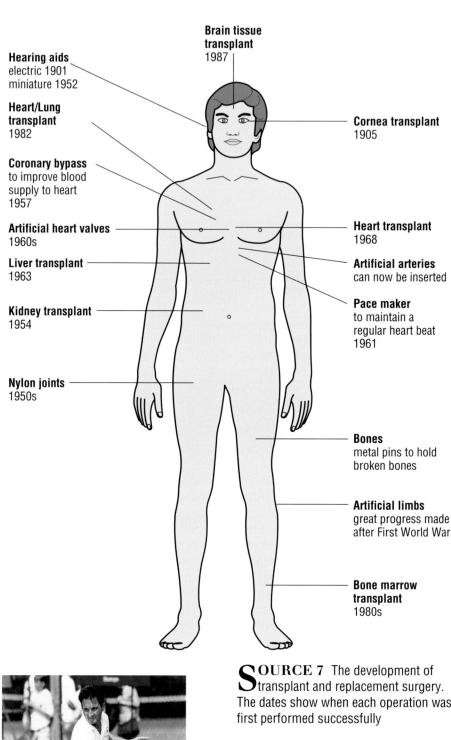

Brain tissue transplant 1987

Hearing aids electric 1901 miniature 1952

Heart/Lung transplant 1982

Coronary bypass to improve blood supply to heart 1957

Artificial heart valves 1960s

Liver transplant 1963

Kidney transplant 1954

Nylon joints 1950s

Cornea transplant 1905

Heart transplant 1968

Artificial arteries can now be inserted

Pace maker to maintain a regular heart beat 1961

Bones metal pins to hold broken bones

Artificial limbs great progress made after First World War

Bone marrow transplant 1980s

SOURCE 7 The development of transplant and replacement surgery. The dates show when each operation was first performed successfully

SOURCE 6 An athlete taking part in the tennis tournament at the Transplant Games, Manchester, August 1995. This competitor had received a heart transplant five years earlier

Teamwork

Major surgery involves many different skills. This is how Dr Christiaan Barnard described the preparations for the first heart transplant in 1967.

SOURCE 8

  Kidney function was checked by measuring urine output … the liver was studied through urine and blood analysis. The heart pattern was plotted by an electrocardiogram. The lungs were X-rayed. Blood chemistry was also checked in the laboratory.

During the operation the specialist surgeon is supported by highly trained anaesthetists and nurses.

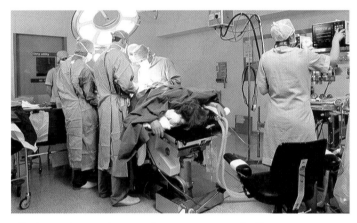

SOURCE 9
A team of surgeons at work. The person on the right is monitoring the life support and anaesthetic equipment

Resources

Major surgery is becoming increasingly costly. The operations themselves involve large teams, and after-care of patients can be long and expensive. Even successful operations may only add a few years to a patient's life. However, such operations are life-saving and, as a result, they capture the public's imagination. Some hi-tech surgeons receive attention and money out of all proportion to the number of people who actually benefit. The media treat the pioneers of transplant surgery as heroes, just as they treated Pasteur as a hero when he made his breakthroughs in developing new vaccines.

2. Why do you think transplant surgery attracts so much public interest?
3. Do you think that transplant surgery is a good use of medical resources?

Keyhole surgery 1901

Rummaging about inside someone's body whilst holding a large knife is not always the most effective way to treat a patient. The patient has to recover not only from the original illness but also from a large wound. In recent years, miniaturisation, fibre-optic cables and the use of computers have meant that surgeons can perform operations through very small 'keyhole' incisions.

Keyhole surgery uses an ENDOSCOPE. This instrument includes all the tools needed to perform an operation.

SOURCE 10
The benefits of keyhole surgery

Microsurgery 1920

Microsurgery is also advancing rapidly. By magnifying the area the surgeon is working on it is possible to rejoin nerves and very small blood vessels. This means that some feeling can be returned to limbs that have been severed or damaged.

4. Draw a timeline from 1800 to the present. Mark on it what you consider to be the major turning points in the development of surgery. You will also need to refer back to pages 116–21.
5. When has the pace of change been most rapid?
6. How have the following factors influenced changes in surgery:

   ■ war
   ■ technology
   ■ individuals
   ■ drug development?

The fight against disease and infection: from magic bullets to guided missiles

DURING THE NINETEENTH century doctors and scientists discovered the causes of many illnesses and infectious diseases. They identified the bacteria and started two lines of research in the hope that they would eventually be able to prevent and cure those diseases.

Line 1: Prevention

Pasteur began the first line of research with his germ theory.

Koch then identified the bacteria which caused specific diseases.

So these are the bacteria which cause anthrax

Using Koch's methods the bacteria causing other diseases were quickly discovered.

Pasteur discovered ways of using weakened forms of bacteria to give the body immunity.

If it works for rabies then it will work for other diseases.

Following Pasteur other vaccines were developed although very slowly.

In 1906 Calmette and Guerin discovered a vaccine against tuberculosis.

In 1913 Behring perfected a diphtheria vaccine.

Line 2: Cure

Koch set off the line of research by discovering that he could stain certain bacteria.

I've stained them purple so that I can see them

Paul Ehrlich searched for a stain that would also kill the bacteria.

If the stain could also kill the bacteria it would be like a magic bullet to shoot the microbe

At first this line of research met with little success. It seemed to be hoping for the impossible. But after many patient experiments...

It works! 606 works!

Following Ehrlich, others continued the search for magic bullets.

SOURCE 1 The two lines of research

The first magic bullet: Salversan 606

Paul Ehrlich was a member of Robert Koch's research team. Koch had shown that certain dyes sought out certain bacteria – that is how he had been able to stain septicaemia bacteria (see page 102).

Ehrlich spent hours staining bacteria and observing the effects of the dye. He worked with Behring on diphtheria, and was fascinated by the way in which the body created antibodies that killed bacteria but did not harm anything else. Ehrlich compared these antibodies to 'magic bullets'; he was convinced that a chemical could be found which might do the same and he set out to find one.

Despite years of research Ehrlich had little success. In 1905 he was looking for a magic bullet to treat SYPHILIS. Instead of using dyes he experimented with a variety of chemical compounds based on arsenic. Ehrlich's team tried 605 variations before they found one that worked. They nearly missed the discovery that variation 606 worked and it was only when it was being retested that another assistant, Sahashiro Hata, realised that it killed the syphilis bacteria.

The drug was named Salversan but it was difficult to use. It could kill not only the microbes causing the disease but the patient as well. The importance of Ehrlich's discovery was that a chemical compound had been used for the first time to destroy bacteria.

1. Explain what Ehrlich meant by the phrase 'magic bullet'.
2. How was Ehrlich's work different from that of Pasteur?

The second magic bullet: Prontosil

Research into the use of chemical compounds was interrupted by the First World War, but in the 1920s it was picked up again.

In 1932, Gerhardt Domagk tried out Prontosil, a red dye. Domagk started a series of tests using mice. The results were good. Prontosil definitely had an effect on the bacteria which caused blood poisoning.

SOURCE 2 The entry in Domagk's laboratory notebook on Christmas Day 1932

66 Prepared D4145 K1 730.
Gave orally at the dose of 0.5 grams. So far [the mouse] is very lively, eats heartily, the swellings on the digits … have disappeared … 99

Domagk got an opportunity to test Prontosil on a human much sooner than he had expected. His daughter Hildegarde was playing with her pet guinea pig near to some medical equipment when she pricked her finger on an infected needle. She soon developed severe blood poisoning. With his daughter near to death, Domagk decided to risk using Prontosil even though he had not tried it on any human before. He gave her a large dose. She recovered. The second magic bullet had been found.

The sulphonamides

The obvious next step was to find out what the active ingredient was in Prontosil. It only took two years for French researchers to find it. It was a sulphonamide derived from coal tar. The discovery was made so speedily as a result of the invention in 1931 of new powerful electron microscopes.

Soon all the major drug companies joined a race to discover cures based on sulphonamides (which meant any drug derived from coal tar). This was a period of great excitement. Within a few years drugs had been developed to cure and control scarlet fever, meningitis, GONORRHOEA and pneumonia.

The new drugs soon improved health. Maternal mortality, for example, was reduced because infections following childbirth could now be controlled (see Source 3).

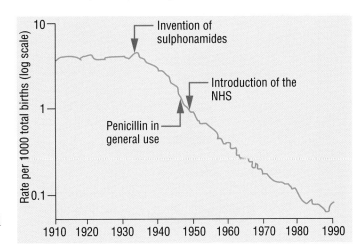

SOURCE 3 MATERNAL mortality in Britain, 1910–90

■ TASK

Draw your own diagram to show the factors which led to the development of sulphonamide drugs, and the results that flowed from their development.

Case study: the development of penicillin

THE STORY OF penicillin begins well before the Second World War as you can see from Source 1.

1928 Fleming discovers mould has killed germs

1929 Fleming writes articles about penicillin

1937 Chain and Florey begin research in Oxford on penicillin after reading an article by Fleming

1940 Experiment with mice

1941 Penicillin first tested on a human being in Oxford

1942 U.S. and British governments co-operate to fund production of penicillin

1944 Enough penicillin to treat all the Allied forces wounded in the D-Day invasion of Europe

THE SECOND WORLD WAR

SOURCE 1 The discovery and development of penicillin

When was penicillin discovered?

Penicillin itself is made from a mould called penicillium. The mould was first discovered in the early nineteenth century by John Sanderson, who found that very little grew near it. In the 1880s Joseph Lister noted these observations and wrote to his brother saying that he intended to try penicillin on infected wounds. Lister successfully used penicillin to treat a young nurse who had an infected wound. However, he did not leave any notes on this case and apparently stopped using the mould. Several other scientists investigated the mould but were unable to produce it in sufficient quantities or discover a way of applying it to a patient.

It was in the laboratory of St Mary's Hospital, London, in 1928, that Alexander Fleming rediscovered the properties of penicillin. This is how Fleming's biographer describes the discovery. Fleming's friend Pryce had gone to visit him in his laboratory.

SOURCE 2 A. Maurois, *The Life of Sir Alexander Fleming*, 1963

66 *Fleming was in his little laboratory as usual, surrounded by innumerable dishes. The cautious Scot disliked being separated from his CULTURES before he was quite certain that there was no longer anything to be learned from them ... Fleming took up several old cultures and removed the lids. Several of the cultures had been contaminated with mould ... 'As soon as you uncover a culture dish,' he said to Pryce, 'something tiresome is sure to happen. Things fall out of the air.'*

Suddenly he stopped talking, then, after a moment's observation, said ... 'That's funny ...' On the cultures at which he was looking there was a growth of mould, as on several of the others, but on this particular one, all around the mould, the colonies of STAPHYLOCOCCI had been dissolved ... 99

On investigation he found that penicillin bacteria had got onto the dish, possibly blown in through an open window. The penicillin was killing the staphylococci. There are other versions of the story of how Fleming discovered penicillin. Indeed, Fleming's own versions varied. When he explained in 1945 how he grew the mould it was a different explanation from his original report for a research paper in 1929. However, the important point is that Fleming observed the results and recognised their significance – that penicillin could be applied to or injected into areas infected with penicillin-sensitive microbes. However, Fleming did not have the facilities or the support to develop and test his idea that penicillin could fight infection.

1. Why is Fleming usually thought of as the discoverer of penicillin?
2. Why do you think that so many people observed the power of penicillin yet did not develop it as a cure?

How was penicillin developed?

It was the Second World War which finally brought about the successful development of penicillin.

In the 1930s two Oxford scientists, Howard Florey and Ernst Chain, became interested in Fleming's 1929 paper about penicillin. In 1939 they gathered together a skilled research team, including pathologists, chemists and BIOCHEMISTS, and three days after the outbreak of the Second World War Florey asked the British government for money to fund the team's research into penicillin.

> **SOURCE 3** Part of the proposal made by Florey to the Medical Research Council, 6 September 1939
>
> ❝ *I enclose some proposals that have a very practical bearing at the moment.*
>
> *The properties of penicillin hold out the promise of its finding practical application in the treatment of infections. In view of the great practical importance of penicillin it is proposed to prepare these substances in purified form suitable for injection and to study their antiseptic action on living creatures.* ❞

> **SOURCE 4** Sir Ernst Chain describing the team's research in the *Journal of the Royal College of Surgeons*, 1972
>
> ❝ *The only reason that motivated me was scientific interest. That penicillin could have a practical use in medicine did not enter our minds when we started work on it.* ❞

Stage 1: growing the penicillin

The process devised by Chain to make penicillin was a combination of the latest freeze-drying technology and some much more traditional equipment: thousands of milk bottles (in which to grow the bacteria), milk churns, a dog bath and a hand pump! Slowly the team gathered a few grams of pure penicillin.

Stage 2: testing the penicillin on animals

There was just enough penicillin to try an experiment on eight mice. They were all injected with dangerous microbes. Four mice were then given penicillin. Four were not. Twenty-four hours later the mice who had not been injected with penicillin were dead. Those who had been given penicillin were fine.

Stage 3: the first human trial of penicillin

The team needed more penicillin for a human trial than they had for the mice. It was not until early 1941 that they had enough to test it on a human patient.

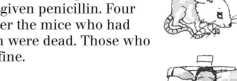

> **SOURCE 5** Professor Fletcher (one of Florey's team) remembering events in Oxford, 19 February 1941
>
> ❝ *The patient had a sore on his mouth a month previously, and the infection had spread to his scalp. He'd had an abscess there. It had spread to both his eyes and one had to be removed. He had abscesses open on his arm. He had abscesses on his lung – he was well on his way towards death from a terrible infection. We'd nothing to lose and everything to gain. So we thought we'd try [penicillin].*
>
> *The shortage of penicillin was such that after the first day I collected his urine and I took it over to where Florey was working so that the penicillin could be extracted from the urine and used again.*
>
> *On the fourth day the patient was really dramatically improved, he was sitting up in bed and his temperature had gone down. On the fifth day the penicillin began to run out and we couldn't go on. Of course when they extracted it from the urine they couldn't get it all back and it gradually ran out … He gradually relapsed and eventually died.* ❞

Although this patient still died, the trial confirmed that penicillin was a powerful drug. Florey was sure that if enough had been available the man would have lived. Production of penicillin remained painfully slow, but as new batches were produced two more patients were successfully treated. A year later, in August 1942, Fleming himself used penicillin successfully to treat a friend who had meningitis.

■ ACTIVITY

Work in pairs. Either write or role play a discussion between members of Florey's team discussing the progress the team has made so far.

How was penicillin mass produced?

It was clear that penicillin could be a very powerful treatment if only it could be mass produced. The growing casualties of the Second World War added urgency to this need. Florey knew that a massive amount of research and investment would be necessary to produce the thousands of doses of penicillin needed.

A setback

Production in Britain was always going to be a problem because of the threat of German bombing, so, in June 1941, Florey travelled to the USA to try to interest drug companies there in developing penicillin. At that stage, the USA was still not involved in the war, there had been only three successful trials of penicillin and there was no proven method for speeding up production.

However, in December 1941 the USA entered the war and this completely changed the situation.

Timetable of success

In 1942 the US government gave $80 million to four drug companies to find a way to mass produce penicillin.

In 1943 production began. The first use in war was by the British army in North Africa (see Source 7).

By June 1944 there was enough penicillin to treat all the casualties suffered on D-Day.

By 1945 the US army was using two million doses a month. It is estimated that another 12–15 per cent of wounded Allied soldiers would have died without penicillin to fight their infection. Penicillin also roughly halved the average time the Allied wounded spent in hospital.

Soon after the war penicillin became available for civilian use – it was called an antibiotic.

Government
- British government funded Florey's research in 1939
- US government gave drug companies $80 million in 1942 to start production of penicillin

Technology

Scientific experiment

Chance

PENICILLIN: WHY THEN?

Industry
Development was undertaken by four major drug companies pooling their experts

War

Communications

Individuals
Florey and Chain were skilled scientists supported by a skilled and committed team of researchers

SOURCE 6   Factors influencing the development of penicillin

S OURCE 7 Lt Colonel Pulvertaft describes the first use of penicillin by the British army in 1943

66 *We had enormous numbers of infected wounded, terrible burn cases among the crews of the armoured cars. Sulphonamides had absolutely no effect on these cases. The last thing I tried was penicillin ... The first man I tried it on was a young New Zealand officer called Newton. He had been in bed for six months with compound fractures of both legs. His sheets were soaked with pus and the heat of Cairo made it smell intolerable. Normally he would have died in a short time. I gave three injections a day of penicillin and studied the effects under the microscope ... the thing seemed like a miracle. In ten days' time the leg was cured and in a month's time the young fellow was back on his feet. I had enough penicillin for ten cases. Nine out of ten of them were complete cures.* 99

Penicillin – why then?

By now you will have identified a number of causes of change in medicine – war, the role of governments, and scientific discoveries by research teams. These causes have often been interconnected, as you can see in this case study of penicillin.

■ TASK 1

1. Describe the main events in the development of penicillin.
2. Explain the part played by Fleming in the development of penicillin.
3. Why was penicillin mass produced in 1942–45, and not before?

How have drugs and treatments developed since 1945?

There are enormous profits to be made for companies who develop successful drugs. Drug companies now spend billions of pounds on research.

The range of new drugs being produced each year is impossible to summarise. There are now many new antibiotics with thousands of variations of 'magic bullets'. They all work in roughly the same way as penicillin – by killing bacteria. However, there are also many diseases they cannot help with. They do not attack viruses, for example, so the search for other ways to prevent and control disease has continued. Since 1945, polio, whooping cough, German measles and measles vaccines have been developed. Other developments have included drugs which use the body's hormones, for example, the contraceptive pill.

Problems

There have also been some tragic failures and mistakes in drug development. Between 1959 and 1962 a drug called THALIDOMIDE was sold to women to help alleviate morning sickness during pregnancy. It had not been adequately tested before it was put on the market. Thalidomide was found to cause severe abnormalities to FETUSES. Children were born with severely deformed limbs. It is now known that these problems can be passed on to their own children. The drug was withdrawn and testing procedures were tightened up. All drugs now undergo rigorous trials before becoming available to the public.

Over the last 40 years researchers have also found that some bacteria have begun to become resistant to antibiotics which could cause great problems in the future.

Genetic engineering

More powerful microscopes have made it possible for doctors to see not just the body's cells, but the genes and chromosomes within them.

This has made possible a whole new type of treatment: genetic engineering (see page 151). Genes can be manipulated to correct problems in a patient's body. For example, DNA can be made to produce the important protein INSULIN, which occurs naturally in most people, but is absent in people with diabetes. Genetic engineering can also artificially produce antibodies which seek out and destroy specific cells within the body – a kind of guided missile!

■ TASK 2

List any treatments which members of your class or your family have used recently. Divide the treatments into groups:
a) those which were available in the nineteenth century
b) those which were developed between 1900 and 1945
c) those developed since 1945.
Use these lists to help you prepare for a class debate on the topic: 'There has been more change than continuity in treatments since the nineteenth century.'

Has public health improved since 1900?

TWO CONCERNS DOMINATED public health campaigns in the twentieth century – housing and air quality.

Healthier housing

As industrial towns grew in the early nineteenth century, houses were built quickly and sometimes to a very low standard.

Stage 1: Back-to-backs banned

In many cities, to pack in as many houses as possible, and to cut building costs, builders had built back-to-back. These houses were badly ventilated; they had no internal water supply; the only toilets were at the end of the row and there were no gardens.

The surveys of the late 1800s and early 1900s revealed that back-to-back houses were a major cause of ill health. In 1909 they were banned by the government. Local authorities had to submit town-planning schemes to the government for approval. Building standards were established which had to be followed by all builders.

Stage 2: 'Homes for heroes'

The British government had asked working men to lay down their lives in the First World War. In return the government pledged it would do something decisive about the housing problem to ensure that, after the war, soldiers came back to 'homes fit for heroes'. In 1919 a new Housing Act was passed, requiring local authorities to provide good homes for all working-class people in their area. The government promised to help fund these schemes during the first four years – thus they hoped to speed up the building work by councils.

'Homes for heroes' helped to create a quarter of a million new homes.

Stage 3: 'Slum clearance'

Even a quarter of a million houses were only a small percentage of what was needed. In 1930 the most ambitious step was taken with the beginning of a five-year 'slum clearance' programme. Large areas of bad housing in major cities and towns were labelled improvement areas. Local authorities were forced to rehouse people in the improvement areas. The old housing was razed to the ground.

In the 1930s 700,000 new homes were built by local authorities, many of them on large housing estates away from the city and town centres. The local authorities claimed to have rehoused 80 per cent of slum dwellers in the 1930s. This was an overestimate and it was often the poorest people who remained in some of the worst housing! Many such slums were not demolished until the 1960s, when they were largely replaced by high-rise blocks of flats which posed as many problems as the old slums.

■ ACTIVITY

Look at Source 1. Write a detailed description of how the new home is an improvement on the old.

SOURCE 1 Artist's reconstruction of houses in Hereford Street, Brighton. The back-to-back house on the left was demolished after the First World War to make way for the new council house on the right

Cleaner air

Well into the twentieth century air quality in many industrial cities was still appalling (see Source 2).

In 1952 London suffered a terrible smog. Chance weather conditions caused dense, smoke-polluted fog to settle over the city. At least 4000 people died of respiratory illness brought on by the smog, making it the worst health disaster in the capital since the flu epidemic of 1919. It speeded up action to do something about air pollution.

In 1956 a Clean Air Act was passed to set up smokeless zones in cities and even to control what fuel could be burned by people in their own homes. By 1971 the amount of smoke pollution entering the atmosphere had been reduced by 65 per cent.

1. What factors were important in improving housing and improving air quality?
2. Why do you think neither of these issues was tackled effectively in the nineteenth century?

SOURCE 2 Air pollution in Stoke-on-Trent in the 1920s. The pottery-making town had literally thousands of coal-fired kilns

■ TASK

Study Source 3. It shows how public health concerns have now shifted into wider, even global issues, which cannot be the responsibility of an individual, or even the government of one country. Environmental pressure groups have taken over the campaigning role of the public health movement.

What do you regard as the three most important priorities for public health today?

1. Everyone in Britain has access to fresh water

but is that water clean and is there enough of it?

2. Sewage is disposed of so that it doesn't spread disease in towns and cities

but it sometimes pollutes beaches and kills wildlife

3. There are laws to control waste disposal and rubbish dumping

TOXIC WASTE

but toxic waste can still leak into our water supply and some things cannot be disposed of safely.

4. Clean Air Acts have stopped factories and coal fires polluting

OFFICIAL Sheffield cleanest industrial city in Europe

but car exhaust fumes create polluted air which can spread from one country to another. Some environmental problems need international solutions.

5. Houses are better built than in 1900 and have services such as rubbish collection and piped water

but there are still some people who have no home at all

6. There are laws to enforce safe working conditions

DANGER ASBESTOS KEEP OUT!

but new dangers to health are always emerging.

7. Food must be carefully labelled and hygienically stored.

but some people may still have an unhealthy diet

8. Public health may have improved in developed countries

but They are only a small proportion of the world's population. The majority of people are still facing the problems which developed countries faced in the nineteenth century.

SOURCE 3 Public health issues today

'From cradle to grave' – the National Health Service

THE SECOND WORLD WAR led directly to the setting up of the National Health Service in Britain. You are now going to investigate in detail why the NHS was established and how it changed medicine and health in Britain.

The story starts at the beginning of the twentieth century.

1911: National Health Insurance introduced

In the early 1900s the government became increasingly aware of the health problems facing ordinary people. Evidence showed that the poor still lived in terrible housing, and that when they were sick they could not afford medical care (see page 165).

In 1911 the government introduced a National Insurance Scheme. Workers and their employers made weekly contributions to a central fund which was then used to give the workers sickness benefit, and free medical care from a panel doctor, if they became ill.

The scheme was limited to those who were employed. This meant that women and children were often not covered by any insurance scheme; nor were the unemployed, the elderly, the mentally ill and the chronically ill.

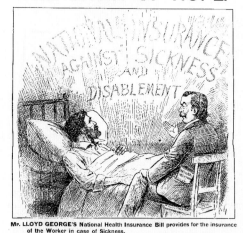

THE DAWN OF HOPE.

Mr. LLOYD GEORGE'S National Health Insurance Bill provides for the insurance of the Worker in case of Sickness.

Support the Liberal Government
in their policy of
SOCIAL REFORM.

S OURCE 1   A poster produced by the Liberal government in 1911

1. Look at Source 1. Who do you think this poster was aimed at?

How did things change in the 1930s?

For many people it became harder to get good medical care during the economic depression of the 1930s. Up to three million people in Britain were unemployed. The government reduced its contribution to health insurance. Many unemployed people could not keep up their contributions and the companies who ran these schemes found that they were not making any profits. In 1934 there were four million insurance policies on which people owed payments. There were alarming statistics to show that in some areas, which were most affected by the economic depression, infant mortality was climbing again.

The government was, however, unwilling to accept publicly that large portions of the population were suffering, and the government's overall contribution to the nation's health care remained small, as you can see from Source 4.

Town	1928	1931	1933
Wigan	93	103	110
Liverpool	94	94	98
St Helens	98	88	116
Bath	47	39	52
Brighton	50	54	47
Oxford	38	44	32

S OURCE 2   The death rate of infants out of 1000 births in selected towns

S OURCE 3   In 1933 the Minister of Health, against the advice of his public health officials and doctors, said:

66 *There is at present no available evidence of any general increase in sickness or mortality as a result of the economic depression or unemployment.* 99

S OURCE 4 Funding for health services in 1938–39, assessed by C. Webster

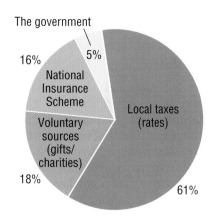

The government 5%
16% National Insurance Scheme
Voluntary sources (gifts/ charities) 18%
Local taxes (rates) 61%

What health care was available to most people?

Despite the National Insurance Scheme many people continued to rely on cheap, easy-to-find remedies or those handed down through families for generations. They relied on neighbours and family for care when they were sick.

SOURCE 5 From an interview in the 1930s with Kathleen Davys, one of a family of thirteen children. She lived in Birmingham. The local doctor charged six pence per visit

66 *Headaches, we had vinegar and brown paper; for whooping cough we had camphorated oil rubbed on our chests or goose fat. For mumps we had stockings round our throats and measles we had tea stewed in the teapot by the fire – all different kinds of home cures. They thought they were better than going to the doctor's. Well, they couldn't afford the doctor because sixpence in those days was like looking at a five pound note today.* 99

SOURCE 6 An advert for a healthy drink from a 1930s newspaper. Such remedies continued to sell well in the 1930s

and keep out of the New Hospital!

SOURCE 7 Oral history interview describing the 1930s quoted in Gray, *The Worst of Times*, 1986

66 *I remember our Brian being born. He was delivered by a doctor up at Oldham, a Scotsman. He got called up and killed in the war, so we never paid for Brian. The doctors were very good. You'd go to the doctor. He had your name and address. And after, you got a bill, and if you couldn't pay it, which very few people could, each doctor had his own collector. The collector used to come round each week and you'd pay sixpence. My wife's father and mother used to say they'd never be straight in their lifetime. The collectors always used to be the same type that were park keepers in them days – they'd be no use today, kids'd throw them in the pond – but they were always wizened little fellers.* 99

SOURCE 8 An interview recorded by R. Roberts in the journal *Oral History*, 1984, describing the 1930s

66 *She wasn't quite 71 [when she got ill] and she was 77 when she died. She was in bed all that time. It paralysed her all down one side. She could get out of bed … but she couldn't get back. So my auntie next door took her and she had her in the front room in the bed downstairs and my mother looked to her in the daytime and auntie looked to her at night.* 99

SOURCE 9 A pharmacy

SOURCE 10 An interview with a pharmacist describing his work in the 1920s in R. Roberts *Health, Disease and Medicine in Lancashire 1750–1950*, 1980.

66
Q: Did people ask you for advice?
A: We had to do a bit of diagnosing in our own way and be responsible for it.
Q: Would they for example bring the children in and say 'What is the matter?'
A: Oh my goodness yes.
Q: What sort of things would be the matter?
A: It might be just nettle rash, it might be measles – very often it was measles and teething trouble, a little feverish, CONSTIPATION or something like that, the usual childish ailments but we had to be very very careful …
Q: You didn't charge for this advice?
A: Oh dear no. Anything had to be cheap … 99

2. List the different types of health care shown or described in Sources 5–10.
3. Does this evidence suggest change or continuity in comparison with earlier centuries?

Why was the National Health Service introduced?

With the outbreak of the Second World War in 1939, the government knew there had to be adequate medical services to cope with large numbers of civilian casualties so it increased its involvement in medical care. By 1942 people were beginning to think about how the system should be organised when the war ended. In that year a leading civil servant, William Beveridge, put forward his ideas about 'a free national health service' as part of a complete rethink of the government's National Insurance Scheme.

O, rare and refreshing Beveridge!

SOURCE 11 The front page and cartoon from the *Daily Mirror*, 2 December 1942

4. Read Source 11. What was the Beveridge Report proposing for health care in 1942?
5. How was this different from the system that existed before 1939?
6. In one year over 600,000 copies of the Beveridge Report were sold. Why were so many people interested in the changes that it proposed?

Timeline showing the development of the National Health Service

1939 The Emergency Hospital Scheme started – it was funded and run by the government.

1946 National Health Service Act provides for a free and comprehensive health-care system.

1900	1910	1920	1930	1940

1911 The National Insurance Scheme was introduced

1942 Beveridge proposes a 'free national health service'.

1944 The government proposes a free and comprehensive health service.

What was the National Health Service? (NHS)

By 1944 the system was being planned to be 'comprehensive in two senses – first that it be available to all people, and second, that it cover all necessary forms of health care'. In 1945 a new Labour government was elected, and in 1946 its Bill to introduce an NHS was passed by Parliament.

SOURCE 12
A The front page of the first leaflet describing the new National Health Service
B Diagram showing the services provided by the NHS

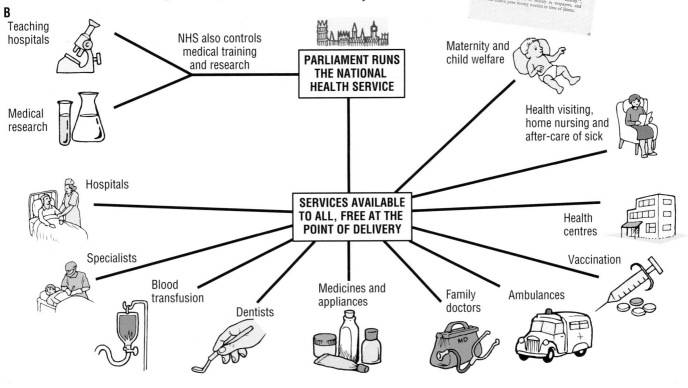

B

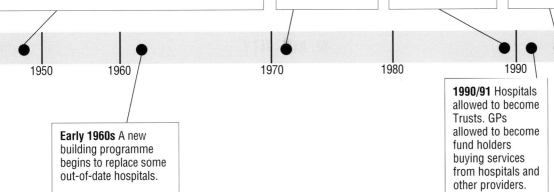

5 July 1948 The first day of the National Health Service:
■ the nationalisation of hospitals
■ the creation of health centres
■ the better distribution of doctors around the country
■ a new salary structure for doctors.

1970s Single-issue health-care campaigns begin – for example, against smoking, or promoting a healthy diet.

1989 'Working for Patients' produced by the government proposes changes to the NHS with the introduction of competition between hospitals.

1992 'The Health of the Nation' initiative sets the NHS five targets to help prevent and reduce death and illness in the following areas: heart disease; cancer; mental illness; HIV/AIDS; and accidents.

Early 1960s A new building programme begins to replace some out-of-date hospitals.

1990/91 Hospitals allowed to become Trusts. GPs allowed to become fund holders buying services from hospitals and other providers.

1950   1960   1970   1980   1990

167

Why did people oppose the NHS?

Most medical changes meet some resistance but the NHS was a major and a sudden change. The minister appointed to introduce it was Aneurin ('Nye') Bevan, an ex-miner from South Wales and a trade-union leader with a reputation for being rebellious and outspoken.

He faced a number of problems.

Local authorities and voluntary organisations

Under the NHS the 3000 hospitals in Britain would be nationalised. This was opposed by the local authorities and voluntary bodies who ran them.

The cost

Argument raged over the enormous costs involved. Bevan agreed that the NHS was going to be an expensive venture, but he argued that the nation had to afford it and could afford it.

The British Medical Association

The stiffest opposition came from the British Medical Association (BMA), which represented the medical profession. Doctors didn't want to be employed by the government and be told where to work, because they would no longer be able to sell their services. They feared that this would result in a loss of income.

HERE HE COMES, BOYS'!

7th August, 1945. Mr. Aneurin Bevan's appointment as Minister of Health is not welcome in certain circles.

SOURCE 13 Cartoon from the *Daily Mirror*, May 1946

How Bevan won

When the BMA ran a survey in late 1946, 54 per cent of its members said they would refuse to co-operate with the NHS, and by January 1948 this had risen to 90 per cent.

However, Bevan had a powerful personality and he won many in the medical profession over to his side. He gained the support of hospital consultants

by promising them a salary and allowing them to treat private patients in NHS hospitals. At the same time, he seemed willing to talk to doctors on the lesser issues. In May 1948 opposition crumbled and when the NHS was finally introduced in July 1948 90 per cent of doctors had enrolled.

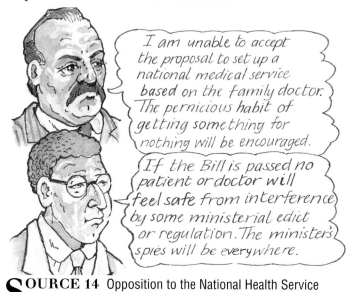

I am unable to accept the proposal to set up a national medical service based on the family doctor. The pernicious habit of getting something for nothing will be encouraged.

If the Bill is passed no patient or doctor will feel safe from interference by some ministerial edict or regulation. The minister's spies will be everywhere.

SOURCE 14 Opposition to the National Health Service

SOURCE 15 From a speech made by Nye Bevan in 1946

66 *Medical treatment should be made available to rich and poor alike in accordance with medical need and no other criteria. Worry about money in a time of sickness is a serious hindrance to recovery apart from its unnecessary cruelty. The records show that it is the mother in the average family who suffers most from the absence of a full health service. In trying to balance her budget she puts her own needs last ... The essence of a satisfactory health service is that the rich and the poor are treated alike, that poverty is not a disability, and wealth is not advantaged.* 99

■ ACTIVITY

Work in pairs. One of you take the side of Nye Bevan, the other take the side of a doctor opposed to the National Health Service. Use the information and sources on this page to help you write down the main points on which your argument is based. Try to persuade your partner that you are right.

In class discussion, pick out the most persuasive arguments on each side.

Achievements of the NHS

Impact on women

The NHS made women's health a priority and has continued to do so. Women are now four times more likely to consult a doctor than men. Life expectancy for women has risen from 66 to 78 since 1948. Maternal mortality had been declining since the development of sulphonamide drugs (see page 157), but under the NHS the rate came down faster still. The NHS also took away the awful worry which women as the main carers in a family often had to bear – helplessly watching the pain or death of a relative for lack of money to do anything about it.

Family doctors

The NHS transformed the role of the family doctor. General Practitioners (GPs) increasingly work as part of teams offering a whole range of health services.

7. Before the NHS was established most GPs worked on their own. What are the advantages of working in a team such as the one in Source 17?

SOURCE 17 Services available through a south London surgery

Problems faced by the NHS

The NHS aimed to provide the best care possible. As medicine has advanced since 1948 the cost of providing that care has increased.

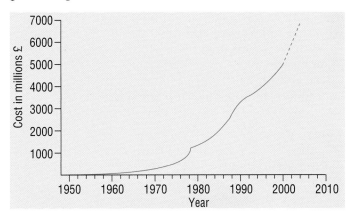

SOURCE 18 The rising cost of the NHS, 1948–92

Compromises have had to be made. Prescription charges were introduced in the early 1950s. Charges for other services such as dental treatment were also introduced. In recent years lack of money has left hospital beds unused even though there is a need for them. Some people have even been refused costly services.

However, the fact remains that the NHS costs less than other systems. For example, the USA has a private health care system which costs 12 per cent of national income while the NHS costs just 6 per cent.

■ TASK

Write your own comparison of health services before the NHS with services since 1948. Use the information on the last six pages and your own research.

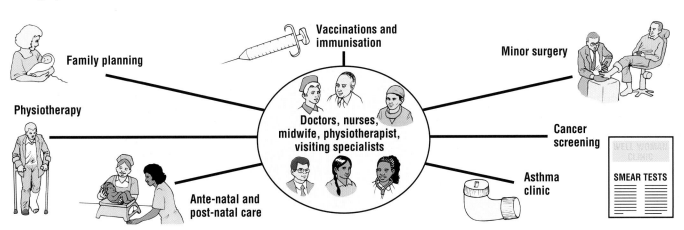

Why did infant mortality decrease so rapidly after 1900?

PARENTS DID ALL they could to protect their children but infant mortality was a normal part of everyone's life in the early twentieth century. In fact in 1901, despite all the progress in science and in public health in the nineteenth century, infant mortality was worse than it had been in 1801. The worst year on record was 1899 when 163 out of every 1000 babies died before they reached the age of one.

In the twentieth century the picture changed completely, as you can see from Source 1.

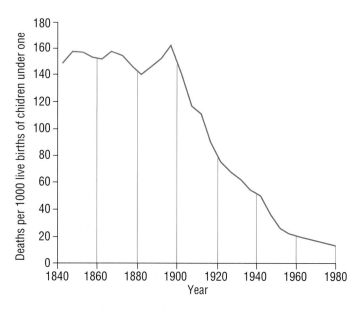

SOURCE 1 Infant mortality, 1840–1980

1. Look at Source 1. When did the infant mortality rate begin to fall?
2. When did it fall most rapidly?
3. Study Sources 2 and 3. List all the factors leading to high infant mortality.
4. Look at Source 2. Why did the government want to improve child health?
5. Pick the three changes in Source 3 that you think would do most to improve children's health. Explain your choice.

SOURCE 2 In 1900 when the army needed recruits for the Boer War, it was found that 38 per cent of volunteers were unfit to be soldiers. The government was so alarmed by the army recruitment problem that it set up a Committee on Physical Deterioration to find out why. These were the main conclusions of the Committee in 1904

Bad health is not inherited. It can be improved by changes in food, hygiene and clothing and by:
a) getting rid of overcrowded housing
b) enforcing building regulations
c) controlling smoke pollution
d) regular medical inspections of school children
e) setting up day nurseries for the infants of working mothers, run by local councils
f) prohibiting the sale of tobacco to children.
The main conclusion of the Committee was:
'The Committee are aware of the enormous sacrifice of infant life due to insufficient or improper feeding. The Committee advocates:
g) the systematic instruction of girls in the process of infant feeding and management.'

From 1907 schools were set up to teach girls and women. The schools taught:

- the importance of hygiene and the danger of diarrhoea for infants
- how flies spread disease from privies and rubbish in the street
- that breast feeding was better than bottle feeding
- that good mothering was a duty women should perform for their king and country.

SOURCE 3 Measures taken by the government 1902–30

1902	*Compulsory training for midwives*
1906	*Meals provided for school children*
1907	*All births to be notified to health visitor*
1907	*Schools to provide medical care and checks*
1909	*Overcrowded back-to-back housing banned. Building regulations to be enforced*
1918	*Local authorities to provide health visitors, clinics for pregnant women and infants, and day nurseries*
1919	*Local authorities required to build new houses for the working classes*
1930	*Five-year slum clearance programme began*

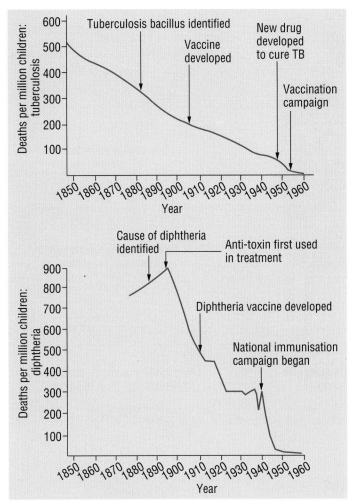

SOURCE 6 Findings of a survey by Elizabeth Robertson into infant mortality in Preston in the early twentieth century

66 *The fall in infant mortality coincided with:*
a) *the replacement of earth privies with water closets*
b) *the introduction of health visitors and qualified midwives*
c) *rise in family incomes at least partly due to a rise in married women's employment*
d) *marked decline in the rate of infectious diseases.* 99

8. List the reasons mentioned or shown in Sources 4–6 which helped to reduce infant mortality. Do you think these reasons were more important or less important than educating mothers about hygiene?

The Second World War

During the Second World War health services were reorganised to cope with the high number of casualties from bombing. This gave everyone much better access to health care.

Food rationing was introduced, together with a healthier eating campaign. The diet of some poorer people improved during the war because the Ministry of Food tried to ensure that rations included the vitamins and calories which many people would not otherwise have had in their diet.

Finally, in 1948, the National Health Service was set up, providing free medicines and treatment for everyone.

9. 'The introduction of the NHS was the most important step in reducing infant mortality.' Explain why you disagree with this statement. Remember to use Source 1.

SOURCE 4 Graphs showing the decline in deaths of children from TB and diphtheria, two major killers of young children in the nineteenth century

6. Study Source 4. Which disease was the biggest killer in 1900 and 1940?
7. Which factors were most important in reducing deaths from these diseases?

SOURCE 5 Details of housing improvements in the 1930s

In the 1930s the government forced local authorities to rehouse 80 per cent of people living in poor housing. The old houses were demolished. By 1939 700,000 new homes with good sanitation and ventilation had been built by local authorities, many of them on large new housing estates away from the city and town centres.

How has the training and role of doctors changed?

Some scientific education but very hands-on training

Dr Smith 1860

Relies on payments from patients for his income

Very limited understanding of the causes of disease

Visits wealthy patients in their homes

Very little equipment

Holds a surgery for the poor in the local dispensary

Highly respected

Sometimes harms patients with dangerous 'cures'

Could not be a woman – there are no female doctors at this time

Has some understanding of the causes of disease

Dr Jones 1930

Relies on payments from patients for his income, but up to one-third of patients cannot pay their bills

Can offer very few cures

Visits many patients in their homes

Has very little equipment – a stethoscope, thermometer, X-ray equipment

Does some charity work

Highly respected

Can refer patients to specialists if they can afford to pay

Could be a woman, although there are very few female doctors at this time

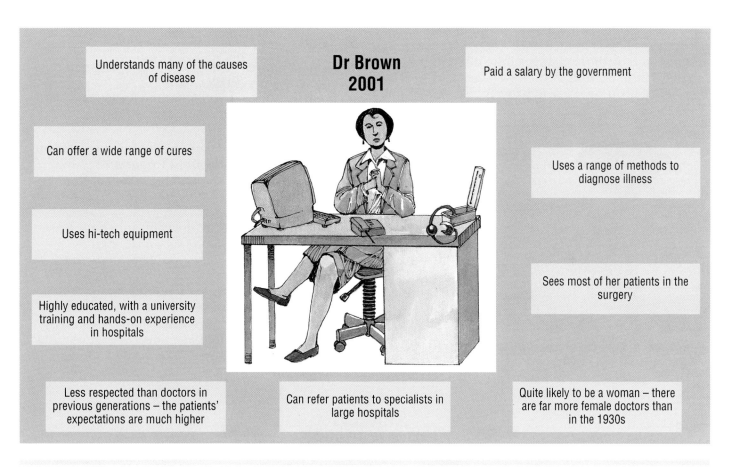

Dr Brown 2001

Understands many of the causes of disease

Paid a salary by the government

Can offer a wide range of cures

Uses a range of methods to diagnose illness

Uses hi-tech equipment

Sees most of her patients in the surgery

Highly educated, with a university training and hands-on experience in hospitals

Less respected than doctors in previous generations – the patients' expectations are much higher

Can refer patients to specialists in large hospitals

Quite likely to be a woman – there are far more female doctors than in the 1930s

■ TASK

1. Make your own copy of the table on the right and complete columns 1 and 2, summarising the continuities and changes in the training and role of doctors.
2. Fill in column 3, suggesting why these aspects either changed or stayed the same.
3. Which of the reasons in column 3 do you think has been most important? Explain your choice.

	Continuities	Changes	Reasons
Training			
Understanding of the causes of ill health			
Equipment			
Respect in the community			
Number of female doctors			
How doctors are paid			
Ability to send patients to a specialist			
Ability to treat the less well off			

Medicine since 1900 – a summary

THERE HAVE BEEN many very important improvements in medicine since 1900. Source 1 shows you how these changes have affected the length of time we live. These two pages look at why there have been so many improvements since 1900.

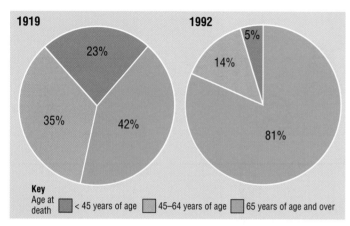

1919 23% 35% 42%

1992 5% 14% 81%

Key Age at death: ▨ < 45 years of age ▨ 45–64 years of age ▨ 65 years of age and over

SOURCE 1 A comparison of age at death of people in Britain in 1919 and 1992

■ TASK

1. Look at Source 1. How has life expectancy changed since 1919?
2. Look at Source 2. Explain how each of the reasons on the left of the diagram helped to change attitudes.
3. Which of the effects on the right of the diagram do you think was the most important?
4. Look at Source 3. Explain how each of the developments since 1900 has been important in improving health.
5. Look at Source 4. List the ways in which wars have affected:
   a) health
   b) medicine.
6. Which of these effects do you think was the most important?
7. 'War has been the most important reason why medicine and health have improved since 1900.' Explain why you agree or disagree with this statement.

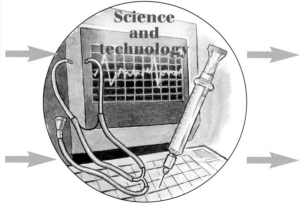

After 1928 everyone over the age of 21 could vote.

Support grew for the Labour Party, which aimed to improve life for ordinary people.

Wars gave people experience of living and working together.

Nineteenth-century reforms had shown how to make people healthier.

Better education meant people could understand how to protect their own health.

Attitudes of people and governments

Improvements in housing, medical care in schools, and training for mothers.

Development of the NHS – free medical care for all.

Much more money spent by governments on medical research, hospitals and day-to-day medical care.

Healthy eating, fitness and anti-smoking campaigns.

SOURCE 2 The impact of changing attitudes

Developments before 1900

Improved instruments and equipment, e.g. microscopes.

Better understanding of the causes of disease.

Methods of prevention, e.g. antiseptics, vaccination, public health.

The beginning of government funding and planning.

Discoveries mainly by individuals, who often faced opposition to their new methods and ideas.

Science and Technology

Developments after 1900

Improved equipment, e.g. computers, cameras, plastics.

Better understanding of the human body, e.g. discovery of DNA.

Understanding of the impact and use of chemicals and medicines, e.g. radium/radiotherapy, antibiotics.

Major spending by drug companies and governments on research.

Discoveries by research teams, working together and building on each other's work.

SOURCE 3 The impact of developments in science and technology

X-rays and blood transfusion
Developments were spurred on by the need to help casualties.

Surgery
Surgeons had to develop new techniques, e.g. skin grafts, and brain, eye and other head surgery.

Diet
Rationing improved some people's diet. Government posters encouraged healthy eating.

Hygiene
Government posters educated people about basic health and hygiene.

MINISTRY OF HEALTH *says*:–
Coughs and sneezes
spread diseases

Trap the germs by using your handkerchief

Help to keep the Nation Fighting Fit

Drugs
Penicillin – the first antibiotic – was developed during the Second World War.

Disease
The government launched its national diphtheria immunisation campaign during the Second World War.

DIPHTHERIA COSTS LIVES

IMMUNISATION
COSTS NOTHING

Ask at your local council offices, school or welfare centre

Housing
In 1914 the low standard of health among recruits to the army made the government very worried about the health of the population generally. It made them more eager to improve health care at home.

The soldiers who fought in the war were promised good housing when they returned – 'homes for heroes'. This speeded up the process of getting rid of unhealthy slum housing in Britain.

The National Health Service
With the threat looming of major civilian casualties from German bombing, the government reorganised health care. In 1942 William Beveridge, a leading civil servant, proposed that these changes should be preserved in a 'free national health service' for all.

SOURCE 4 The impact of war

The health jigsaw: AD2001

THIS IS THE last in a series of pictures which show how doctors in each period have tried to help patients towards better health and longer life. The others are on pages 36 and 90. On page 142 you were asked to draw your own version for the nineteenth century.

1. Describe how the changes shown in this picture have helped to improve health.
2. Do you think this picture gives an accurate impression of the state of medical knowledge and skills today? Explain your answer.
3. How significant do you think the contribution of doctors was in improving medicine and health in the twentieth century? Explain your answer.

chapter 5

CONCLUSIONS: EXPLAINING CHANGE AND CONTINUITY IN MEDICINE AND HEALTH

CONGRATULATIONS! You now know and understand much more than you did a few months ago about the history of medicine and health. This final section will help you to revise the information you have already covered so that you remember it better. It also gives you an opportunity to look at the concepts that are vital to understanding the history of medicine and health.

Pages 178–81 give you an overview of how methods of treatment and explanations of disease have changed over the entire period you have studied.

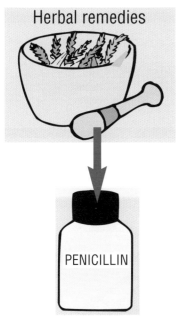

Pages 182–194 look at some of the main factors which have led to changes or have prevented change in medicine and health.

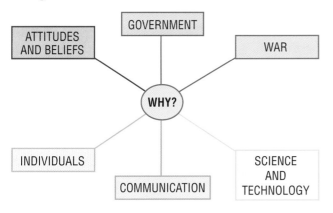

Finally, **pages 199–207** investigate the different patterns of change that have characterised medicine and health through case studies of:
a) surgery   b) hospitals and training
c) the role of women.

Things get steadily better

OR LIKE THIS...?

Sometimes things get better, sometimes they get worse.

177

How have methods of treatment changed through history?

THIS PAGE SUMMARISES some of the main treatments that have been used across the centuries.

1. Which treatments have been used for the greatest length of time?
2. Why were they used for so long?
3. Which treatments used in earlier times are not used today?
4. Why are they no longer used?
5. Which treatments used today were not used in earlier times?
6. Why were they not used in earlier times?
7. When was the period of greatest change in treatments?

IMMUNISATION

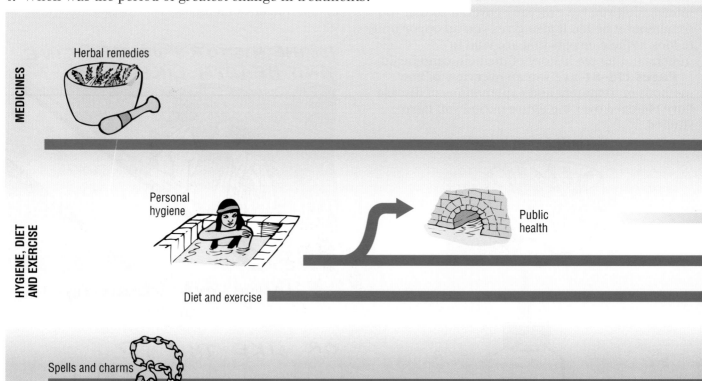

MEDICINES

Herbal remedies

HYGIENE, DIET AND EXERCISE

Personal hygiene

Public health

Diet and exercise

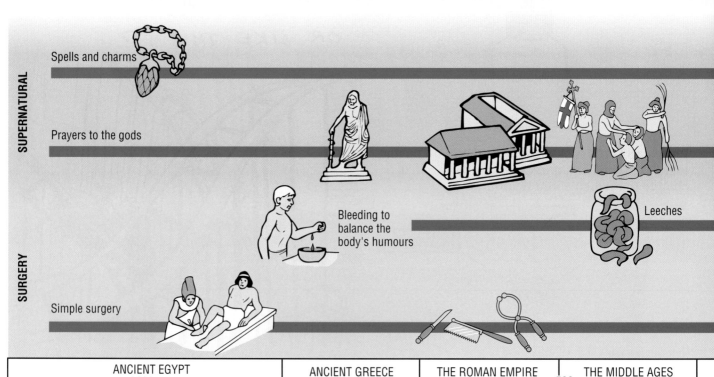

SUPERNATURAL

Spells and charms

Prayers to the gods

Bleeding to balance the body's humours

Leeches

SURGERY

Simple surgery

ANCIENT EGYPT 3000BC	ANCIENT GREECE	THE ROMAN EMPIRE AD500	THE MIDDLE AGES

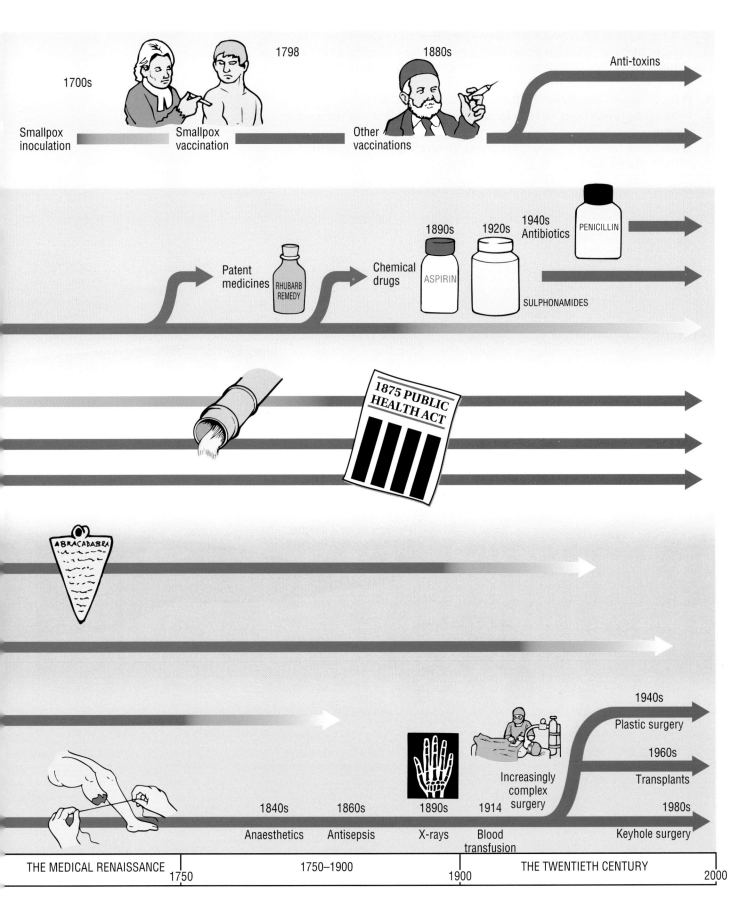

1700s

1798

1880s

Anti-toxins

Smallpox inoculation

Smallpox vaccination

Other vaccinations

Patent medicines

RHUBARB REMEDY

Chemical drugs

1890s

ASPIRIN

1920s

1940s Antibiotics

PENICILLIN

SULPHONAMIDES

1875 PUBLIC HEALTH ACT

ABRACADABRA

1940s

Plastic surgery

1960s

Transplants

1980s

Keyhole surgery

1840s

Anaesthetics

1860s

Antisepsis

1890s

X-rays

1914

Blood transfusion

Increasingly complex surgery

THE MEDICAL RENAISSANCE

1750–1900

THE TWENTIETH CENTURY

1750

1900

2000

How has understanding of the causes of disease changed through history?

FOR CENTURIES HEALERS have struggled to understand why people become ill. This page summarises the different explanations for illness and disease that healers have given through history.

1. Which ideas were believed for the longest period?
2. Why were ideas believed for long periods even though they were wrong?
3. When was the most important breakthrough in understanding the causes of disease?

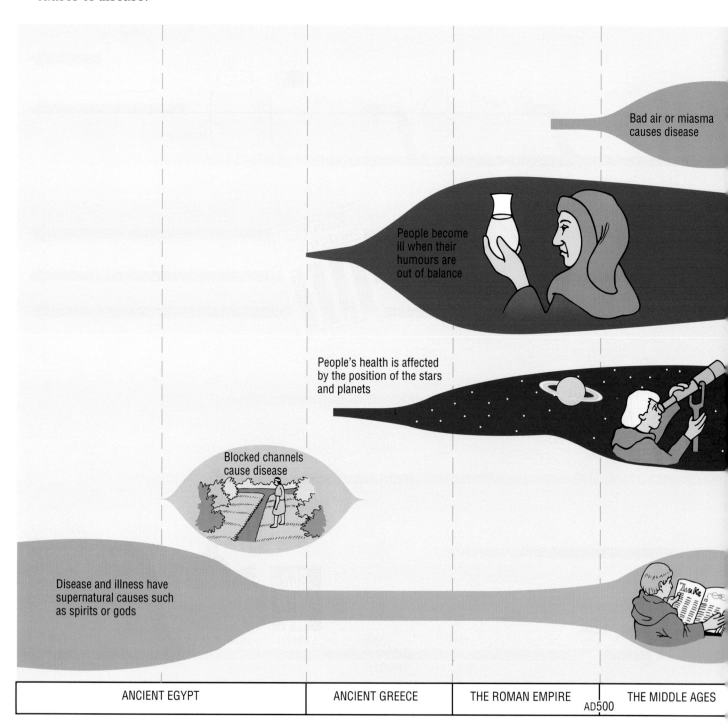

Bad air or miasma causes disease

People become ill when their humours are out of balance

People's health is affected by the position of the stars and planets

Blocked channels cause disease

Disease and illness have supernatural causes such as spirits or gods

| ANCIENT EGYPT | ANCIENT GREECE | THE ROMAN EMPIRE | THE MIDDLE AGES |

AD500

Germs cause disease

MEDICAL RENAISSANCE
AD1750

1750–1900

AD1900

THE TWENTIETH CENTURY

AD2000

Why? The factors that have caused change and continuity in medicine and health

WHILE YOU HAVE been working on the history of medicine and health you will have noticed a number of factors cropping up again and again, and if you didn't notice them by yourself some of the questions made sure you did! These factors have included war, governments and the others shown opposite.

These factors are important because our task in history is not just to list or describe the events of the past – it is also to explain why they happened. Therefore, these factors have not kept appearing by accident. They are the causes that have 'made things happen' in the history of medicine. Sometimes they have made things change. Sometimes they have prevented change.

The next thirteen pages help you to think about the factors you can see opposite. You begin by studying in detail the impact of three separate factors – governments, war, and attitudes and beliefs – to see how they affected the development of medicine and health. Then you should examine some of the other important factors more briefly.

However, you must realise from the start that investigating each factor in isolation is misleading because they almost always work together to produce change or continuity. It would be extremely unusual for a single factor by itself to force change or to stop development. So the final aim of this section is to see how these factors worked together.

Our first task is to identify the different factors.

Why did infant mortality go down quickly in the twentieth century?

Science: because of the discovery of germs and the development of vaccinations against killer diseases.

Education: by the 1900s the message about germs was finally getting through to ordinary people.

War led to improved health care.

Religion and individuals helped too. Religious leaders made the government aware of the problems.

Government: healthier housing was built by local government.

Then we must see how these factors worked together.

Were any of these reasons linked?

War and government worked together. The Boer War made the government worried about health in the first place. The First World War was what made them do something about housing. The Second World War made them reorganise the health service and try to improve people's diet.

Finally, we try to work out which factor or factors were the most important reasons for change or continuity.

Which reason did you think was most important?

I think war was most important. If it hadn't been for war no one would have taken action.

Science was most important. If Pasteur hadn't proved his germ theory, then people would never have realised the importance of hygiene, and they would never have developed vaccines.

Look at the factors shown in the picture below.

1. Attitudes and beliefs have had a major effect on the development of medicine. Which two people in the picture are both examples of attitudes and beliefs?
2. List two ways in which each factor affected the history of medicine.
3. For each factor explain whether it led to change or continuity or both in the history of medicine.
4. Which factors do you think have been the most important in the history of medicine for:
a) causing change
b) maintaining continuity?

Factor 1: Governments

THE SIMPLEST WAY to begin investigating the causes of change and continuity is to study the impact of individual factors. On the next six pages you can investigate three major factors which have affected medicine and health, although they are not in order of importance. You may decide that although we have started with governments they have been less influential than other factors.

■ TASK

1. List as many examples as you can of governments changing medicine or health for the better. Sources 1–7 will get you started but you can also look at the page references on the timeline.
2. In which periods did governments not try to change medicine or health?
3. What methods have been used by governments to change medicine or health?
4. Have governments ever caused change by themselves or have there always been other factors at work?
5. Describe one example of change where factors worked together.
6. How important have governments been in improving medicine and health? Explain your answer.

Doctors will not have to pay taxes. In every town there shall be doctors who treat the poor.

SOURCE 1 An announcement by a Roman emperor

SOURCE 2 K. Branigan, *Roman Britain: Life in an Imperial Province*, 1980

❝ In Roman Britain, in towns like Chichester, Leicester and Wroxeter in Shropshire, probably as many as 500 people a day used the public baths, even if they only visited them once a week.

One of the finest suites of public baths in Britain was at Wroxeter, which also included an outdoor swimming pool and a massive exercise hall. ❞

SOURCE 3 From a letter by Edward III to the Mayor of London, 26 September 1371

❝ Edward by the grace of God etc to the mayor and sheriffs of London, greeting. The air in the city has lately been greatly corrupted and infected by the slaughtering of animals in the city, because of the putrefied blood running in the streets and the dumping of entrails in the river Thames, and as a result appalling abominations and stenches have been produced, and sicknesses and other maladies have befallen residents and visitors to the city. ❞

ANCIENT EGYPT	ANCIENT GREECE	THE ROMAN EMPIRE PP. 30–31, 42–43

3000BC

SOURCE 4 From regulations introduced by the Mayor of London to stop the spread of plague in 1665

66 ... *The Government appointed public prayers and days of fasting, to make public confession of sin and implore the mercy of God to avert the dreadful judgement that hung over their heads ...*

... in every parish there be one, two or more persons by the name of examiners to enquire and learn what persons be sick. And if they find any person sick of the infection, to give order to the constable that the house be shut up.

... to every infected house there be appointed two watchmen, one for every day and the other for the night [so] that no person go in or out of such infected houses. 99

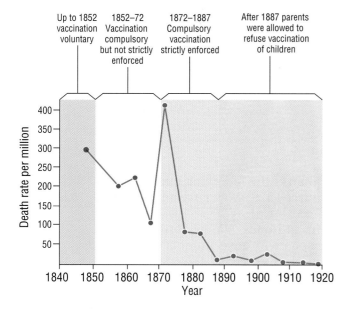

SOURCE 5 Graph showing deaths from smallpox, 1848–1920

SOURCE 6 Measures taken by the government in Britain, 1900–45

1902 Midwives Act, compulsory training and the setting of standards.

1906 Education (Provision of Meals) Act, local authorities allowed to provide meals in elementary schools.

1907 Notification of Births Act, so that health visitors could be sure they visited all new babies.

1907 Education (Administrative Provision) Act, medical services provided for children at school.

1911 National Insurance Act, free medical treatment for workers who paid a contribution, but not for their families.

1918 Maternal and Child Welfare Act, allowed local authorities to provide free clinics for pregnant women and infants.

1930 Housing Act, slum clearance undertaken.

1940 Diphtheria immunisation campaign.

1940s Funding for the development of penicillin.

SOURCE 7 From a speech by Nye Bevan, the Minister of Health who introduced the NHS in Britain in 1948

66 *Medical treatment should be made available to rich and poor alike in accordance with medical need and no other criteria. Worry about money in a time of sickness is a serious hindrance to recovery apart from its unnecessary cruelty. The records show that it is the mother in the average family who suffers most from the absence of a full health service. In trying to balance her budget she puts her own needs last. The essence of a satisfactory health service is that the rich and the poor are treated alike, that poverty is not a disability, and wealth is not advantaged.* 99

THE MIDDLE AGES PP. 42–43, 50–51, 54–56	THE MEDICAL RENAISSANCE PP. 71–72, 89	1750–1900 PP. 97, 106, 110–15, 127, 141	SINCE 1900 PP. 144, 159–71, 174–75

0   AD1750   AD1900

Factor 2: Attitudes

Attitudes! What do we mean by attitudes?

The attitudes of governments to caring for the people
Why did Charles II and his government not try to protect people from the plague?

The attitudes of people to the way medicine and health can be improved
Why did people in the 1840s oppose the building of sewers and other public health improvements?

The way the work of individuals affected other people's attitudes
How did an individual like Florence Nightingale change attitudes to nursing?

SOURCE 1 Three examples of attitudes

Real change in medicine and health cannot take place unless:

■ people see a need for change and want change

■ governments force change to happen and pay for change.

I've thought of a new way to treat the sick.

New way! We do not need new ways. Galen told us everything we need to know about medicine.

We need to improve people's health. The way to do that is to spend money on new sewers and clean water and to pass laws forcing towns to make these changes.

SOURCE 2 Why are attitudes so important?

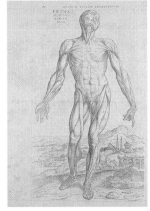

SOURCE 3 In 1543 Vesalius published his book *The Fabric of the Human Body*. Vesalius proved that Galen had been wrong about important details of anatomy. He proved this through dissections. Vesalius' work encouraged other doctors to experiment to test and challenge old ideas

■ TASK

Look at Source 1. Now answer the following questions.
1. a) Which **three** of Sources 3–9 show governments' attitudes to caring for people?
   b) How did governments' attitudes change between 1600 and 1900?
   c) Make a list of the reasons why governments' attitudes changed. Use the timeline index to help you.
2. a) Which **two** of Sources 3–9 show people's attitudes to improvements in medicine?
   b) Explain why the people in **one** of these sources opposed improvements.
3. a) Which **two** of Sources 3–9 show how individuals affected other people's attitudes?
   b) Use the timeline index to find **one** more example of individuals changing other people's attitudes.
4. Look at Source 2. Why are attitudes so important in the history of health and medicine for
   a) preventing change
   b) making change happen?

ANCIENT EGYPT PP. 9, 12	ANCIENT GREECE PP. 14, 16	THE ROMAN EMPIRE PP. 26, 28–29, 43

3000BC

186

SOURCE 4 When plague struck London in 1665, Charles II and his nobles left the city. Charles and his ministers only once discussed the impact of the plague on the people

SOURCE 5 From an article published in *The Times*, 1 August 1854 (see page 111, Source 19 for the full text)

66 *We prefer to take our chance with cholera than be bullied into health. There is nothing a man hates so much as being cleaned against his will. Mr. Chadwick set to work everywhere, washing and splashing, and Master John Bull was scrubbed and rubbed till the tears came to his eyes and his fists clenched themselves with worry and pain.* 99

The 1875 Public Health Act
This laid down in detail all the duties that were expected of a local council. All towns were forced to perform these tasks. They included the provision of clean water, proper drainage and sewerage, and the appointment of a Medical Officer of Health.

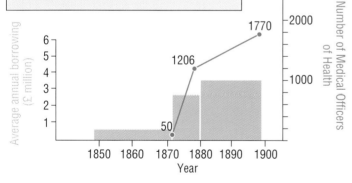

SOURCE 6 Numbers of Medical Officers of Health and average amount borrowed by councils for public health and improvements. In the late 1800s both national governments and local councils were spending much more money on public health schemes to improve the health of the people. The 1875 Public Health Act forced local councils to make great changes

SOURCE 7 Measures taken by the government, 1902–30

1902   *Compulsory training for midwives*
1906   *Meals provided for school children*
1907   *All births to be notified to health visitor*
1907   *Schools to provide medical care and checks*
1909   *Overcrowded back-to-back housing banned. Building regulations to be enforced*
1918   *Local authorities to provide health visitors, clinics for pregnant women and infants, and day nurseries*
1919   *Local authorities required to build new houses for the working classes*
1930   *Five-year slum clearance programme began*

SOURCE 8 Florence Nightingale's work changed many people's attitudes to nursing. Before her work in the Crimea and her reforms, nurses were poorly trained at best and people did not respect nurses. By the early 1900s nurses were well-trained and nursing was a job many people wanted to do

I am unable to accept the proposal to set up a national medical service based on the family doctor. The pernicious habit of getting something for nothing will be encouraged.

If the Bill is passed no patient or doctor will feel safe from interference by some ministerial edict or regulation. The minister's spies will be everywhere.

SOURCE 9 When the National Health Service was set up in 1948 there was a lot of opposition from doctors. These quotations show their attitudes

THE MIDDLE AGES PP. 43, 48–51, 54–55	THE MEDICAL RENAISSANCE PP. 64, 67–69, 70–81, 88	1750–1900 PP. 93, 97–98, 104, 106, 115, 132, 140–41	SINCE 1900 PP. 144, 162–71, 174

Factor 3: War

■ TASK

War has affected medicine and health for a number of reasons. You can see the key reasons in the table below.

A. Governments invested money in improving the health of soldiers and the people	B. Doctors and nurses could practise and make new discoveries as they battled to deal with high casualties and new types of injury or emergency	C. Research was increased to solve medical problems or to give a country a lead over its rivals	D. Research was disrupted because doctors were needed to cope with casualties

1. Draw your own copy of this table. Look at Sources 1–5 and decide which column each belongs in.
2. Use the timeline index to add more examples to your table.
3. War has sometimes:
   a) accelerated change
   b) led to new discoveries
   c) slowed down developments.
   Which sources show each of these effects of war?
4. Do you think that war has done more to **help** or **hinder** medical developments? Explain your choice.

SOURCE 1 Ambroise Paré first treated soldiers in 1536. He copied the methods of other doctors, using boiling oil and cauterisation on wounds. He was forced to experiment with other treatments when supplies of the traditional treatment ran out

66 … eventually I ran out of oil and I had to use a mixture made of yolks of eggs, oil of roses and turpentine. That night I could not sleep, fearing that the wounded would die or be poisoned because they had not been cauterised. I rose very early to visit them. Beyond my hope, I found those on whom I had used my mixture in little pain, their wounds without inflammation and having rested well. The others whom I had treated with boiling oil, I found feverish, with great pain and swelling around their wounds. I resolved with myself never more to burn thus cruelly poor men wounded with gunshot. 99

SOURCE 2
A cartoon showing Robert Koch slaying the tuberculosis bacillus. Koch, a German, and Louis Pasteur, a Frenchman, made many discoveries in the late nineteenth century. The two men were bitter rivals because France had lost a war to Germany in 1870–71 and Pasteur wanted to show that his country was not falling behind Germany, in science at least

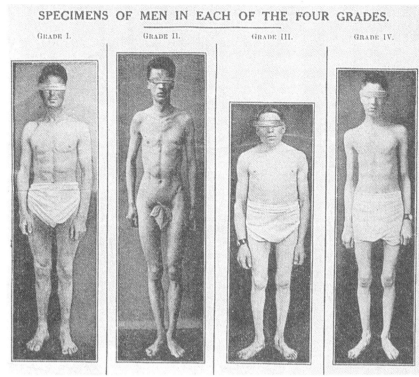

SPECIMENS OF MEN IN EACH OF THE FOUR GRADES.

GRADE I.   GRADE II.   GRADE III.   GRADE IV.

SOURCE 3 Photographs of army recruits in the First World War, taken by National Service Medical Boards. The poor physical standard of recruits to the Boer War (1899–1902) had resulted in the rejection of 38 per cent of potential soldiers. In 1914 recruits in the First World War had similar health problems. They suffered from heart complaints, poor sight, inadequate hearing and rotten teeth. This evidence of poor health led to the establishment of the Committee on Physical Deterioration which made far-reaching proposals to improve health

SOURCE 5 Penicillin was discovered in 1928 but by 1940 was still only being used in trials on mice. However, in 1941 the USA entered the Second World War and this led to a rapid acceleration in the research and use of penicillin

- In 1942 the US government gave $80 million to four drug companies to find a way to mass produce penicillin.
- In 1943 production began. The first use in war was by the British army in North Africa.
- By June 1944 there was enough penicillin to treat all the casualties suffered on D-Day.
- By 1945 the US army was using two million doses a month. It is estimated that another 12–15 per cent of wounded Allied soldiers would have died without penicillin to fight their infection. Penicillin also roughly halved the average time the Allied wounded spent in hospital.
- Soon after the war penicillin became available for civilian use – it was called an antibiotic.

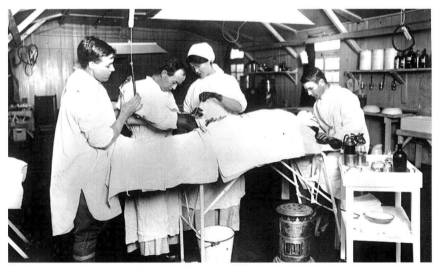

SOURCE 4 A makeshift operating theatre during the First World War. During this war 14,000 British doctors were taken away from their normal research work because more doctors were needed to deal with the huge number of casualties

00   AD1750   AD1900

The role of key individuals

SOME INDIVIDUALS made great discoveries that improved people's health. Others had ideas that were used for centuries, even though they were not correct.

1. Who are the six people shown below?
2. With which breakthrough in medicine and health do you associate each person?

3. On your own copy of the timeline below add the names of these individuals at the appropriate points.
4. 'Individuals are not really important in the history of medicine. Sooner or later someone would have made the key discoveries. Changing attitudes and the work of governments are far more important.' Do you agree with this statement?

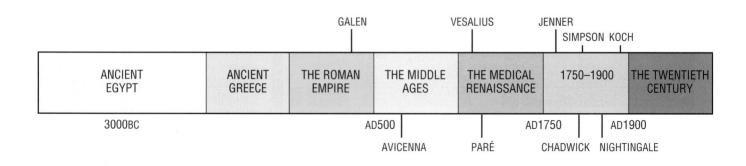

What other factors have affected medicine and health?

THE SOURCES ON this page give you some clues about four other factors:

■ chance
■ science and technology
■ communications
■ conservatism.

1. Which factor does each source show?
2. Find one other example of each factor at work using the reference box below.
3. Explain whether each factor:
   a) helped to create change
   b) prevented change
   c) did both at different times.
4. These are not the only factors which have been important in the history of medicine and health. Look back through this book and list examples of other factors creating or preventing medical change. You could look at education, industry or another factor which interests you.

Reference box
Page 65, Source 1
Page 118, Source 9
Page 146, Source 2
Page 188, Source 1

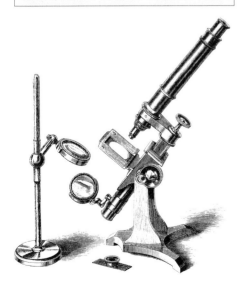

SOURCE 1 The microscope was improved in the 1800s. As a result scientists could study micro-organisms in detail

SOURCE 2 R. Jackson, *Doctors and Diseases in the Roman Empire*, 1988

❝ … At the same time as knowledge and techniques were spread by the Roman army, fresh information was collected … the mobility that the army provided allowed doctors to learn of and collect new herbs … It is probably fair to say that the Roman army was the single most powerful agency in the spread of Graeco-Roman medicine. ❞

SOURCE 3 Pasteur's researcher, by chance, used an old batch of bacteria. He found it worked as a vaccine

SOURCE 4 The response of two doctors to the proposals for a National Health Service

How did different factors work together to produce change?

THE FIRST STEP in explaining why an event happened is to identify the causes. Then you need to decide how the causes worked together and which, if any, were the most important. As an example you are going to look again at the medical breakthroughs at the time of the Renaissance between 1350 and 1750: Vesalius' discoveries in anatomy, Paré's work in surgery and Harvey's discovery of the circulation of the blood, which you studied in Chapter 2.

The chart on page 193 identifies five major reasons why these discoveries were made.

Individual genius

The individual scientists and doctors themselves were important. They were highly intelligent and observant people who had original ideas.

War and chance

In the case of Paré (see pages 60–61) war and chance were also an important part of the explanation. Paré was an army doctor who had learned his skills on the battlefield, as had many other surgeons. However, if he had not run out of the hot oil he usually put on wounds he would never have tried his own mixture of eggs, oil of roses and turpentine, which turned out to be both more effective and less painful.

Beliefs and attitudes

Changing beliefs and attitudes also played a vital part in these discoveries. For the first time in centuries many religious beliefs were being challenged. Even the Pope and the Roman Catholic Church were being criticised and challenged by Protestants who were eager for a purer, simpler kind of Christianity. It seemed as though none of the old ideas was safe.

Science and technology

The loosening of the power of old religious ideas opened the way for science. New scientific methods were applied to solve old problems.

Copernicus, a Polish astronomer, said that the Sun did not orbit the Earth but that the Earth orbited the Sun. In medicine, Galen's ideas were being challenged. His theories on anatomy and treatments had been the basis of medicine for over a thousand years but, if the Catholic Church could be challenged, then why not Galen? When Vesalius discovered through careful scientific observation that Galen's ideas on some parts of anatomy were wrong he was able to say this. Before the new atmosphere brought about by the Renaissance it would have been almost impossible to dare say that Galen was wrong.

Technology was being improved or invented. One improved machine was the water pump, which Harvey had in mind when he wrote 'When water is forced through pipes we can see and distinguish the individual compressions of the pump (perhaps at a considerable distance) in the flow of the escaping water. It is the same from the opening of a cut artery ...'

Communications

Finally, communications were vital in these discoveries. The greatest invention of the period was the printing press which spread ideas and information far more quickly than had been possible before. New theories reached other scientists and doctors quickly so that they could test and build on the work of Vesalius and others. Printing was especially important for the illustrations of anatomy in Vesalius' work. The detail was captured with a new kind of engraving onto blocks of wood or copper.

These illustrations would also have been impossible without major developments in art. Medieval illustrations often seem unreal compared to the work of Renaissance artists such as Leonardo da Vinci. Da Vinci's work was based on careful observation and even dissection of human bodies because he believed that he needed to study bodies in detail before he could draw them accurately. Other artists copied da Vinci's methods of research and this meant that Vesalius could find good artists who were able to illustrate his discoveries.

Which of these causes was the most important?

Perhaps the most important factor was the change in beliefs and attitudes, which created a spirit of enquiry. Without this, it was almost impossible for new ideas to be developed, however clever an individual was, because no one else would take them up. Communications were vital because they spread ideas rapidly. Chance, war, the work of individuals and developments in science could not have had an effect without the changes in beliefs and communications.

■ TASK 1

1. Explain the links shown by three of the arrows in the chart below.
2. Do you think other links should be shown?
3. Which factor or factors do *you* think were most important in causing change between 1350 and 1750?

■ TASK 2

Draw a similar chart to show how factors worked together to beat the killer diseases of the nineteenth century.

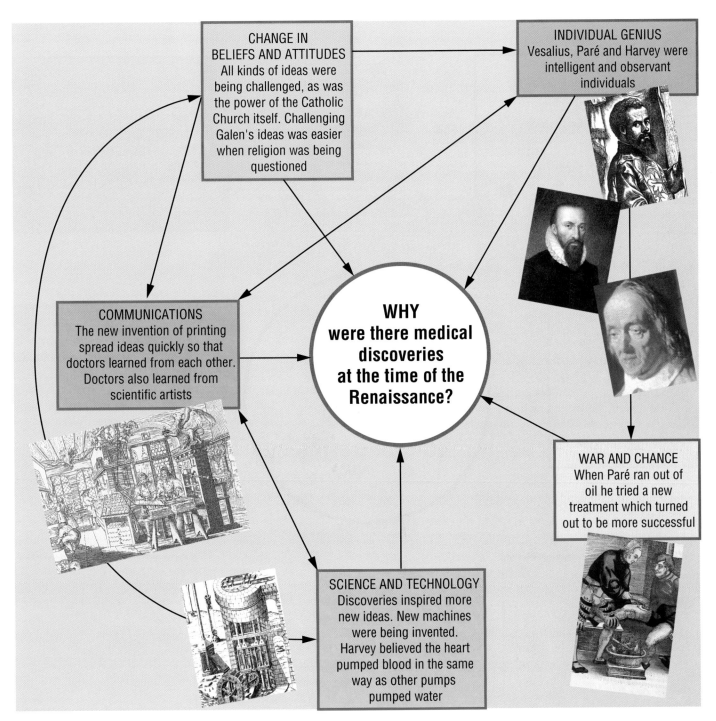

CHANGE IN BELIEFS AND ATTITUDES
All kinds of ideas were being challenged, as was the power of the Catholic Church itself. Challenging Galen's ideas was easier when religion was being questioned

INDIVIDUAL GENIUS
Vesalius, Paré and Harvey were intelligent and observant individuals

COMMUNICATIONS
The new invention of printing spread ideas quickly so that doctors learned from each other. Doctors also learned from scientific artists

WHY were there medical discoveries at the time of the Renaissance?

WAR AND CHANCE
When Paré ran out of oil he tried a new treatment which turned out to be more successful

SCIENCE AND TECHNOLOGY
Discoveries inspired more new ideas. New machines were being invented. Harvey believed the heart pumped blood in the same way as other pumps pumped water

How did different factors work together to prevent change?

AFTER THE ROMAN period there was little improvement in medical knowledge in Europe for centuries. For some people, particularly the wealthy, this was actually a time of regression. Health became worse because the Roman public health facilities were destroyed, and some of the methods and skills of the Roman doctors were lost.

In this case the different factors worked together to prevent change. War, for instance, which helped to bring about new medical discoveries in the previous example, had a harmful effect on medical progress during this period.

1. Look back to the chart on page 193. It has arrows showing the links between the factors that caused change. Make your own copy of the chart below and draw arrows showing how the factors that *prevented* change were linked. For example, if you think that war harmed communications you should draw an arrow from war to communications.
2. Choose two of the arrows you have drawn and explain why you have drawn them.
3. Which factors were most important in preventing change?

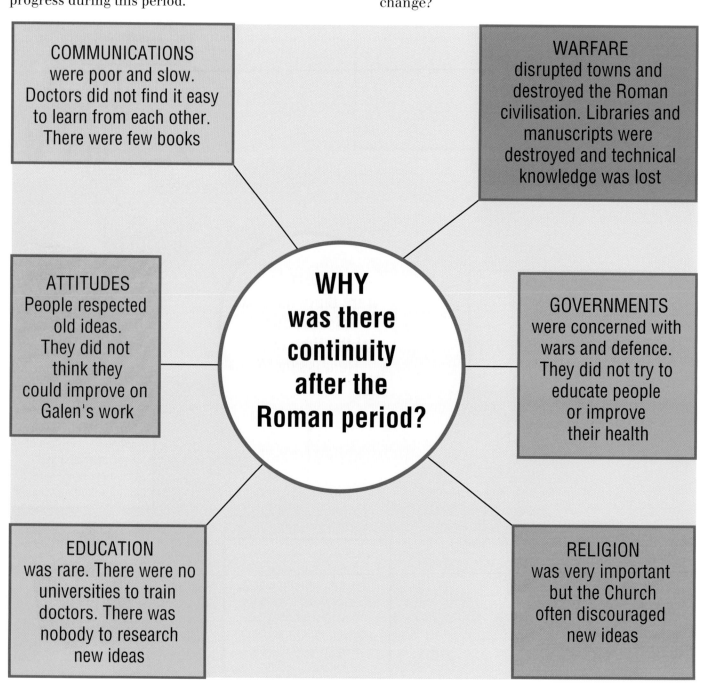

COMMUNICATIONS
were poor and slow.
Doctors did not find it easy
to learn from each other.
There were few books

WARFARE
disrupted towns and
destroyed the Roman
civilisation. Libraries and
manuscripts were
destroyed and technical
knowledge was lost

ATTITUDES
People respected
old ideas.
They did not
think they
could improve on
Galen's work

WHY
was there
continuity
after the
Roman period?

GOVERNMENTS
were concerned with
wars and defence.
They did not try to
educate people
or improve
their health

EDUCATION
was rare. There were no
universities to train
doctors. There was
nobody to research
new ideas

RELIGION
was very important
but the Church
often discouraged
new ideas

Patterns of change

EVER SINCE YOU began studying history you have been investigating changes and continuities, and their causes. Now is the time to think in more detail about the pattern of change and continuity in the history of medicine and health.

1. Look at the gravestones below. Is this an accurate picture of how life expectancy has changed since Roman times? Explain your answer.

2. Find one more example of each of these patterns of change.

Some aspects of medicine stayed the same for many centuries

At some times there were rapid changes in medicine and health

CHILDREN CLINIC

Sometimes medicine and health grew worse, not better

A brief history of surgery from 1350 to the present

The impact of Paré

■ TASK 1

Look at Sources 1–3.
1. What can you learn from each source about surgery in the Middle Ages?
2. Where did many surgeons gain their experience?
3. Why were operations quick and simple?
4. Why was there no significant improvement in surgery in the Middle Ages?

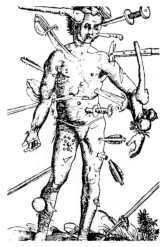

SOURCE 1 A 'wound man', showing the kinds of injury a surgeon would try to treat. Pictures like this were probably used for teaching surgeons

SOURCE 2 A fourteenth-century illustration showing a surgeon at work on the battlefield

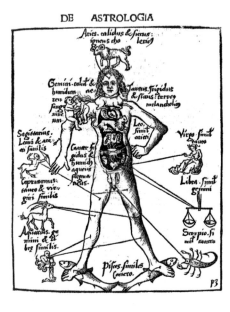

SOURCE 3 A Zodiac Man. Charts like this showed how and when each part of the body was affected by the planets and the stars. Surgeons checked the chart to see if the time was right for operating on a particular part of the body

Medieval surgery – a summary

Training of surgeons
- Surgeons trained as apprentices to older surgeons, not at universities.
- Master Surgeons had to pass tests to get their licences.
- Some women trained to be surgeons.

Types of surgery
- Simple, quick, external surgery, e.g.
  - setting broken bones
  - amputating limbs
  - removing external tumours or cataracts from eyes
  - stopping bleeding and sealing wounds with cauteries (red-hot irons).

Problems
- Pain – there were no safe, effective anaesthetics. Surgeons did use painkillers but they were dangerous if they mixed the wrong balance of ingredients.
- Pus – infection killed many patients and there was no way of stopping it spreading. Surgeons believed that putting boiling oil on wounds was the way to stop infection spreading.
- Blood – it was difficult to stop bleeding and patients could not be given more blood artificially.

Do you want more detail? Then turn to page 53.

Change on the way?

There were people who questioned the normal methods used by surgeons. One of them was Theodoric of Lucca in the thirteenth century. His father had been a famous surgeon. Theodoric said 'Ancient surgeons and their disciples teach that pus should be generated in wounds. There could be no greater error than this. Pus prolongs the disease and prevents healing. My father used to heal almost every kind of wound with wine alone and he produced the most beautiful healing without any ointments.'

Did other surgeons listen to him? No, they did not! Theodoric's idea that pus was bad for the patient went against the ideas of Galen, the great Roman doctor and no one believed that Galen could be wrong. So no one believed Theodoric for another 200 years until …

Ambroise Paré (1510–90), the great French surgeon

Do you want more detail?
Then turn to pages 60–61.

What did Paré do?

■ Paré did not use boiling oil to heal open gunshot wounds.
■ He used simple, clean bandages and a mixture of egg yolks, oil of roses and turpentine on gunshot wounds.

Why did Paré do it?

■ He was a surgeon with the French army in the 1530s. During a battle he ran out of boiling oil and had to use another treatment.
■ Next day his patients were recovering well but some of the patients who had been treated with boiling oil were in agony or had died. Paré carried on using his new method.

Why was Paré important?

Short-term – his ideas spread quickly around Europe because:
■ by the 1500s many doctors were challenging old ideas and methods, even those of Galen
■ he published his ideas in his book, *Works on Surgery*. Now that books could be printed, ideas spread rapidly. Paré wrote in French and more surgeons could read French than Latin. His book was also translated into many other languages.

Therefore Paré's work was **important** because the spread of his ideas encouraged others to try **new** methods and **challenge** old ideas.

Long-term – Paré made a second discovery. He used ligatures made of silk thread to stop bleeding instead of using the red-hot iron called a cautery. The ligatures were tied around individual blood vessels to stop the bleeding. This did stop bleeding but patients still died because the ligatures carried germs into the wound and thus helped to spread infection. This discovery only became really useful 300 years later when Lister discovered antiseptics.

■ **TASK 2**

War has often led to advances in surgery.

1. How did war lead to changes in the 1500s?
2. Which other factors played a part in improving surgery at that time?

The surgical revolution, part 1: 1800–1900

■ TASK 1

James Simpson, a famous surgeon in the 1800s, said 'The man laid out on the operating tables of our hospitals has more chances of death than the English soldier on the fields of Waterloo.'

1. What were the three reasons why operations were so dangerous?
2. What evidence can you find in Source 4 to support Simpson's belief?
3. Which medical breakthrough is shown in each of Sources 5 and 6?
4. Which doctor was responsible for each breakthrough?
5. How does each discovery help to explain the changes in surgery between 1800 and 1900 (see Source 7)?

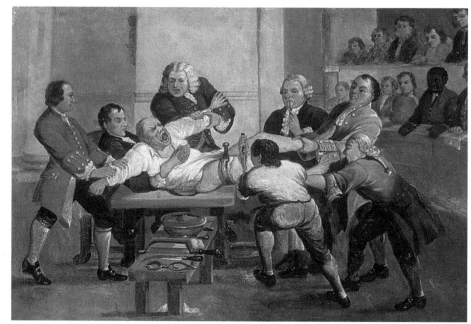

S OURCE 4 An operation around 1800

S OURCE 5

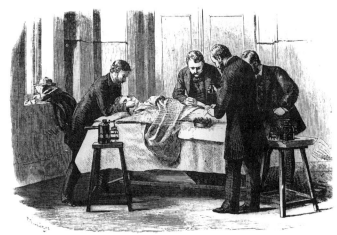

S OURCE 6

What kinds of surgery took place?

1800	1900
Quick and simple surgery: – setting broken bones, removing cataracts from eyes Desperate surgery: – amputations, removal of tumours	Longer, more complex surgery, deeper inside the body, e.g. – removing appendix – operations on the heart

S OURCE 7 Changes in surgery, 1800–1900

■ ACTIVITY 1

Why did people oppose these new ideas in the 1800s?

Here is list of reasons why people opposed the new ideas shown in Sources 5 and 6 on page 198. However, you need to sort them out.

1. List the objections to the discovery in Source 5.
2. List the objections to the discovery in Source 6.

Overdoses led to deaths.

Doctors could not see the germs.

The method was unnatural.

It slowed down the operation and caused extra work.

It was God's wish that people suffer pain.

The idea was new and it took time for people to accept a new idea.

■ ACTIVITY 2

Why did this revolution happen THEN?

1. Draw a diagram like the one on page 193 for the discovery in Source 5. Draw in the arrows showing the links between the reasons. Use the reasons below to get you started but beware – they may not all be relevant!
2. Draw a similar diagram for the discovery in Source 6.

The discoveries of Pasteur and Koch

Improved understanding of chemistry

Improved technology, e.g. better microscopes and other equipment.

Doctors were well-trained in research and methods of experiment.

Individual inspiration

Improved communications spread ideas very quickly.

■ TASK 2

1. 'The discovery of effective anaesthetics was a turning-point in medicine.' Explain why you agree or disagree with this statement.
2. How important was Lister's development of antiseptics for the future of surgery? Explain your answer.

Do you want more detail?
Then turn to pages 116–22.

The surgical revolution, part 2: 1900 to the present

War and surgery

The twentieth century was dominated by wars. The First World War of 1914–18 was fought not long after the great breakthroughs in antiseptics, X-rays and the discovery of blood groups. War helped to change surgery and then, twenty years later, the Second World War of 1939–45 brought more changes. Among these was the development of plastic surgery to deal with burn injuries, particularly of pilots and other aircrew. How exactly did war affect surgery?

New techniques developed during the two world wars

Setting broken bones

Treating head wounds, especially to eyes and ears. Brain surgery

Plastic surgery to treat and repair burned skin. This kind of treatment was a result of a new kind of injury, caused by planes and tanks catching fire

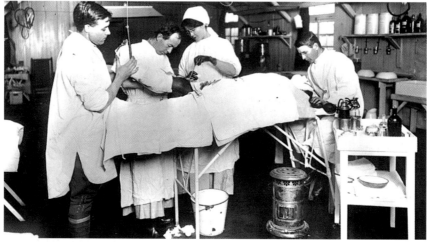

Improved methods of dealing with infection after operations, particularly the development of penicillin during the Second World War

Effective use of blood transfusion, which improved in both wars

Improved use of X-rays, which had been discovered in the 1890s

SOURCE 8 A makeshift operating theatre during the First World War

Why did war help to improve surgery?

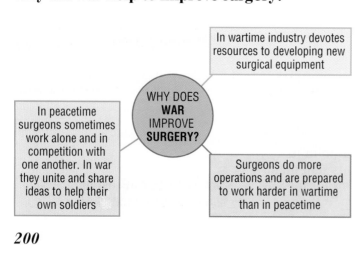

In wartime industry devotes resources to developing new surgical equipment

WHY DOES **WAR** IMPROVE **SURGERY?**

In peacetime surgeons sometimes work alone and in competition with one another. In war they unite and share ideas to help their own soldiers

Surgeons do more operations and are prepared to work harder in wartime than in peacetime

SOURCE 9
A summary of the views of Heneage Ogilvey, a British surgeon, on the relationship between war and surgery

Do you want more detail? Then turn to pages 152–55.

The pace of change accelerates!
Although wars had a great effect on surgery, even greater and faster changes took place after 1945. By 2000 surgery was taking place that no doctor in 1900 would have thought possible!

New developments

■ Transplant surgery

■ Keyhole surgery

■ Microsurgery

■ Improved anaesthetics and antiseptics

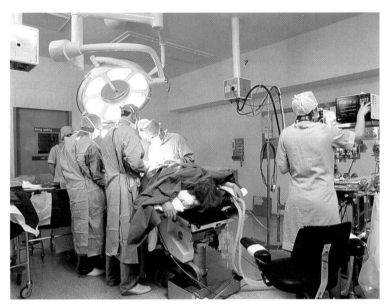

SOURCE 10 A team of surgeons at work in the late twentieth century

Reasons for rapid change

■ Improvements in science and technology

■ Specialist training of doctors

■ Higher levels of funding from governments

■ New and improved equipment

■ TASK 1

1. Choose one advance in surgery and explain how war helped to bring it about.
2. Choose one advance in surgery and explain how new scientific knowledge helped to bring it about.

■ TASK 2

An overview of surgery
Use pages 196–201.

1. What examples of continuity can you find in the history of surgery?
2. Was the pace of change always the same in surgery? Explain your answer.
3. Choose the **two** turning-points that you think were the most important in the history of surgery. Explain your choice.
4. What were the most important factors in bringing improvements in surgery?

Do you want more detail?
Then turn to pages 152–55.

A brief history of hospitals and training from 1350 to the present

The changing face of hospitals

■ TASK

Use Sources 1–4.

1. What kinds of work did nurses do in each of the periods shown?
2. What dangers to health can you see in each ward?
3. These sources give you an overview of the history of hospitals and nursing. When did the greatest changes happen?
4. 'Without Florence Nightingale's work, hospitals would not have changed in the 1800s.' Explain why you agree or disagree with this statement.
5. 'The history of hospitals and nursing has been one of steady and gradual improvement.' Explain why you agree or disagree with this statement, using evidence from these sources.
6. How valuable are these sources for historians investigating the development of hospitals since 1350?

■ ACTIVITY

Get into groups. Each group must take one of the sources. Your task is to devise the training programme for the nurses on your ward. List all the things they need to study and decide which items are the most important. Then do a three-minute presentation to the whole class explaining the training programme.

SOURCE 1 A ward in one of the largest medieval hospitals, the Hôtel Dieu in Paris, which opened in 1452

Do you want more detail?
Then turn to pages 86–87.

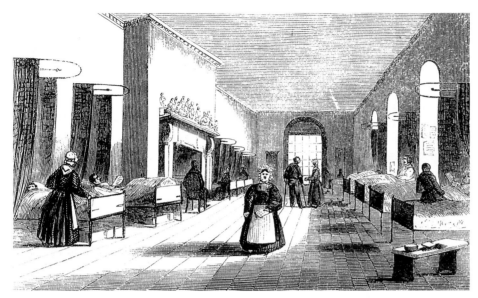

SOURCE 2 A drawing of Rahere ward at St Bartholomew's Hospital in London, made in 1844

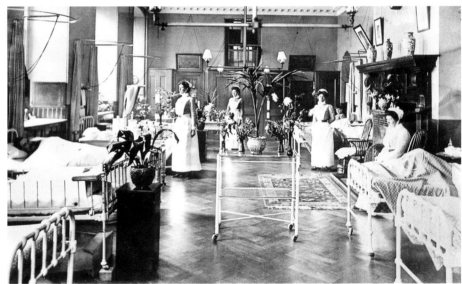

SOURCE 3 A ward at St Bartholomew's Hospital in 1909

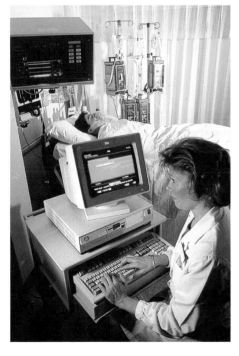

SOURCE 4 A patient is monitored in a modern cardiac intensive care unit

The training of doctors: 1350 to the present

■ ACTIVITY

Divide into groups. Each group must devise the training programme for new doctors in one of 1350, 1650, 1900 or 2000. Use the sources on this page as a starting point and then look at the other pages listed in the pink cross-reference boxes. Then give a three-minute presentation to the whole class explaining the training programme.

It may help you to think about:

- ■ causes of disease
- ■ treatments
- ■ equipment
- ■ other skills required.

■ TASK

Why did the training of doctors change in:

a) the sixteenth and seventeenth centuries

b) the late nineteenth century?

Use the factors below to help you – there may be others and not all of these may be relevant!

- ■ Developments in science/technology
- ■ Great discoveries about the way the body works
- ■ Improvements in communications
- ■ Epidemics and new diseases
- ■ Changing attitudes and beliefs

The Middle Ages *c.* 1350

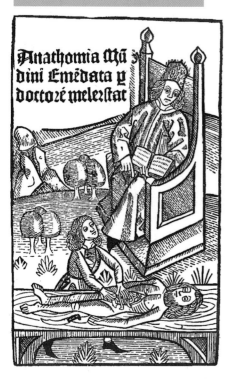

SOURCE 5 A teacher presiding over a dissection at a medical school. At these schools students listened to lectures in which the teacher read out passages from the work of Galen and other ancient writers. At Montpellier, after 1340, the students were allowed to study one corpse a year, but the dissection was done by the teacher's assistant, not by the student

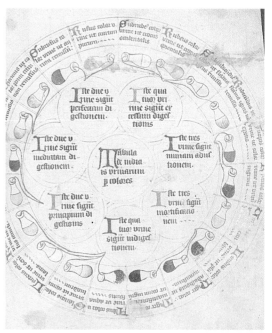

SOURCE 6 A urine chart. This was one of the basic tools which doctors used to diagnose illness. Wealthy families regularly sent urine samples to their doctor so he could look for signs of illness. The text around the outside of the chart describes the colour and quality of the urine (whether it is cloudy or clear). The text in the middle tells the doctor about the patient's digestion. The best digestion is bottom left. Death (black urine) is bottom right

… and see pages 82–83.

The sixteenth and seventeenth centuries

SOURCE 7 Physicians were fully qualified doctors who had studied for fourteen years at university, seven of those studying medicine. They were all men. They knew the work of Galen and many other ancient writers, as well as that of Vesalius, Harvey and other more modern doctors. They charged large fees for their work, especially in London. Even the fee of a country physician could be a month's wages for a labourer

SOURCE 8 When Charles II was ill in 1685 his doctors tried the following treatments – bleeding, purging, and giving him a medicine made from 40 drops of spirit of human skull, taken in an ounce and a half of Cordial Julep

... and see pages 80–81.

1900

SOURCE 9 From an article in *The Lancet*, 1869, by Joseph Lister, Professor of Surgery, Glasgow University

When it had been shown by the researches of Pasteur that the septic property of the atmosphere depended on minute organisms suspended in it, it occurred to me that decomposition in the injured part [following an operation] might be avoided by applying as a dressing some material capable of destroying the life of the floating particles.

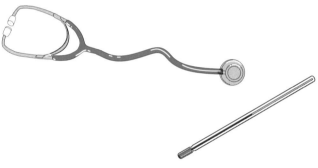

SOURCE 10 A modern thermometer and stethoscope

... and see pages 128–29.

2000

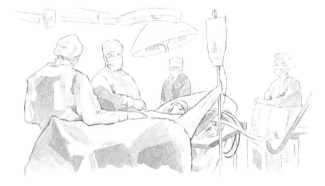

SOURCE 11 A patient being given a blood transfusion

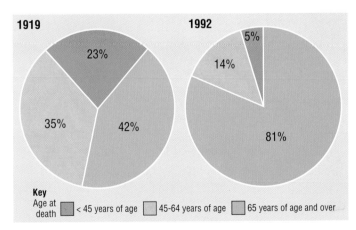

Key
Age at death ☐ < 45 years of age ☐ 45-64 years of age ☐ 65 years of age and over

1919: 23%, 35%, 42%
1992: 5%, 14%, 81%

SOURCE 12 A comparison at age of death of people in Britain in 1919 and 1992

... and see page 172.

Women in medicine – healers, nurses and midwives

■ TASK

Answer these questions first for nurses, then for midwives.

1. Describe the main changes in training since 1350.
2. When was the greatest change in their roles?
3. Why did these changes happen when they did?

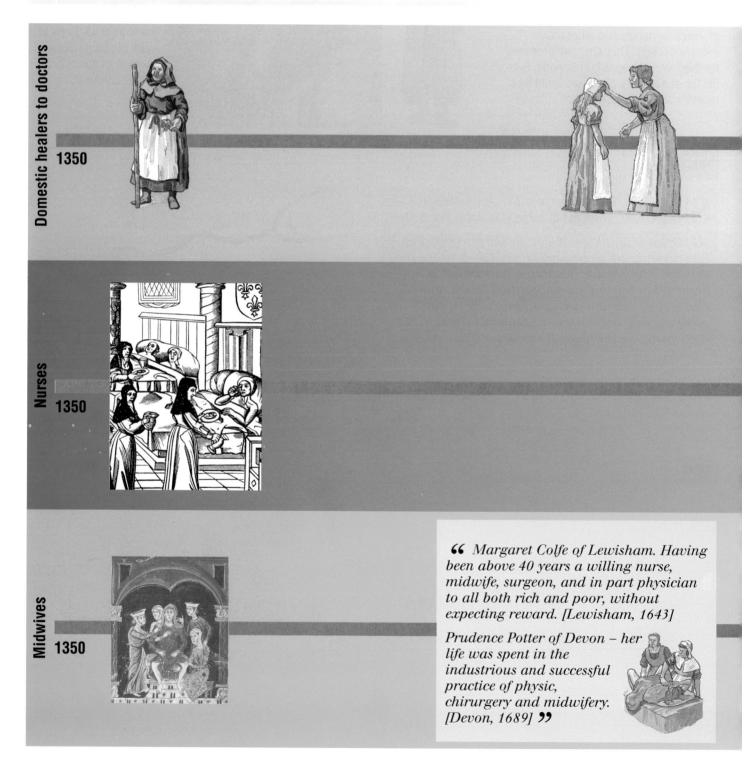

Domestic healers to doctors

1350

Nurses

1350

Midwives

1350

> 66 *Margaret Colfe of Lewisham. Having been above 40 years a willing nurse, midwife, surgeon, and in part physician to all both rich and poor, without expecting reward.* [Lewisham, 1643]
>
> *Prudence Potter of Devon – her life was spent in the industrious and successful practice of physic, chirurgery and midwifery.* [Devon, 1689] 99

Invention of forceps by Chamberlen

Use required knowledge of anatomy

| Only men studied at university and so only men could claim to understand theory of anatomy | Wealthy families thought it was fashionable to have an expensive male doctor, instead of an experienced wise woman who charged them little or nothing for helping at births |

Men took over delivering babies

SOURCE 1 Why were women excluded from delivering some babies in the 1600s?

Do you want more detail? Then turn to pages 83, 85 and 130–39.

Glossary

abscess a collection of pus caused by an infection

ague an old-fashioned term for any disease causing a fever

ailment an illness that is not serious

amputation the removal of a limb by surgery

amulet a charm that the wearer believes gives protection from disease

anaesthetic a drug or drugs given to produce unconsciousness before and during surgery

anatomy the science of understanding the structure and make-up of the body

antibiotics a group of drugs used to treat infections caused by bacteria, e.g. penicillin

antisepsis the prevention of infection by stopping the growth of bacteria by the use of antiseptics

antiseptics chemicals used to destroy bacteria and prevent infection

apothecary a pharmacist or chemist

arteries blood vessels that carry blood away from the heart

arthritis the painful swelling of joints

Asclepion temple of the Greek god of healing Asclepius (or Asklepios)

astrology the study of the planets and how they might influence people's lives

bacterium (pl. bacteria) *see* **germ**

balm *see* **salve**

bezoar stone a ball of indigestible material found in goats' stomachs

biochemist a scientist who studies the make-up of living things

Black Death a phrase used in the Middle Ages to describe bubonic plague. (The 'blackness' was caused by bleeding under the skin. Over 50 per cent of all cases were fatal)

bleed/bleeding the treatment of opening a vein or applying leeches to draw blood from the patient. Also means the loss of blood caused by damage to the blood vessels

cauterise using a hot iron to burn body tissue. This seals a wound and stops bleeding

cell the basic unit of life which makes up the bodies of plants, animals and humans. Billions of cells are contained in the human body

cesspool/cesspit a place for collecting and storing sewage

chirurgery/chirurgeons surgery/surgeons

chloroform a liquid whose vapour acts as an anaesthetic and produces unconsciousness

cholera a disease passed on in water contaminated with faeces. It causes violent sickness and diarrhoea, leading to dehydration and death

chromosomes thread-like structures in the nuclei of cells that contain genetic information

constipation difficulty clearing the bowels

constitution the physical make-up of a person

consumption/consumptive fever tuberculosis which was observed as the wasting away of the body

contagion the passing of disease from one person to another

contaminated/contamination something that is infected

cordial a non-alcoholic drink

coronary referring to the blood vessels around the heart (coronary thrombosis, a blood clot in the coronary artery)

culture/culturing the growth of micro-organisms in the laboratory

diarrhoea frequent, fluid bowel movements, a symptom of a disease

dissection the cutting up and examination of a body

DNA deoxyribonucleic acid, the molecule that genes are made of (*see* **gene** below)

dropsy an old-fashioned term used to describe fluid collection in the body, often used to account for death

dysentery a severe infection causing frequent, fluid bowel movements

effluvia/effluvial unpleasant smells from waste matter. Blamed for disease in the eighteenth and nineteenth centuries

electron microscope a powerful microscope that uses electrons rather than light to produce a magnified image

embalm the treatment of a dead body to preserve it

endoscope an instrument used to view inside the body

faeces waste material from the stomach and digestive system

flux a flow, watery discharge or diarrhoea

fetus a baby before it is born

gangrene (gas gangrene) the infection of dead tissue causing, in the case of gas gangrene, foul-smelling gas

gene part of the nucleus of a cell that determines how our bodies look and work. Genes are passed from parents to children

genetic engineering the investigation of genes and how they can be used to change how the body works

germ a micro-organism that causes disease

germ theory the theory that germs cause disease, often by infection through the air

gonorrhoea a sexually transmitted disease that can be treated with antibiotics

haemorrhage the medical term for bleeding

hi-tech surgery surgery using the most modern techniques, including computers, new skills and new drugs

Hippocratic Oath the principles by which doctors work, for the best health of the patient and to do no harm, named after Hippocrates who wrote it

humours four liquids – phlegm, blood, black bile and yellow bile – in the body, which were believed for centuries to cause illness when they became unbalanced

immune protected against a disease

immunise the process of giving protection from disease through the body's own immune system

immunity protection against disease through the body's own defences or immune system

incision a cut made with a knife in surgery

infant mortality deaths of babies

infection the formation of disease-causing germs or micro-organisms

infirmary a place where the sick are treated, a hospital

inoculate to put a low dose of a disease into the body to help it fight against a more serious attack of the disease

insulin a hormone (chemical) produced by the pancreas that controls the amount of sugar in the blood

King's Evil *see* **scrofula**

laissez-faire belief that governments should not interfere in people's lives. It hindered the development of public health schemes in the nineteenth century

leech a blood-sucking worm used to drain blood from a wound

leper   someone suffering from leprosy, an infection that causes damage to the nerves and skin

ligament   tough elastic tissue that holds joints of the body together

ligature   a thread used to tie a blood vessel during an operation

lunatic   an old-fashioned word for someone who is insane

malady *see* **ailment**

mastectomy   removal of a breast, as a way of preventing the spread of cancer from a tumour

maternal   concerning motherhood and looking after children

medical officer   a person appointed to look after the public health of an area

meningitis   inflammation of the brain caused by an infection by micro-oganisms, a virus or bacterium

miasma   smells from decomposing material that were believed to cause disease

microbe   another name for a micro-organism

micro-organism   a tiny single-celled living organism too small to be seen by the naked eye. Disease-causing micro-organisms are called bacteria

osteoarthritis *see* **arthritis**

papyrus   early 'paper' made from the papyrus plant

parasites   animals that live on or in other animals

penicillin   the first antibiotic drug produced from the mould penicillium to treat infections

physic   a medicine *or* the skill of healing

physician   a doctor, and particularly a doctor of medicine who trained at university

physiology   the study of how the body works

plague   a serious infectious disease spread to humans by fleas from rats and mice

pneumonia   the inflammation of the lungs due to an infection

Poor Law Commission   three commissioners who controlled the work of parishes which provided help for the poor. They were influential in public health reforms

poultice   a warm dressing made of layers of fabric and moist paste

prognosis   medical judgement about the probable course and result of a disease

public health   refers to the well-being of the whole community

purging   giving a medicine to cause a patient to empty their bowels

pus   a pale yellow or green fluid found where there is an infection

putrid   decomposing

quack   a person who falsely claims to have medical ability or qualifications

quinine   the drug treatment for malaria

remedy   a drug or treatment that cures or controls the symptoms of a disease

rheumatism   a term describing stiffness in muscles or joints

rickets   a disease caused by a poor diet resulting in a misshapen skeleton

salve   a soothing ointment

sanatorium   a place where people who are chronically (very) ill can be cared for

scrofula   sometimes known as the King's Evil. It is tuberculosis of a gland in the neck. At one time it was believed that being touched by the king could cure the disease

septicaemia   blood poisoning caused by the spread of bacteria from an infected area

sinew   a tendon or fibrous cord that joins a muscle to a bone

spontaneous generation   the theory that decaying matter turns into germs

staphylococci   bacteria found on the skin that can cause infection if the bacteria become trapped

sterilise   to destroy all living micro-organisms from surfaces and surgical instruments, e.g. on a scalpel before an operation

stye   a small pus-filled abscess near the eyelashes caused by infection

sulphonamide   an antibacterial drug used to treat bronchitis and pneumonia

supernatural   something that cannot be given an ordinary explanation

superstition   an unreasonable belief based on ignorance and sometimes fear

suppuration   the formation and/or discharge of pus

suture   the closing of a cut or wound by the use of stitches (sutures)

syphilis   a sexually-transmitted disease that was common from the late fifteenth century until the introduction of penicillin

tetanus   a disease causing violent muscular spasms

thalidomide   a drug to prevent morning sickness that was withdrawn in 1961 after it was found to cause limb deformities in babies born to women who had taken it

transfusion   the use of blood given by one person to another when a patient has suffered severe blood loss

trephining   the drilling of a hole in the skull

tuberculosis (TB)   a disease that causes severe coughing and chest pains. It is passed on by droplets of moisture during coughing, or from unpasteurised cow's milk

tumour   a swelling caused by cells reproducing at an increased rate. An abnormal growth of cells which may or may not be cancerous

typhus   a disease passed on by bites from body lice, which causes fever and headaches. It can be fatal

ulcer   an open sore on the skin

vaccination   the injection into the body of killed or weakened organisms to give the body resistance against disease

virus   a tiny micro-organism, smaller than bacteria, responsible for infections such as colds, flu, polio, etc.

wise woman   a person believed to be skilled in magic or local customs

witch/witchcraft   a person who practises magic and is believed to have dealings with evil spirits

worms   an infestation where worms live as parasites in the human body

Index

Acknowledgements

Photographs:
Cover: Bridgeman Art Library, London/Royal College of Surgeons, London; **p.8** *bl* Hirmer Fotoarchiv, München, *br* Ancient Art & Architecture Collection Ltd; **p.9** *t* Mansell Collection/Katz Pictures Ltd, *b* Still Pictures/Christian Aid/ Elaine Duigenan; **p.13** *t* Mansell Collection/Katz Pictures Ltd; **p.14** *t* Peter Clayton, Hemel Hempstead; **p.18** British Museum; **p.19** *r* British Museum; **p.20** *t* Mansell Collection/ Katz Pictures; **p.27** Wellcome Library, London; **p.40** York Archaeological Trust For Excavation and Research Ltd; **p.41** *b* York Archaeological Trust For Excavation and Research Ltd; **p.46** *t* British Library (MS Egerton f.53), *b* City of Hereford Archaeological Committee and Mappa Mundi Trust; **p.47** *t* Hulton Getty; **p.49** Hulton Getty; **p.52** *t* British Library (MS 42130, f.61r); **p.53** *l* Bridgeman Art Library/ Biblioteca Marciana, Venice, Italy, *r* Wellcome Library, London; **p.57** *tl* Mary Evans Picture Library, *tr* Mansell Collection/ Katz Pictures, *b* Reproduced by kind permission of Royal College of Physicians of London; **p.58** *l* Mary Evans Picture Library, *r* Wellcome Library, London; **p.60** *t* Mansell Collection/ Katz Pictures, *b* Frederico Abora, Milan; **p.61** Mansell Collection/Katz Pictures; **p.62** *tl* Reproduced by kind permission of Royal College of Physicians of London; **p.65** *t* Wellcome Library, London, *b* Ann Ronan Picture Library; **p.66** *br* Nigel Cattlin/Holt Studios; **p.67** *bl* Ann Ronan Picture Library; **p.68** *b* Bodleian Library, University of Oxford (MS Ashmole 399, f.34r); **p.69** *r* Wellcome Library, London; **p.73** *both* Bridgeman Art Library; **p.74** V & A Picture Library, Victoria & Albert Museum; **p. 75** Corbis UK Ltd; **p.76** Reproduced by kind permission of the President and Council of the Royal College of Surgeons of England; **p.77** Philadelphia Museum of Art, Purchased: SmithKline Beckman Corporation Fund (1949-97-11c); **p.80** *l* Mary Evans Picture Library, *r* Hulton Getty; **p.82** Ann Ronan Picture Library; **p.83** *t* Bodleian Library, University of Oxford (MS Ashmole 391, part V, f.10r), *b* Österreichische Nationalbibliothek, Vienna; **p.88** *portraits (clockwise from top)* Mary Evans Picture Library, Reproduced by kind permission of Royal College of Physicians of London, Mansell Collection/Katz Pictures; **p.94** *b* Science & Society Picture Library, Science Museum, London; **p.95** *t* Science & Society Picture Library, Science Museum, London, *b* Mary Evans Picture Library; **p.96** Wellcome Library, London; **p.98** *t* Wellcome Library, London, *b* British Museum; **p.99** *b* Mansell Collection/Katz Pictures; **p.101** *cl* Institut Pasteur, Paris; **p.102** Hulton Getty; **p.104** *t* Mansell Collection/ Katz Pictures, *cr* Institut Pasteur, Paris; **p.105** *t* Institut Pasteur, Paris; **p.106** *l* Mansell Collection/Katz Pictures; **p.107** Guildhall Library, Corporation of London; **p.109** *b* Wellcome Library, London; **p.110** *r* Mary Evans Picture Library; **p.116** Bridgeman Art Library, London/Royal College of Surgeons, London; **p.117** Wellcome Library, London; **p.118** Ann Ronan Picture Library; **p.120** Hulton Getty; **p.121** Mary Evans Picture Library; **p.122** *t* Mary Evans Picture Library; **p.123** *tc* Mansell Collection/Katz Pictures, *cl* Mary Evans Picture Library, *cr* Hulton Getty; **p.126** Science & Society Picture Library, Science Museum, London; **p.130** *t* Mansell Collection/Katz Pictures, *b* Science & Society Picture Library, Science Museum, London; **p.133** Mansell Collection/Katz Pictures; **p.134** *tr* Mansell Collection/Katz Pictures; **p.135** *tr* Mansell Collection/ Katz Pictures; **p.136** Wellcome Library, London; **p.137** Science Photo Library; **p.138** Mary Evans Picture Library; **p.140** *bl* Wellcome Library, London; **p.146** *r* Imperial War Museum Q52408; **p.147** *c* Science & Society Picture Library, Science Museum, London, *b* Science Photo Library; **p.149** *l, r* Science Photo Library, *c* Corbis UK Ltd; **p.152** *l* Hulton Getty, *r* Corbis UK Ltd; **p.153** Hulton Getty; **p.154** *b* Manchester Evening News; **p.155** *l* Science Photo Library/Tim Beddow; **p.163** *l* Courtesy Gadstone Pottery Museum, Stoke-on-Trent; **p.164** *l* Hulton Getty; **p.165** *r* Mansell Collection/Katz Pictures; **p.166** *tl & tr* Syndication International; **p.167** *t* Public Record Office Image Library, Kew; **p.168** *l* Associated Newspapers/Atlantic Syndication Partners; **p.175** *tl and cl* Public Record Office Image Library, Kew; **p.175** *c* Imperial War Museum; **p.175** *br* Hulton Getty; **p.186** *bl* Wellcome Library, London; **p.187** *tr* Wellcome Library, London, *cr* Mansell Collection/ Katz Pictures; **p.188** Hulton Getty; **p.189** *b* Imperial War Museum E(Aus)1304; **p.190** *tc* Reproduced by kind permission of Royal College of Physicians of London, *tr* Mary Evans Picture Library, *bl* Institut Pasteur, Paris, *bc and br* Mansell Collection/ Katz Pictures; **p.193** *clockwise from top* Mary Evans Picture Library, Mansell Collection/Katz Pictures, Reproduced by kind permission of Royal College of Physicians of London, Philadelphia Museum of Art, Purchased: SmithKline Beecham Corporation Fund, Ann Ronan Picture Library, Mary Evans Picture Library; **p.196** *l* Frederico Abora, Milan, *c* Bridgeman Art Library/Biblioteca Marciana, Venice, Italy, *r* Wellcome Library, London; **p.197** Mansell Collection/Katz Pictures; **p.198** *bl* Wellcome Library, London, *br* Hulton Getty; **p.200** Imperial War Museum; **p.201** Science Photo Library/ Tim Beddow; **p.203** *all* Science Photo Library; **p204** *l* Ann Ronan Picture Library, *r* Bodleian Library, University of Oxford (MS Ashmole 391, part V, f.10r); **p. 205** *tr* Mary Evans Picture Library; **p.206** *bl* Österreichische Nationalbibliothek, Vienna; **p.207** *tl and cl* Mansell Collection/Katz Pictures Ltd, *tr and cr* Science Photo Library, *c* Imperial War Museum, *br* Sally & Richard Greenhill/Sally Greenhill.

(t = top, b = bottom, r = right, l = left, c = centre)

Written sources:
p.19 H. von Staden, *Herophilus, The Art of Medicine in Early Alexandria*, Cambridge University Press, 1989; **p.23** Lindsey Davis, *The Silver Pigs*, Arrow Books, a division of Random House UK Ltd, 2000; **p.165** N. Gray, *The Worst of Times*, Scolar Press, a division of Ashgate Publishing Ltd, 1986.

While every effort has been made to contact copyright holders, the publishers apologise for any omissions which they will be pleased to rectify at the earliest opportunity.